**Jah Wobble** was born John Wardl~ ~ 
1958. He was one of the founde 
along with John Lydon, former 
met, along with Sid Vicious, a 
left the band, he embarked on 
collaborations, including the Inv 
Condition. His album *Rising Abc* ........ated for the 
Mercury Music Prize (1992). His latest project, *Chinese Dub*, is one 
of the great world music hits of recent years. He is a bass guitarist, 
singer, composer, poet and music journalist. As well as all that he 
runs his own record company, 30 Hertz Records. More information 
on Jah Wobble can be found at www.30hertzrecords.com.

**Praise for** *Memoirs of a Geezer*

'Like his bass, the lows are low and the style upfront' Ludovic 
Hunter-Tilney, *Financial Times*, Music Books of the Year

'Blackly comic' Helen Brown, *Daily Telegraph*

'He writes as well as he plays...entertaining and uplifting' Tom 
Widger, *Sunday Tribune*

'An exhilarating journey...he is an agreeable and thoughtful tour 
guide' Tony Russell, *Mojo*

'Eminently readable account of the affable East Ender's journey... 
perfectly mixes open humility with cavalier swagger. In this 
engaging dichotomy, Wobble's personality shines through every 
anecdote and insight as he matches Devil-may-care visceral 
grit with cerebral self-analysis...Hilarious, unflinching, self-

deprecating...therein lies this particular geezer's twinkle-eyed, likeably roguish charm' Ian Fortnam, *Classic Rock*

'There's plenty to talk about with John Wardle...his honesty and forthrightness is the book's greatest strength...Wobble is an engaging narrator' Joe Shooman, *Record Collector*

'He writes with a punchy honesty and has a good ear for insult... an enjoyable romp through three decades of pop culture as well as an occasional meditation on working-class life and the changing face of London' Toby Lichtig, *TLS*

'Passionate, digressive, angry, philosophical and full of (often jet black) humour...If the idea of getting as close as you can to having your ear bent by this talented but awkward customer appeals, you're likely to find things to enjoy here' Jamie Renton, *Roots*

# MEMOIRS OF A GEEZER

THE AUTOBIOGRAPHY OF JAH WOBBLE
MUSIC, MAYHEM, LIFE

## JAH WOBBLE

A complete catalogue record for this book can
be obtained from the British Library on request

The right of Jah Wobble to be identified as the author of
this work has been asserted by him in accordance with
the Copyright, Designs and Patents Act 1988

First published in 2009 by Serpent's Tail

First published in this edition in 2010 by Serpent's Tail,
an imprint of Profile Books Ltd
3A Exmouth House
Pine Street
London EC1R 0JH
website: www.serpentstail.com

ISBN 978 1 84668 720 4

Designed and typeset by folio at Neuadd Bwll, Llanwrtyd Wells

Printed and bound in Great Britain by CPI Bookmarque Ltd,
Croydon, Surrey

10   9   8   7   6   5   4   3   2   1

The paper this book is printed on is certified by the © 1996 Forest
Stewardship Council A.C. (FSC).

# Contents

# Acknowledgements

Thanks to everyone featured in this book, especially 'my enemies'. Without you lot, it would have been anodyne and meaningless, so thank you very much for giving me something to push against. And anyway, none of you could ever be a worse enemy than I have been to myself. Special credit goes to John Williams, my editor. He was like a good dentist; I was fearful before we started and yet felt little pain during the process. Thanks to all the friends who gave me their unconditional and enthusiastic support. In particular thanks to Pete Holdsworth, Pat Macardle (especially for getting stuck into the 'first wave' of typos), John Freeman, Jon Savage, Jim Driver, Dave Maltby, Helen Maleed, Scott Murphy and Jim McCarthy. Thanks to Niamh Murray, Anna-Marie Fitzgerald and everybody else at Serpent's Tail for going the extra mile on my behalf. I must also express my gratitude to Clive Bell for giving this book its title (I didn't really like it, to be honest, but just about everyone else did). Lastly, thanks to Zi-Lan and my sons, John and Charlie, for keeping me firmly 'in today', because, as we all know, too much looking back isn't healthy.

# Chapter One: Childhood

## THE BELL (SECONDS OUT, ROUND 1)

A bell rang loudly. My mum Kathleen was as alarmed as the bell. As if giving birth isn't scary enough, she was now fearful that the bell signified that I was a 'blue baby'. In fact it merely indicated that I was a 'witnessed birth'. In those days every twelfth birth had to be witnessed by the student midwives, and trainee doctors. The bell was summoning all to witness my birth. So even then I had an audience. As was the practice then, the midwife held me upside down and smacked my bum, causing me to issue forth a loud and furious wail. She laughed and said, 'This one got a temper!' Well, she wasn't wrong there. My entrance into the world was made at the East End Maternity Home on Commercial Road, Stepney, London, E1. The date was 11 August 1958. I was christened John Joseph Wardle.

At that time my family were living in Locksley St, E14. When I was still a baby we moved to Smithy St, E1. The house had been home to a woman who was a spiritualist. She had held regular spiritualist meetings there. The house had a very dark and weird vibe. My mum found that she was afraid there, especially when she was alone with me and my sister Catherine, during the day.

She was very unnerved by the place. I now realise that what many would term poltergeist activity was taking place there. My mum's resolve finally broke when my sister, who was about six at the time, told her about the conversations she was having with the 'old man at the piano' (the place came with an old out-of-tune pub piano). That was it... my mum freaked out and got my dad's brother Terry, who is a Roman Catholic priest, to come and bless every room in the house. He didn't do a 'full-on' pukka exorcism (I think that at that time the Catholic Church in the UK sort of unofficially left full-on exorcisms to a group of monks based in Highgate).

I recollect him going from room to room, splashing holy water about while mumbling prayers in Latin. I think the feeling, for my mum, was akin to having sorted out an insurance policy; a few evil spirits cannot argue with the cover provided by the Holy Ghost. My most vivid memory of that house is falling ill with a very high temperature (something that I was prone to throughout childhood). I started to hallucinate, seeing gaudily coloured snakes on both animate and inanimate surfaces. I was screaming, ''nakes!' ''nakes!', but could not be consoled, because those snakes were everywhere, even on the bodies and faces of my mum and dad.

They fetched the Jewish doctor from across the street where his practice was situated. When summoned, Dr Abrahams said, 'If I didn't know better, I would swear that this boy had the DTs.' Well, funnily enough years later I did indeed suffer from the DTs, but I never saw anything quite as powerful as that childhood hallucination. Years later, when I looked at Van Gogh's later paintings, his vibrant swirls of colour reminded me of that vision.

Another memory of Smithy Street is of the rather shadowy tenant that came with the house. In those days having to share accommodation with others was by no means an unusual situation in the East End. The bloke in question was a Canadian, who went by the name of Constantine. He lived up in the attic. He kept pile upon pile of old newspapers. My mum felt that was a fire risk. No one saw much of him. He was often away. Years later my family

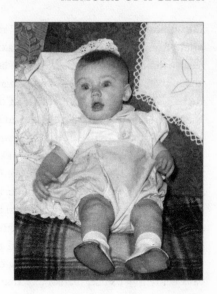

Blokes like me start out in life in similar fashion to how they finish; lying back on the settee à la Homer Simpson

found out that he had amassed a fortune on the stock market. Mysterious marginal characters like that were typical of the East End. My mum to this day suspects that he used to wee down the sink in his room rather than use the outside privy (a wise choice, to be honest; it was three storeys down to a cold yard, and I know I'd rather use the sink). At this time nearly all my extended family lived within a ten-minute walk of each other. There were always lots of cousins to play and fight with. I had many violent clashes with a cousin of mine who was also called John. He was a few months younger than me, so he was called 'Little John' and I was called 'Big John'. I recall getting into big trouble for hitting him with a brick on one occasion; I really whacked him. Then again I'm sure that he whacked me a few times. My mum had three sisters, Nora, Mary and Edie, and two brothers, John and Joey. Joey was severely handicapped. I take my middle name from Joey. He died in a 'home' when he was in his twenties; I believe that he choked to death. My dad, Harry, had a sister, Agnes, and two brothers, Terry and John. I am named after John. John fell in the river by

3

Limehouse Cut when he was eight. He was fished out but died a few days later in the old Poplar Hospital from 'complications' (pneumonia, I would imagine). My dad's family still feels bitter about the circumstances surrounding John's death. They believe that the treatment he received, from the doctor at the hospital, was appalling. This was in the era prior to the formation of the NHS. You didn't want to be poor and poorly. (It looks to me like those days are coming back.)

FAMILY HISTORY

The maternal side of my family (the Fitzgibbons and Haggertys) had been coming over from Ireland in dribs and drabs since the time of the potato famine. This culminated in my mum's mum and her mum coming to Britain a few years into the twentieth century. My maternal great-grandfather, who was an alcoholic, came with them. However, he soon ended up living rough on the streets. Most of the family settled in Wapping, where their boats docked. A regular steam packet ran from Cork to Wapping; consequently most of the Irish in East London at that time hailed from the vicinity of Cork. Indeed, both sides of my mum's family came from west Cork. Her mum's clan came from a coastal town called Durrus. Funnily enough, I still work at a music studio that is situated right on the site they settled at, in Pennington Street, Wapping.

My dad's first name is Harry, his second is Eugene; his side of the family had made their way over from Schull in west Cork, as a result of the potato famine. Their family names were Leahy and Connolly. The exception to this Irish lineage was a bloke called Wardle, my great-grandfather, who was a Scouse Protestant. Apparently, as long as any offspring were bought up as Catholics, no one in my staunchly Catholic family minded my great-grandmother marrying him. He was a good man by all accounts, who died young, as so many did then. My dad's family were known as a Limehouse family; i.e. that was their parish. My mum told me that as a kid she remembers her family being of a strong republican persuasion; her mum would get very nervous when the men of the family started singing rebel songs too raucously, in case they were overheard and trouble ensued. My Uncle Terry says the same thing about my dad's side of the family. Here we are two generations later, and any sense of Irishness has long since petered out, apart from my mum and a couple of cousins who married back in with the Irish. I only caught the dying embers of that Irish stuff, so rest assured I'm not going to go all 'plastic Paddy' on you. Anyway, the East End Irish were so long established that they became a strange hybrid, even more so than the London Irish generally. In their heyday they were probably similar to the Welsh in Patagonia.

All the same, when I hear good Irish music it really does tend to connect and resonate with me. It was because of my mum that I was exposed to the music of The Dubliners at an early age, as well as one or two other Irish artists. I loved the Dubliners. Tracks like 'Travelling People' and 'Weila Waila' still make the hairs stand up on the back of my neck. I went on to make a record with the late Ronnie Drew, from that band, in the mid-nineties. Words cannot convey what a great feeling that gave me. Ronnie was truly a great man, a very cultured bloke. He is one of the giants that I have met along the way.

In regard to instrumental Irish music I particularly favour slow mournful airs, especially when played on uillean (elbow) pipes. I must admit that does tend to stir my blood, as well as my tears, but that's about it as far as any degree of Irishness goes with me. I was mad for the drink at one time, of course, so maybe that was partly genetic – after all, only a fool would say that the Irish don't like a drink.

Anyhow, never mind this Irish ancestry stuff, because I strongly suspect that there is a bit of Slav or even Oriental in both sides of the family. You only have to look at the cheekbones and the eyes.

5

As a young kid I would loudly point out that out. I would be firmly admonished and told to shut up. My mum and dad were worried that the members of the extended family that I accused of being Chinese would take offence. Although, to be fair, they would, on the quiet, have a laugh about what I said.

Anyway, whatever, I consider myself to be English, despite the ridiculously entrenched class system, which often leads you to feel that you are playing a rigged game. I have certainly never felt like a 'full citizen' of the UK. Even so, I am a supporter of the England football team. However, I don't sing the national anthem (apart from an occasion in Lisbon a few years ago), because I'm not a monarchist in any way, shape or form. England is a funny old country and it's far from perfect, but all the same it is still my country.

*Of course, ultimately I know that patriotism is a load of old fanny, a mere construct. Furthermore the same can be said of our own individual identity – ultimately there is nothing there of any true substance. However, I do think that we should be of our time and place (fully participating in the relative and conditional world), wearing the karmic cloak of this particular life lightly, but wearing it nevertheless, while we are here, with good heart, and then eventually, when our number is up, moving on. I mean, what do you want of me; to dress and behave like a seventeenth-century French peasant? Isn't it enough that I now cook with olive oil? Actually I quite fancy being Brazilian in the next life. Then finally I can see 'my team' in another World Cup final.*

I only ever knew one of my grandparents, Jack (John) Wardle, my dad's dad. The other three passed away well before I could know them. Jack was a Thames lighterman. I thought the world of him. He was often a bit tipsy, singing and playing the spoons, and the like. A very spirited man, so he was. When I was a kid he was always quick to give me a florin, a Bounty bar or an orange. I felt assured that I was his favourite. They all used to say that I was like him. Certainly it's true that 'in drink' we both tended to behave very badly. Anyway, he was definitely a good geezer to my mind, even though he was seen as a bit of an embarrassment, increasingly so in his later years, to some in the family.

He used to take my dad and Terry to work with him on the barges. However, neither of them had the inclination to follow in Grandad's footsteps. Not surprising really, it was a hell of a tough job, 'driving' the barges, as they used to call it, using massive oars. My old man enlisted in the Tower Hamlet's Rifles at the advent of the Second World War; like so many of those old soldiers he lied about his age in order to be enlisted. *(I have never heard of a recruiting sergeant accusing a boy of lying about his age – surely they must often have had suspicions?)* He ended up as a sergeant in the 8th Army and was at El Alamein.

Apart from the combat itself my dad liked the army. It gave him a sense of purpose and belonging. He kept his spoon and blanket as mementos, of this, the happiest time of his life. Although as far as I know he was never a bloke to attend army reunions. I'm not surprised that he liked the army; from what I understand life was pretty tough for him, as it was for so many, growing up in what we would now see, judging from our contemporary perspective, as pretty extreme social deprivation. After the war he worked as a tea clerk for the East India Company. He was made redundant in his fifties and ended up working as a postman. Although he was a strong man, it was important to his self-image that he did not, unlike all the other men in the family, do some form of manual labour. He liked to see himself as a cut above everyone else around him. Paradoxically, however, he was a staunch Labour voter.

I think that he really missed the army. Apart from the sense of meaning that it gave his life, it had also opened up new vistas for him socially. He got friendly with some of the lower-ranking officers. I think that he aspired to be, in some respects, like them. Thanks to the army he was able to meet men who in Civvy Street were schoolteachers, accountants and the like. He thought that they were 'good men'. I think that he thought that they were cultured.

My dad on leave after the battle of El Alamein. He is standing on the far right of the picture as you look

If it wasn't for the army he would not have met people like that. I think that he wanted to be like them. I have some sympathy for him. The working-class experience can get a bit claustrophobic at times.

My mum's dad Joey was one of the poor sods who went off to fight in the First World War. He was gassed, and saw all sorts of horrors. He was in the trenches right until the end of the war. This was the antithesis of my other grandad's experience in the First World War. Because of his lighterman skills he ended up working on the River Seine. I'm pretty sure that while he was there he saw a lot of girls and drunk a lot of red wine. I know he told everyone that he had a great time; he was by all accounts quite sad to come home. That was some result, to avoid the Royal Navy, let alone the trenches. That was typical of him.

Apart from his job in the tea trade my dad worked part time for a Polish mate of his called Wojciech, who was one tough geezer. Wojciech had two wooden legs; his real ones had got blown off as he escaped from a German prisoner-of-war camp. Somehow, against all the odds, he had survived, nursed, covertly, by peasants and a patriotic doctor. Wojciech never seemed sorry for himself. He had married an Irish woman when he came to this country but she had died. I think they had one daughter. He remarried, to a Polish woman, and again had a daughter. He drank vodka as if it was water.

I believe that Wojciech owned a small factory making handbags somewhere in the East End. I think that my dad helped Wojciech to set up his company and looked after his books, but I'm not certain about that. To be honest, as far as I know my dad never really told anyone anything. You certainly never would have thought that my dad had two jobs, because (unlike me) he never flashed his cash about. We never had a car or took flash holidays. We certainly never went abroad. Butlins holiday camp in Bognor Regis was the most salubrious establishment that we ever stayed at. But then again for the East End that wasn't that unusual; in fact many of the families that we knew took working holidays in the hop fields of Kent.

By chance Wojciech and my dad were both in The Blind Beggar public house on the night Georgie Cornell got shot by Ronnie Kray. They had left the pub a good while before the shooting occurred, and I can categorically state that they had absolutely nothing to do with organised crime, or criminals in any way, shape or form, that much I do know. But they had been drinking in the Beggar so they had to get their fingerprints taken, to aid the police in their process of elimination.

Outside of the house or on the phone (it took my mum ages to get him to agree to get a phone) he would try his best to speak without a cockney accent. Upon getting demobbed, as well as training as a clerical worker, he had also, as part of the course, taken elocution lessons. His voice, under this constraint, was actually rather reminiscent of Alf Ramsey, the old England football manager (another East Londoner uncomfortable with his origins); over-controlled, and therefore cold – you could feel the impatience, frustration and anger just underneath the surface.

On occasion he could display a strange rather surreal sense of humour. I remember him having a long conversation with a visiting priest. Throughout the conversation he held his pointed index finger at right angles against his nose (elbow sticking out). He was amused when the priest eventually followed suit. I now suspect that this was some kind of insane spontaneous mudra, rather than a random bit of piss-taking. He always considered himself to be above 'the rabble' that surrounded him in the East End (however, like so many of the eccentrics who lived in the area, he couldn't drag himself away to the new towns in Essex). Guinness and whisky were his preferred tipples. He could be a pretty ugly drunk, especially after a night of drinking vodka with Wojciech and the Poles. Oh yes, I nearly forgot, he would habitually holler, quite randomly, 'never marry an Irish colleen!' once or twice a day.

However, on the whole I found him to be a morose, isolated, bad-tempered and unapproachable man. By the time I was seven or eight we had no relationship, other than mutual antipathy. We hated to even be in the same room as each other. Incredibly I never had anything like a proper conversation with him, and I eventually became completely estranged from him. I came to view him as a sort of an 'anti-father'. He did not get on with his own father; their temperaments were totally different. I was similar to his dad, even in the way of my mannerisms, and I think that compounded our difficulties; every time my dad looked at me, he saw his own father. Having said that, he didn't get on that well with anybody, and he became increasingly isolated over the years. He suffered badly from tinnitus, probably due to damage sustained in the war; not surprisingly this had a detrimental effect on his mood. Really he just wanted to be left in peace to have a drink and brood. The overriding image I have of my dad is of him sitting, alone, in the darkened kitchen at Paymal House, while Beethoven blared from the radio/cassette player.

## MUM

My mum's maiden name was Kathleen Bridget Fitzgibbon. Her parents died within weeks of each other, her mum, Catherine, aged fifty-eight, and her dad, Joey, aged sixty-one. By the age of fourteen Catherine was working in the 'rope grounds' making ship's rope. She developed a bad cough because of the fibres of the rope irritating her airways. My grandad Joey did all manner of jobs. He eventually ended up as a street sweeper. Apparently, he was a very good drummer in the parish drum and fife band, as was his cousin, also called Joey Fitzgibbon, but referred to by everyone as Joey Fitz. They would all dress up in their best suits when they marched; they looked very stylish. At that time every Roman Catholic parish in the East End had a drum and fife band. They would march against each other every year in a large procession. There was a great deal of competition and rivalry between those bands. The men used to hold up big statues of Our Lady above their heads. I remember going on a couple of those processions. The Italians of Saffron Hill used to participate. Sadly, as far as I know, only the Italians still have a procession. Somehow, like the Latin mass, it was one of the things that disappeared after the Vatican II council.

*I realise now that the culture that I was born into was on its last legs as I was born. The docks were on their way out, and the culture that grew up alongside them was fast going as well. Government housing policies certainly helped in regard to finishing it off.*

My mum talks of her parents as if they were saints. Truly, I have never heard a bad word uttered by her in relation to them. Some of my mum's family put me right on that one, assuring me that while they were essentially good people, they certainly weren't without faults. However, they were, by all accounts, a very sociable

My mum supervises the
girls on an East End
Catholic procession

couple. My mum inherited that sociability, and thankfully, passed
it on to me. As well as having an ability to get on with people, my
mum can be a bit manipulative. She would often work on bringing
me and the old man head to head. There were many unholy rows
at home. I can remember her coming at me with a pan full of hot
chip oil at Paymal House. I bet there is still a massive oil stain
on the wall there. (I narrowly got out of the way when I saw it
coming; I moved as quickly as those dudes in the Chinese martial
arts films.)

When she was a bit younger she often used to play the martyr.
You risked her wrath, as I and others in the family found out, if
you dared point out this trait. However, if she wasn't in the mood
to be wrathful she would simply continue to play the martyr, while
maintaining (in between deep sighs) that yet again her motives
had been misinterpreted, when all she wanted was the best for
everyone else (rather than controlling everyone else to the nth
degree, of course).

She has a fiery temper; however, if she is really upset, she will simply stop talking to you. Blanking one another is the chief weapon of choice in her family. In fact, among her clan, she is possibly not the chief protagonist of that tactic. Her brother Johnny 'cut off' most of his sisters over thirty years ago. They don't know why. The Fitzgibbon family history is littered with that kind of behaviour.

Mum could represent England at the Olympics, if non-stop talking was an event, as could her younger sister Edie. I remember the kitchen at Paymal House when all her sisters would be around; there'd be my mum, Nora, Mary and Edie all nattering away in a deep fug of cigarette smoke. The only place I ever saw cigarette smoke as thick as that was at AA meetings many years later. Mum worked as a school secretary and she also worked at the old County Hall for a while.

She had been an evacuee in the war. An experience she didn't enjoy one bit. She was sent to Somerset, and was treated appallingly. Her dad came to visit out of the blue. He sussed the situation out immediately, put his foot down, and took her and Edie back to London. The authorities had in their wisdom split the family up, which was, inexplicably, common practice. It's funny, I've talked to a quite a few evacuees over the years, and I've never met one who was happy about the experience; ill treatment was, by all accounts, a regular occurrence. They were seen as a source of slave labour. I'm sure there were exceptions; however, I've never come across one. It seems those country dwellers would often view the London 'slum kids' with disdain. Good old middle England, heh?

## THE CLICHY

The late fifties, early sixties landscape of Stepney that I inhabited was a jumble of old Victorian two-up-two-downs, alternating with 1930s tenement blocks. There were still plenty of bomb sites remaining from the war. These were great, and sometimes dangerous, playgrounds for all us naughty boys. More than one boy fell through rotten old floors, or got hit by bricks thrown by rival gangs. I can still strongly recollect the odd unexploded bomb being found.

This is how it seemed to me at the time. The bomb disposal squad used to come round to check out the unexploded bomb. They would put up some tape a hundred yards or so away from the bomb. Then they would sit smoking fags, chatting to each other, legs dangling over the edge of the crater, while bilious amounts of steam rose up from the process of 'steaming the bomb'. We would chance our arm, ducking our head under the tape. There was normally a police constable, normally near to retirement age, in the vicinity who would casually threaten the naughty boys with a clip around the ear unless they cleared off. If you were a member of the bomb squad at that time please don't take umbrage... it is how I remember it.

There were very many Jewish people in the East End in those days. I had a shock of blond hair at that time. (I'm an old bald bloke now, of course.) Apparently the old Jewish ladies took to me. I must have reminded them of the Poland and Russia of their youth. I would have thought that a Slavic- or Aryan-looking kid would have given them the horrors. Coincidentally my Uncle John who drowned also had a shock of blond hair similar to mine.

There was a synagogue just across the road from our house on the other side of Jubilee Street. Stalin and Lenin had addressed a meeting there in 1903, when the site was also used for political meetings; indeed, Stalin stayed in lodgings just a few yards farther up Jubilee Street. At the turn of the century the East End (Whitechapel especially) was a political hothouse. It was still a highly politicised area in the fifties and sixties. To this day I believe it is one of the few areas of the country ever to have elected a communist Member of Parliament.

By 1963 a massive rebuilding programme of social housing was under way. We left Smithy Street, and moved to a new estate, the Clichy, that was already half built on the bomb site adjacent to our row of houses. I vividly remember the day of the move. I was beside myself with excitement. I was full of that mad puppy-dog energy that is so typical of little boys. So understandably I was kept out of the way. At the end of Smithy Street lay one of three tower blocks, Bradmore House, which was also newly built, where my mum's elder sister Mary lived with her husband Ted, and my cousins Pat and Marie. I watched the move from Mary's flat. It was all so mind-blowing, to be up that high, looking down at my mum and dad getting on with the move. I looked down at them through the snowflakes that swirled around in the strong wind. The winter of 1963 is still remembered as one of the harshest ever. Aunt Mary gave me a Cornish pasty to eat. It was the first time that I had ever had one, and it seemed rather exotic to me.

The Clichy estate quickly grew and within days our house had also disappeared, another victim of the new estate's rapacious conquest of the local streets. The tree that was in our backyard still survives, against all the odds, to this day, in the middle of that estate. The council gave the 'houses' (the individual blocks of the estate) French names that are associated with Clichy, the working-class suburb of Paris. We lived in Paymal House, right on the corner of Stepney Way and, aptly enough for me, Jamaica Street. The 'house' next to us was called 'Charles de Gaulle'.

Of course, ours was not the only new estate. It seemed like the new flats were springing up everywhere. Everyone was so excited. We were so proud of our new flats, each of which had its own bathroom (that was such a big deal at the time). It was like a revolution was taking place. The generation before me had suffered a lot during the war; they had also had a lot to put up with in the post-war years. It had been a pretty austere time for most of them, so understandably many of them felt that Utopia was imminent. That was the time of the Wilson Labour government;

Clichy House,
The Clichy Estate

©Tower Hamlets Local History Archive

the ruling class were on the back foot, the Profumo affair had hit the headlines, and working-class icons like Michael Caine were coming to the fore. It felt like our time had come.

*There was a film made on and around the Clichy at that time called* Sparrows Can't Sing. *It starred James Booth and Barbara Windsor of* EastEnders *fame. It's not a great film (some would say that's an understatement); it does, however, capture the exuberance of its time and location. This is probably due to the fact that many of the cast were locals; present, for instance, was Stephen Lewis, who played 'Blakey' from* On the Buses *('Get that bus out, Butler!'). Even the Kray twins made a cameo appearance.*

Unfortunately our dream home was not what we expected. It turned out that the Clichy was jerry-built. Before long water was literally pouring down the inside walls when it rained. It was damp and freezing. My mum ended up with a bad case of bronchitis. They never did completely cure the damp problem in our flat. I should add that whoever built the Clichy decided to use, in their wisdom, bright yellow bricks. The word lurid comes to mind when I think of the newly built estate. The effect was similar to some sort of demented holiday camp. Before long there were massive dark patches in the yellow brickwork. Our utopian dream soon turned into a bleak landscape, closer to the barren

Odette Duval
House, The
Clichy Estate

outskirts of Katowice than some neo-Renaissance version of Florence, which was, supposedly, the vision that inspired many of the redevelopers of that age (the corrupt politician T. Dan Smith comes to mind). Opposite our flats were three tower blocks. Right in the middle of these was a massive, brutal, modernist sculpture. No one knew what to think of it, other than it was meaningless and ugly. People just laughed at it. It's incredible to think of the massive gulf, spiritually and philosophically, that existed between the 'planners' and the people who actually lived in those estates (and by God it got even worse later on in the decade). Of course, the modernist dwellings that the architects of the day lived in were spacious, full of natural light and were often based close to Hampstead Heath.

*All that's not to say that I don't feel indebted to the great socialist reformers, such as Herbert Morrison, for the great strides forward that they and the Labour movement achieved, in regard to housing, health and education for the working classes. My generation was the first to really get the benefits of all those socialist-induced post-war reforms. Don't worry, though, I'm not a fool. I know that in one of the old Eastern Bloc-style communist or socialist societies I would have been be one of the first to be sent off to the gulag, because I just can't keep my mouth shut.*

## WE DIDN'T MOVE TO ESSEX

Another option at that time, other than being moved into a council flat within the borough, was to move out to new towns in Essex like Harlow or Harold Hill. Many of my relatives did just that. I clearly remember visiting my dad's sister Agnes's family out in Essex. Her husband John O'Donovan, or 'John O'D' as he was known, was a docker and one of my favourite uncles. He was a very tough bloke who was immensely likeable. The O'Donovans had moved to Harold Hill with their five children, Keena, Carmel, Pat, Kevin and John. I was impressed by their climbing and gymnastic skills; I think they were all double jointed. And typical of my dad's side of the family, they were all bright. In order to visit them we used to get the Green Line coach from Mile End Road. It was (to me) as if we were travelling far into uncharted territory.

Within a few years most of the family lived in Essex; in fact just about everybody that I know from the East End lives there now. In 1999 I belatedly (and reluctantly) became a member of the cockney diaspora. However, I didn't move to Essex. When I was around fourteen I made a pact with my sister that neither of us would ever live there. She came close to breaking the pact by moving, for a while, to East Ham; however, crucially she never moved that extra few miles east, so I can't say that she reneged on our agreement. At that time I viewed Essex as a sort of Siberia. I saw it as a conformist suburban hell, where people lived in quiet desperation. I thought that moving there was 'taking the path of least resistance', and therefore cowardly, and to be avoided. Don't get me wrong; eventually I came to love much of Essex for its bleakness. In a way it's a desert where one can find God. Somehow ambient music and techno are the natural soundtracks for Essex. I think that the underrated film *Essex Boys*, although not quite perfect, captures very well the strange light of Essex, as well as the unique characteristics of the Essex landscape and its people.

*I became fixated with one of Essex's main arteries, the A13, and the culture that lies beside it. I have a prediction in regard to (south) Essex's cockney diaspora. It was Bob Hoskins, the actor, who first compared the fate of cockneys with that of the North American tribes. Well, I predict that, similar to Native American Indian reservations, special dispensation will be given for casinos to be constructed, as part of what they are calling the 'Thames Gateway scheme' (that's 'marshland construction' to you or me, or 'building on a flood plain', if you like). They could say it's a sort of semi-autonomous zone, home to the displaced cockney tribe, and that these once noble people need be recompensed by the state for the humiliations and hardships that they have endured, and that the only way to do that is to let them rake 1 per cent (OK, then, half a per cent; oh, all right, a quarter of a per cent it is, then) off the top. I for one will quite happily return 'to my roots' and play the part of 'theme cockney docker' and dress in a gaily coloured neckerchief, hobnailed boots and flat cap, and circulate through the casino handing out complimentary jellied eels to the assembled gamblers, in return for £250 per night, while humping a papier-mâché mock-up of a large bunch of bananas on my shoulder. Essex is the nearest thing we have in this country to New Jersey in the States. We should honour the fact.*

## THE SIXTIES

My memory of the mid-sixties is a pretty clichéd one. I remember it, as so many seem to do, as a sunny time, inherently optimistic and youthful. An iconic picture of Bobby Moore, in West Ham away strip, hung in Wally's the tobacconist. He became a national hero (Bobby, not Wally) after leading England to victory in the 1966 World Cup. I can vividly remember that tournament; I was glued to the screen. West Ham were the best-supported club in the area; indeed, most of the family are West Ham fans, and even my sister had a Hammers pennant on her bedroom wall. Millwall also had a

Me on Stepney
Green

fair bit of support in the area. Indeed, my dad and his brother Terry both favoured Millwall over West Ham.

Contrary as ever, I became a Spurs fan, partly because of Jimmy Greaves, that other great sixties football icon, as well as a (super) natural affinity with the club. I was by no means alone in the East End. To this day I still avidly follow Tottenham. I'm a 'Shelfside' season ticket holder. As I always say, you change your house, you change your motor, you even change your wife, but you never change your team. You're stuck with the useless bastards through (bits of) thick and (lots of) thin.

From the age of five I loved to play football; we would play for hours on end given a chance. Sometimes there would be forty a side, right in the middle of the estate. Looking back, it was reminiscent of those medieval games some of those country villages still play where all the geezers fight over a dead badger or a large piece of cheese or something. I still enjoy a game of football. Obviously I am an old boy now; however, I still have an eye for a 'killer pass', and I'm a pretty assured finisher. I have a good temperament for taking penalties. My youngest boy Charlie is a better player than I was at his age. He's got two good feet, plays with his head up and covers every blade of grass. Like my older boy John he is also a musician.

Tamla Motown was the popular music of the day in that mid-sixties period. Farther down Stepney Way, the older boys hung around outside the Artichoke pub in mohair mod suits, whistling at giggling girls in miniskirts. This feeling of sixties youthful optimism was very much at odds with the essentially pre-Vatican II doctrines of the Sisters of Mercy who ran my primary school, St Mary and Michaels's on the Commercial Road. I found the Sisters of Mercy to be a pretty neurotic group of women. I remember that whenever there was a thunderstorm one of the nuns would sit under her desk sobbing. Of course, her behaviour was never explained to us kids. If you drew attention to it you would get a clip around the ear, and be told to 'shut up!'

As well as being neurotic the Sisters were also, in my experience, spiteful and vindictive. Their spite was more than matched by one of the two Catholic lay teachers. I had the misfortune of suffering this particular person in my last year there. If you incurred his displeasure he would utilise one of his 'offbeat punishments'. He would, for instance, lift you a few inches from the ground, while you were still seated in your chair, and then drop you. This would jar your back, a very risky manoeuvre. He used to make a point of picking on me. He also used to pick on a particular girl in the class as well. I recall that the girl's mum was a single parent, which was not as common then as it is nowadays. He was a pretty sinister individual.

Getting caned with a bamboo stick on the palm of your hand was, for me at least, a pretty regular occurrence at Mary and Michael's. I was an altar boy by the age of seven. I was often pulled out of my class to go and help with the funerals. I would get the church ready for the service. Sometimes it used to be just me and the deceased in the big dark gloomy church. I would imagine the lid of the coffin being prised open from within, and the corpse slowly emerging. Quite a few of those funerals were like paupers' affairs with hardly any mourners present.

I remember rushing in a state of high anxiety, to do the Saturday evening mass, the one people went to after confession. Apparently I forgot to genuflect before the altar on my way to the sacristy.

St Mary &
St Michael's
Church

Unfortunately there was a nun spying on me from somewhere in the dark recesses of the church. Nothing was said at the time. They waited until assembly on the Monday, at which time I was hauled before the school and given six on each palm. In retrospect I can really see where the mindset behind the Spanish Inquisition came from. After a while those sorts of punishments mean little or nothing to the recipient. You become inured to it. I think I was picked on more than most owing to the fact that my mum had on occasion stood up to the nuns and the priests. A mere parishioner should not have dared to question the authority of the Church, or its representatives, and therefore had to be punished in some way, albeit indirectly. Having a go at me was the best they could do, as they were afraid of my mum.

A lot of the girls who became nuns didn't really want to. Most of them, especially the Sisters of Mercy, came from rural Ireland, which in those days could still be quite feudal in its outlook. So, consequently, they had little or no say in the matter. If it was decided that they would join an order, that was it, they did what their families wanted. It's no surprise that they developed a tendency to be bitter and twisted. In effect most of them had been given a life sentence with no chance of parole. What is surprising is that not one of them seemed to have any degree of warmth or compassion. Normally in a group situation like that there will be at least one 'nice one'. I'm sure it wasn't like that with all orders of Catholic nuns. So there you go, the Sisters of Mercy had no mercy.

By comparison, the priests next door were a pretty docile bunch. A couple of them were pissed all of the time; however, as far as I know, none of them were nonce cases (so that was a result anyway). Thankfully the days of trying to explain the metaphysics behind the Holy Trinity to five-year-olds have now passed, as has the practice of school assemblies where the gory sufferings of saints would be recounted (literally blow by blow), along with graphic descriptions of Hell and purgatory. Basically, the message that I picked up, aged five, was this; if you weren't prepared at some point to suffer like the great saints for your faith (and I wasn't), then you would either go to Hell or burn in purgatory for an aeon. (*The real purgatory for me was the Irish dancing that we had to do every week. I absolutely loathed it.*)

I should add that there are people I went to Mary and Michael's with who are less negative than me about our shared experience, and I must say, I did learn my three Rs very well indeed at M&M's, so it could be argued that the end justified the tough means. I mean, look, by the time I left I had already, thanks to the various neuroses that surrounded me, developed an obsessive-compulsive personality, but by God I was a good reader. This was just as well because I could, therefore, continue to read obsessively. A circular argument of sorts, but it works for me.

## REGGAE AND OTHER CULTURAL MATTERS

The late sixties was the skinhead era, and ska was the popular urban music of its time. In the East End it was called 'blue beat'. Indeed, Paul's, the local record shop, had a blue beat chart, a lot of which was made up of blue beat versions of contemporary pop hits. I often tended to like the blue beat versions more than the originals. I continued to buy 'specialist' records and CDs at Paul's right up to the mid-nineties. In the seventies I would go along there every Friday (funds permitting), around lunchtime, by which time they would have had a delivery of reggae 'pre-releases' as well as the best of any soul imports. If you were late you would miss out on the best stuff. There would often be twenty or so in the know, local DJs and punters, in the shop jostling up at the counter checking out the new stuff. Back in the sixties and seventies Paul's also used to run a stall directly outside Whitechapel station on Fridays and Saturdays. The stretch of market there was known locally as 'the waste'. Every week from the age of six or so my mum would take me there to buy a single. I think that Jim Reeves' 'Welcome To My World' was the first single that she bought me. Jim Reeves was very popular in Jamaica, as was Perry Como for that matter. You used to see their albums stacked up in reggae shops. Another record that my mum bought for me was 'Froggy Went A Courting', a bluegrass tune that, for some strange reason, I fell in love with; apparently I played it to death. I think it's a Burl Ives composition, but I'm not sure who sang the version I had.

I did like some pop; for instance, 'Strawberry Fields' transfixed me. I remember being puzzled why this pop band that all the young girls liked had suddenly made something so deeply strange and pleasurable after pap like 'She Loves You', yeah yeah yeah. I never liked anything, either before or since, that the Beatles released as much as 'Strawberry Fields'. I don't think that I was allowed to buy it. I think that my mum and dad considered it to be druggy music. Up to that point they and my aunts and uncles were quite approving in regard to the Beatles. However, from about '67 onwards that changed, especially when John Lennon got involved with Yoko Ono. They thought that the four youthful and clean-cut Scousers had been corrupted, and led on to a wayward path by an oriental temptress. One of my first memories of watching television consisted of seeing a performance by the Rolling Stones (maybe it was a broadcast of the *Ready Steady Go* show). My dad and my mum's brother Johnny were in the living room having a beer. Their eyes were drawn to the TV. They both went totally mental. I think they came quite close to smashing the thing up (I don't think Radio Rentals would have been too happy). I don't know why they didn't just turn the thing off.

It may surprise you but I do have some sympathy with their response. I have never warmed to Mick Jagger. Of course, my dad and Uncle John were affronted by the campness of the Stones' performance. I think that's why they were shouting things like 'I'm not paying ten bob a week to watch a load of unwashed queers prancing about', and 'I'd use them to clear mines'. Incidentally, the other early memory of TV is watching Dr Who and the Daleks, and yes, I was another of Britain's kids who hid terrified, peeking from behind the settee when it was on.

It was my sister (who's four years older than me) who first bought stuff on the Trojan label (the 'Tighten Up' volumes). When I heard that music I went absolutely nuts for it. I liked the instrumental stuff the most. In a move typical of younger brothers/sisters, I would claim those records for myself, and therefore, as usual, we would fight like cat and dog. My mum would sort us out by attacking our legs with a thick wooden coat hanger. That would soon separate us. When I think about it now, it's incredible to think of my sister being into reggae but, as I say, it was the popular urban music of its time. Unlike most people I knew, I stayed with reggae all the way through to the eighties, by which time it had gone, with the odd exception, off the boil. Throughout the seventies I used to listen to BBC London's reggae hour on a Sunday lunchtime, and then around 1974–75 Capital Radio began a terrific Friday night show, hosted, in its early days, by, inexplicably, Tommy Vance, the heavy rock DJ. It was on that show that I first heard 'Marcus Garvey' (and the dub version) by Burning Spear, one of the seminal moments in my life.

# Chapter Two: Teenage Years

BIG SCHOOL

When the time came to leave Mary and Michael's, men landed on the moon. We were allowed to watch that event on television (a few hours after it actually happened). *The only other time they got the telly out was when Celtic won the European Cup final, staged in Lisbon, in 1967. My teacher was a Celtic fan, as were most of the priests and nuns.* My mum wanted me to go to a Catholic boys' school in South London. It was an old-style state grammar school, and was considered to be one of the best state schools in London. So I went for my interview, which was conducted by some creepy monk-type individual. He had an anaemic complexion and a cruel-looking mouth. God, I remember he gave me the creeps. Joy and bliss! They rejected me. My mum, of course, went mental. She had managed to get my sister into a Catholic girls' equivalent of that sort of place. My mum blamed the Sisters of Mercy for queering our pitch. She went on and on about it. To be fair I was far from thick, I always got very good exam results; in fact I was top of the class, so it was understandable that Mum was angry and hurt.

However, for me it was a result; I was beginning to view most nuns and priests as dark, morbid individuals, and I wanted to avoid all further contact with them if at all possible, so God knows what I would have made of monks. Anyway, my old man interceded when he'd finally had enough of her going on about it, and told her to drop it. I was to choose my own school, as long as it was Catholic. So, the scene was set for me to go to St Bernard's, the local Catholic boys' school, where my dad had attended. However, on the ILEA schools list I'd noticed that there was a boys' comprehensive, called the London Nautical School, which was in Southwark, not far from Waterloo station.

As well as teaching normal subjects they taught navigation and other subjects of a nautical nature. The idea was to train young men for a career in either the merchant or royal navies. At that time I had a strong desire to join the merchant marine and go to sea (in retrospect it's fitting that I became a musician... it seems that one way or another I was destined to end up on the piss in foreign countries).

The London docks were well and truly past their heyday when I was a kid, but I still found them a fascinating place. I used to love to stand by the bridge in Glamis Road, waiting for it to go up, so I could watch the battered old tramp steamers going in and out of Shadwell Basin. LNS had a separate assembly for Catholic boys, and a priest to oversee their spiritual development, so I just managed to swing it with my mum and dad to let me go there. Before long I opted out of anything to do with organised religion and daft old priests, but neglected to tell my mum and dad, of course. (*By the time I was fourteen I refused to attend Mass any more, which caused terrible ructions at home.*) Not so long after that I opted out of anything to do with boats. Eventually I would opt out of school all together. Well, to be honest they ended up expelling me. Not only that, they said that if I ever entered the school premises again the police would be called. I wasn't bothered in the slightest.

I was an absolute nuisance when I was at school, so I can't say that I blame them; however, I didn't actually do the things that

I was expelled for, which were driving a motorbike around the school corridors, vandalism and being drunk and abusive. In fact I wasn't even in school that day. However, I had committed countless misdemeanours before then, so I had no complaints.

Immediately my dad told me that if I wanted to stay at home, I had to go to work and pay him £20 per week rent. I had no argument with that, so I went and got a job up at Leadenhall Market in the City of London. However, within a few weeks the early morning starts did my head in so I went down to Bournemouth with a mate of mine from school, and stayed there until our money ran out. I was only fifteen. Looking back, I must have caused my mum a lot of worry; I was a very headstrong kid. My mum and dad were very keen for me to get the sort of education that had been denied them. However, I really wasn't bothered. I found sitting in class a total drag. I felt that I learnt more outside the classroom, reading books of my choosing, and listening to my records. Additionally, I used to watch a lot of the 'schools programmes' that used to be on in the afternoons during the week, as well as the Open University programmes late at night.

## I WAS FRAMED

*It's funny, in regard to getting expelled, to think that the same pattern of getting blamed for things I hadn't done persisted over the years; I would take the piss left, right and centre and get away with it, while others carried the can. And yet every once in a while I would get the blame for something that had nothing to do with me. To this day I am blamed for hitting Sid Vicious on the head with an axe, at John Lydon's house in Gunter Grove. And that is total bollocks. (I mean, think about it, if you hit somebody on the head with an axe, it's a bit serious, isn't it? Chances are they will suffer more than just an abrasion on their scalp, and consequently it's doubtful that I would have retained my liberty.) In fact I know what happened in regard to that 'axe incident' with Sid. I was having a kip upstairs, out for the count, recovering from a binge, when Sid came round trying to kick the front door in. Another geezer, not John Lydon, went downstairs with an axe, thinking it was something serious. When he saw Sid, he told him to go away. When Sid continued to rant and rave, the bloke in question prodded him backwards with the axe. Sid then, by all accounts, lost his balance, and took a tumble. At the bottom of the stairs he whacked his head, on one of those metal boot scrapers (the kind that you used to get outside some old houses). That is how he cut his head open, and as a consequence of that ended up receiving hospital treatment for, I believe, mild concussion as well as a laceration on the head.*

## MUSICAL TASTES DEVELOP

During my wasted time at secondary school, my musical taste deepened, and broadened. Stevie Wonder released *Innervisions*, and I was totally obsessed with that album; I knew all the songs by heart. I still love that record today. The Who released their *Quadrophenia* around the same time as *Innervisions*. The funny thing is, I hated *Tommy*, and yet loved *Quadrophenia*, which by and large was disliked by fans of The Who. I was very moved by that record. I thought that the artwork was fantastic as well. Admittedly it's something of an adolescence angst record, but come on, we were all adolescents, were we not (some of us more intensely than others). Whatever, it's a terrific record, and since they remastered it you can really hear Entwistle's bass runs, which are very nifty. My other big love was Rod Stewart's album *Every Picture Tells A Story*. I particularly liked the mandolin playing on that record, which I think is by the bloke Jackson from Lindisfarne, another of the groups from that era that I liked.

Another sound that I developed a taste for was short-wave radio oscillations. I used to find that those oscillations put me into a trance, and I would be able to sleep better. It was as if I was listening to infinity. (I suspect that the mantra 'Ohm'

describes and encapsulates this cosmic background resonance.)
The oscillations would ebb and flow all night; sometimes you
hear microtones moving around like fireflies within the sound. I
think that Tibetan Buddhist chanting, Mongolian throat singing
and Ligeti's 'Requiem' have a similar effect. The influence of
those phasing, shifting oscillations can still be heard in a lot of
my music.

I continued to read like a crazy man all through this early
seventies period. I remember that Hemingway, Steinbeck, Camus,
Greene, D. H. Lawrence, Zola, Ballard and Orwell were among
my favourites. Even at that age I had a strong spiritual bent, and
had discovered the Upanishads at Bancroft Street library. I was
captivated by those ancient teachings.

On the telly I liked Monty Python, and the BBC's 'Plays for
Today'. Also at that time the BBC had a penchant for showing classic
film noirs, from both the French and American schools. They would
put these on as late night features at the weekends. I particularly
liked the French films, not only the noirs, but also the later stuff
with Delon and Deneuve; I really thought that they had style. I liked
the way the main characters in the French films, like Melville's *Bob
the Gambler*, for instance, often had a lonely, stoical, resigned-to-
their-fate sort of vibe. I also remember seeing Truffaut's *400 Blows*
around that time. There is a scene at the film's climax where the
main character, Antoine, a juvenile delinquent, runs towards the
sea, with the police in close pursuit behind him. He has nowhere
to go. The film left me with an incredible sense of desolation and
hopelessness. I was very moved by it. I quite identified with it. I saw
it again recently, and I still found it very poignant.


RONNIE

My best mate in those days was a boy called Ronnie Britton.
Ronnie had been a schoolmate and was out of Haggerston (a
lot of the boys at school were from the Hoxton/Haggerston/

Bethnal Green area. They would get the 149 or 76 to school). I felt comfortable with Ronnie. Whenever it was a bit 'hot' for him to go home, I'd sneak him into Paymal. And when it was a bit hot for me (at home) he would reciprocate. There were times when it was hot at both venues, and we would be forced to improvise. We were pretty streetwise, and over the course of the next few months became a pair of soul boys. All we wanted to do was buy records and clothes, and then go dancing and chatting girls up. It was wonderful to dispense with the awful flared trousers that everybody wore at the time, they were so cheap and tacky looking. We used to get baggy tapered trousers made up at a Greek tailor's in Dalston. They would be severely tapered. The idea was to get as many pleats in as possible. We would wear those trousers with what was a sort of cross between a sandal and a shoe (they were great for dancing in). We would also wear capped-sleeve T-shirts (no logos in those days). Baggy army trousers were all the rage as well. You would get them from a surplus store in Valance Road, Whitechapel, or from Lawrence Corner in Camden. We thought that we were the bee's knees.

In order to finance all this I got a job as a messenger boy in the City of London. I used to get the jobs through the Alfred Marks agency in Aldgate. Eventually I got the sack for going into the BP building without a jacket on (it was a very hot day), plus I was wearing army surplus trousers. Apparently a BP director saw me and complained. It was the head of the postroom, a jock who was also a Korean War veteran, who told me the bad news. He was all solemn and acted like it was a big deal. I told him they were all cunts who would get theirs when the revolution came. He was flabbergasted and went into a tirade against communism.

Me and Ronnie would go up to the West End, and blow what little money we had left over getting into soul clubs. The Sound of Philly was really getting into its stride (I especially liked everything that the O'Jays did). The big hit in the clubs of that era was 'The Hustle' by Van McCoy. There were also some terrific hard US soul imports at that time. In particular I loved tunes like 'E Man Boogie' and 'Potential' by the Jimmy Castor Bunch, as well as 'Fight The Power' by The Isley Brothers. I used to buy those seven-inch imports from a rather incongruous location: an electrical supplier in Petticoat Lane.

By the mid-seventies clubs like Crackers in Wardour Street were just starting to get into their stride, as were places farther east like the Lacy Lady in Ilford, the Lively Lady in Leyton and Charlie Brown's in Tottenham. The 100 Club in Oxford Street also had a good soul night every Tuesday. That club was a mainstay for me over the years, and within a couple of years they were putting on some great reggae nights there. They were also one of the first venues to put the Sex Pistols on. An old Jewish couple used to run the soul and the reggae nights, and they were as good as gold. I used to stand upstairs having a chat with them, when I fancied a breather, and some cooler air. They used to serve Chinese food there at that time as well. If I had any money I would have a spring roll and chips. One way I used to raise money in those days was to tightly wrap thin elastic bands around ten-pence pieces. The cigarette machines would 'read' those ten-pence pieces as fifty-pence pieces. I would surreptitiously empty the machines, and then flog the packs of cigarettes at a modest profit. That would give me money for my chips, buses and other extras. I still do performances at the 100 Club; thirty-three years after I first walked in the place.

Me and Ronaldo (as I sometimes called him) discovered less salubrious clubs, like the Eagle in Wardour Mews; that place was a real eye-opener, all the real hardcore West End night-time people would be there. At the end of the night me and Ronnie would often be boracic so we couldn't even afford to get the (highly irregular and unpredictable) N98 night bus back to the East End, so we used to walk it. Sometimes the night buses would deliberately drive past you and leave you standing at the bus stop. Sometimes the drivers would make obscene gestures to you as they passed.

Chasing girls became the number-one priority. Sometimes we would go and hang out in Southend. There was some sort of home for delinquent girls down there, and we started knocking about with a couple of them; sometimes they would come up to meet us in the West End. We started running with a pretty multiracial crew of boys, mainly out of Hackney. There was a Greek Cypriot geezer called Leon who had a massive smile, and a few black geezers and a couple of Turkish Cypriots. They were all older boys that Ronnie knew from youth clubs like Oxford House in Bethnal Green. Sometimes we would accompany them out to towns in Essex. We would sometimes have violent clashes with the local youths, who became inflamed with jealousy when they saw boys from London chatting to their girls. I soon tired of that scene.

*I would never really befriend lots of people in the same fashion that someone like Ronnie would. I always tended to make just a few close friendships. I'm still very much like that. I am a very sociable bloke, I'll have a chat and a laugh, but I'm not really one of the gang, I am more of a loner at heart really. A lot of people would probably dispute that, nevertheless it's true. I'm not a natural herd or pack animal. In the Caucasus I bet they would call a bloke like me 'the mountain eagle'. OK, all right, let's pretend I didn't say that and move swiftly on.*

Me and Ronnie both became fascinated with the blues parties that would be run out of those big old (and at the time run down) Georgian houses in Hackney. It was the bass sound that would lure me in. Those big old bass bins would literally make your trousers flap. I was in heaven. At the time the vogue was to play 'the tune' followed by 'the version', sometimes a straight instrumental, but more often than not a stripped-down dub version, with bass and drums to the fore, and all the echoes going off into infinity and all that. I would be in seventh heaven. The experience was something beyond music for me. A limitless, tension-free world was created. I also liked the food very much, particularly curried goat. I don't ever remember getting grief from the Jamaicans at those places, just a few quizzical looks. In fact I'm still partial to a bit of curried goat and rice and peas. I sometimes go to a Jamaican café in Tottenham before Spurs games.

## KINGSWAY

I started attending Kingsway College of Further Education in King's Cross. The idea was that I would get some O-levels. Kingsway had a reputation, among other things, for taking on kids that had encountered 'problems' at school. It was a pretty liberal institution that was both cosmopolitan and pluralistic. King's Cross was a very down-at-heel area in those days, full of prostitutes and drunken Scotsmen (mainly Glaswegians) who had got off at the station, but not made it any farther. There was a large contingent of Cypriots, both Greek and Turkish, in attendance at Kingsway. There was a fair degree of friction between those two camps, owing to the outbreak of war on Cyprus. But all in all there weren't many racial problems, even though all creeds and colours were represented. (I'm not sure if that would be the case nowadays, there seems to be a lot more racial tension about in this era.)

For the first time I met hippies and some well-to-do bohemian types. Kingsway had quite a degree of cachet (for a college of further education). It had a large catchment area, which meant that it attracted some well-heeled students from places like Hampstead and Highgate, and a few make-believe beatnik types from Islington (whose parents were social workers, college lecturers or similar). Don't get me wrong, I took the piss a bit, but actually I liked meeting new sorts of people, my horizons were starting to broaden. To be honest I wasn't at Kingsway for the right reasons, i.e. to pass exams. I was just killing time.

Also starting at Kingsway at that time was John Lydon. There have been a few meetings in my life that I term 'Stanley/Livingstone moments', and meeting John was definitely one of those moments. John, of course, was another reprobate; he was someone who

thought 'everything was bollocks', to an even greater extent than
I did. I thought that was great. I remember 'dismal' was his most
used word. He was actually pretty quiet and shy. He often wore a
deadpan expression on his face. Apparently he had missed a lot
of schooling after having contracted meningitis, which is why he
was making up lost academic ground at Kingsway. He was out of
Finsbury Park in North London, which in those days was a proper
manor. Even then he could sometimes be a quite nasty, sarcastic
and moody customer. Nevertheless, I was very taken with him; he
was about three years older than me. A mutual love of Hawkwind
helped cement the friendship; in fact we went to see them play at
the East Ham Odeon not long after we met.

I think I came to see John as an older-brother-type bloke,
because three years' difference at that age means a lot. And in a
way he did take me under his wing. It was nice of him; remember,
I was just turned sixteen, and could be quite gauche. John had his
own style, sporting long shoulder-length hair (hennaed, I seem to
remember). He was a good mix: part yob and part arty sort of a
geezer. He was an Arsenal fan, whereas I was a Spurs fan of course.
Not that he took the football itself too seriously. He was more into
what you could call the 'cultural' aspects of the game.

John introduced me to the butt end of the hippy scene over at
the Roundhouse in Chalk Farm on a Sunday night. He thought it
was a jolly good wheeze to go and poke fun at the hippies. It was
a different world to anything I had ever experienced before. They
were probably the first proper gigs that I had ever been to, and to
be honest I don't think that I ever saw a band there that I came
near to liking. However, I quickly picked up on the habit of going
to gigs.

John Lydon and his mate from his schooldays, John Gray,
took me along to see Dr Feelgood out in Dagenham somewhere.
Lee Brilleaux and Wilko Johnson were spellbinding, absolutely
electric, like a pair of caged tigers. The two Johns also took me
along to an all-nighter at London University. Kokomo and Osibisa

were among the groups that played. Osibisa, who were part of London's burgeoning 'Afro Rock' scene, really impressed me.

However, the best gig that I went to at that time, in fact the best gig that I have ever seen, by a country mile, was Bob Marley and the Wailers at the Lyceum in 1975. I went with Ronnie B. The album *Natty Dread* had been in circulation for several weeks before the Lyceum show, and we were nuts for it. So we went along with great expectation to the Lyceum that night. It was a glorious sultry summer evening, and Marley was really on top of his game that night.

*All the musicians in the band were top notch, but for me it was the rhythm section of Aston and Carlton Barrett who really impressed me. I had never before seen a rhythm section play so tightly together, and with such imagination in regard to enhancing Bob Marley's song structures. There was a fantastic sense of space and unhurriedness in their playing. You get a similar feeling when watching great footballers. I'm thinking of players like Hoddle, Cruyff, Platini and Beckenbauer, they always seemed to have more time than those around them. I bet that fans of ballet say the same about their heroes and heroines; it's as if time slows down for them (or even like they step outside of time).*

## VINCE AND SID

Before long me and John were joined at Kingsway by John Beverley. Yet another bloody John! John Lydon had nicknamed him 'Sid', of course. He had met him at Hackney College the year before. There were now four Johns. Over the years that has got a bit mythologised, and people talk about 'the four Johns', but we didn't really hang out as a quartet much. However, we did make a point of drinking in the Four Johns public house in Islington on a couple of occasions, because it would have been going against the natural laws of the universe if we hadn't. I also remember us all getting our hair cropped and dyed by a bloke called Keith at

Me as Vince's best man in 2007, when he married his longterm partner Kim

Smile in Knightsbridge. I remember being surprised that Gray got that done, because he wasn't particularly into clothes. He was a total nut about music, however. I always found him pretty easy to talk to. I generally got on all right with Sid because he liked taking the mick a lot, the same as me. Sid had a mate called Vince, who was out of Hoxton. I can remember John Lydon telling me that he couldn't wait for me to meet Vince (yet another piss-taker), because it would be entertaining to see who came out on top in the mickey-taking stakes. Well, he was right, me and Vince verbally steamed into each other from the off. To this day we are good mates. He lives in Bethnal Green with his wife and two kids, and he's a postman. He says he spends his days in confrontations with 'geezers wearing gravy-stained vests, standing angrily at their front doors'. Me and Vince were a pair of what I would call 'super-nuisances'. You really didn't want to invite us to your wedding or anything like that. And the girls we would hang out with were as bad as we were.

ROMANCE

There was another person who I met at Kingsway who also had a massive impact on my life. Her name was Margaux. I always called her Marg, or Margy (with the 'g' pronounced as it is in the word 'gun'). We fell passionately in love. Somehow there was that immediate and easy familiarity between us, of the type that seems to characterise my close personal relationships. To me she was in a different league compared to the other girls I knew. She was really rather chic, instinctively knowing how to make the most of her hair and make-up. She looked and moved in similar fashion to the girl who played the part of the young bride-to-be in *Time of the Gypsies*. Margaux dressed really well, getting her clothes from Sex, as well as from its predecessor, Let It Rock, the shop that Malcolm McLaren had before Sex.

She was also a regular shopper at the famous Biba store in Kensington. Every girl I knew on the London soul scene acquired their clothes at Biba. Actually quite a few of them shoplifted from there, not because they were hardened criminals or anything, but simply because, by all accounts, it was so easy. Security for some reason was virtually non-existent apparently, and those girls could not resist the temptation. Most of them were in poorly paid clerical jobs, or still at school, so Biba's prices were exorbitant as far as they were concerned. The news rapidly spread through the trendy girls' grapevine that easy pickings were to be had. Well, the rest is history, and maybe it's no surprise that Biba went out of business.

On the day that we met Margaux invited me to her home, which lay just off Middlesex Street by Petticoat Lane. She surprised herself by doing that, because like myself she didn't readily invite anybody back to her home, as her mum would often be on the warpath, shouting the place down. I was more than happy to reciprocate and invite her to my place. The easy familiarity between us meant that I felt no embarrassment at her coming to my home either. A girlfriend I'd had before Margaux made herself scarce after seeing my dad attack me after I snuck her in to Paymal one night for a snog and a bacon sandwich. I was so mortified with embarrassment that I had vowed never to take a girl home again.

I considered Margaux to be sophisticated. Her mum, a Catholic, was originally from the Lebanon. French was her first language. Margaux's dad was a Mancunian exiled in London. He was a copper with the City of London Old Bill. I must admit I was a bit worried about that at first, because the 'City Police' could be the worst in London, even more reactionary than the Met. It was always worth taking a detour around the City boundary if you were driving from the East End to the West End at that time, otherwise you could find your car being turned upside down and inside out, without good reason. If you were black it was even worse. I used to think that black people who drove through the City at that time were nuts, they were bound to get hassled. However, to my surprise her dad Tony was as good as gold with me

*At that time I would also be stopped very regularly by the police, sometimes two or even three times in a night. I can remember a couple of scary occasions when the police who stopped me were drunk and belligerent. On one of those occasions a police van approached driving extremely erratically down Middlesex Street. Suddenly it veered off the road and on to the pavement, trying to knock me down. I had to jump out of the way. A big, burly Met sergeant got out of the van and walked menacingly towards me. He stunk of booze and could hardly stand up. He wanted to fight me. Of course, I was on a hiding to nothing; if I had tried to hit him his colleagues would have slaughtered me. I kept calm, and in the end his colleagues restrained him. On those occasions, and there were a few, it was handy to mention that I had just taken my girlfriend home and that she was a policeman's daughter. They would then search me, verify my story, and reluctantly send me on my way. Operation Countryman was the news of the day. Many viewed large segments of the Met as corrupt and out of control.*

Now that I was at college I wasn't working, and consequently was broke much of the time. Margaux was in the same boat. We faced the classic problems that young lovers without much money face: how could we find some privacy, so that we could be intimate with one another, and how could we get the money to go and do the things we wanted to do, like go to nightclubs, and, far more prosaic this one, stay out of the cold.

We couldn't really spend time at her place in the evening, because of her mum mainly, plus Margaux would be driven nuts by her sisters if we sat in there for more than five minutes. It would often be best for me to give my mum and dad a wide berth, at least for a few days, after one of our frequent family disturbances, so that meant that me and Margaux would spend an inordinate amount of time sitting around in the freezing cold at Liverpool Street station while nursing a solitary cup of tea. We used to regularly get moved on by the police when they made sweeps of the station clearing the dossers (who were always very sweet to us). Even in those days (a year or so before the punk thing got going), teddy boys were a nuisance in the area around Liverpool Street. They used to frequent the Jack the Ripper pub in Commercial Street, so you had to keep your eye out for them, as well as for the police.

*I would always see Margaux home after we had been out together, to ensure that she got in OK. It was a very dodgy area for a young girl to walk in, alone, late at night. (Many people would have made the assumption that a lone woman was a prostitute.) I would then often use Shanks's pony to get home, owing either to the lateness of the hour, or lack of funds for the bus or tube (or sometimes owing to the lack of a bus). The late night walk back to my place used to take me through Spitalfields and Whitechapel. There were quite a few hostels in the area for homeless men, and one in Middlesex Street for homeless women. Sometimes the dossers would be kicked out of the hostels if they caused trouble, and sometimes they chose not to stay in them, preferring to stay in derelict buildings. It was common for them to light fires to try and stay warm. Sometimes they would inadvertently cause the buildings to catch light, and the fire brigade would be called out. Sometimes dossers would die, or be badly injured, as a result of those blazes. Some of the sights I would see walking back at night were truly pitiful. Lost souls walking about talking to themselves while covered in thick layers of grime. You could often smell them from yards away. Dossers often had a knack for finding strange hats and clothes, and would revel in wearing them in bizarre fashion. Sometimes they could look incredibly stylish, in their own way. They are nowhere near as visible in those streets as they once were. The photographers Don McCullin and Alex Slotzkin took some incredible pictures of the East End street people at that time. If I walked back from Margaux's late on a Saturday night/Sunday morning, Petticoat Lane market would already be setting up. A lot of the dossers would have a regular gig helping to set up the*

Down-and-outs in the East End circa mid-seventies

©Alex Slotzkin

stalls, and going to get teas for the stallholders and all that. You would have lots of old Jewish blokes trundling handcarts about. It would all look a bit how eastern Europe probably looked before the Second World War. I must mention the funky smell of pickles; pickled fish, pickled eggs, pickled gherkins. There were a number of pickling places around the East End. I think the most pungent one was down the other end of Stepney Way from where I lived. Your eyes would water. However, I must admit that I love pickled food, especially Chinese pickled preserved vegetables, which are vaguely like sauerkraut, only spicier. Shellfish was a big thing in the East End, especially cockles. That would be your Sunday night tea, well seasoned with white pepper and condiment-style vinegar (never malt), and accompanied by brown bread and butter. That would be the only time that you took brown bread. Tubby Isaac's late night cockle-stand stall is still going strong at Aldgate, I notice. I used to go there in the early hours of Sunday morning for cockles or jellied eels. The Sunday papers would be on sale by the next corner. I would then go up Brick Lane to the Bagel Bake for a salt beef sandwich (on white with mustard), a cup of tea and a dozen warm bagels. Newspapers, cockles, bagels and tea; I was 'sorted', as the E generation would say. Of course, if Spurs had lost badly I wouldn't buy the Sundays. I'm still like that.

Margaux and I both dressed very stylishly. When we had money we would go up West, mainly to soul clubs. We would also go to the movies pretty regularly. That was a golden age for film. I remember that we went to see, among many others, *One Flew Over the Cuckoo's Nest* and *Dog Day Afternoon*. We also went to see *Last Tango in Paris* a couple of times. It had already been out for a couple of years; however, it was still considered a very risqué film, and all the provincials would flock in to London see it. We both loved that film. I saw it again recently and it still moved me. Paris in winter, bitter cold, dull afternoons with the street lights coming on, a vacant apartment and an aching empty sadness that can only be relieved by sexual contact.

We used to make regular sojourns over to West London to go shopping. We would get a bus, a number 11 or 22 from Liverpool Street, and enjoy from the top deck the long journey that wound its way through the City and West End and on into West London. Chelsea, Fulham and Putney were really different in comparison to the East End. Those areas were not as gentrified as they are now, and like every area of London they all had their fair share of council flats, firms and wide boys. Nevertheless, there wasn't the same depth of poverty that was to be found in the East End. The funny thing is I couldn't stand to be away from the East End for any length of time; I never felt like I belonged anywhere else and that feeling persisted right up until I was forty or so.

As well as looking in the shops up King's Road we would have a little stroll by the Thames in Putney, which for me was quite pastoral. Actually the vibe in all those West London manors, especially by the water, is decidedly tranquil. You can certainly see why Whistler liked it (although of course in his day even some of the shores, both north and south, of the West London reaches of the Thames were quite industrial).

*I like the London sky over the Thames. I particularly like it in spring and autumn, just before dusk, when it can seem so wistful and yearning. It brims with a dark luminosity. It's as if the sky is meditating. When you look at it you have to do the same.*

I have to admit that Margaux was, considering her tender years, incredibly ahead of the game in some respects. She took me one night to a gay club called Rod's in the New King's Road. I think it was a Sundays-only club. In those days the gay and straight scenes were not as mutually exclusive as they are today. I was slightly dubious to start with but soon loved it. The music was great (the best soul and Philly) and there were no beer boys, or growlers on the door for that matter. I also thought that a lot of those gays had style (a clichéd observation, I acknowledge, but true nonetheless). This was well before the 'clone' look appeared. Good suits and haircuts seemed to be the order of the day. There was an easy-going vibe; they didn't seem to mind a few girls and straight blokes coming in.

I reciprocated by taking Margaux to a rough old strip pub up the Bethnal Green Road called the Greengate. She was fascinated by it. Can you imagine that: a couple, her still sixteen, and me barely turned seventeen, sitting watching strip shows surrounded by a load of drunken geezers? Funny thing is I don't think anyone ever said boo to us there. I'm probably showing my age here but I thought that the strippers that you used to get around the pubs and clubs in the seventies were, generally speaking, super-sexy. They would slowly tantalise, removing each garment with perfect timing. Sometimes they were a bit chubby; however, that just made them seem even more attractive and womanly, as they seductively peeled off their costumes. I'm really not taking the mick. Some of those girls were real performers, it was an art; the vibe was nothing like the rather anodyne and cynical lap-dancing clubs of today. The comics that also performed on the strip nights were also by and large top-notch performers. Like the strippers they had to be, or they simply would not have lasted in that tough environment. Of course, I acknowledge that all that belongs firmly in another era. This is a different time, and most young people today would be appalled at the levels of sexism and racism that were inherent on that scene.

# Chapter Three: Punk

## JOHN JOINS THE PISTOLS

In 1975 John Lydon announced to me that he was going to join a band, as a singer. Well, he may just as well have told me that he was going to open his own practice as a psychiatrist, or that he was running away to join a circus. I didn't know anyone who had ever been in a band. At that time very few working-class kids would have considered forming a band. We all loved music, and most of us regularly purchased records; however, there was no prevalent culture of playing musical instruments.

The initial contact between John Lydon and the other Pistols has been well documented (the jukebox audition, etc.). I think it was Sid who had made the initial introductions. Sid was a bloke who would busy himself knocking about trendy shops and boutiques all day, and had become a regular at Sex. He was absolutely obsessed with clothes and fashion. I think that Sid had mixed feelings about John getting the gig with the Pistols. I think he was excited that his mate had somehow got inside of what seemed an interesting scene, because he felt it boded well for himself in the future. Another part of him was simply green with envy. John Lydon understandably ducked out of Kingsway not long after getting his break with the Pistols. I therefore spent a fair bit of time hanging around with Sid at that time. To be honest I would never feel entirely comfortable with him. I would often avoid him, or find an excuse to leave his company. Without John Lydon to hang out with he was a bit of a lost soul. He would often end up playing gooseberry if I was with Margaux. He seemed unable to talk to girls, which was strange in a way because his prime interests were quite girlie, i.e. pop stars (Brian Ferry, Bowie et al.) and fashion. In fact he struggled to connect with anyone on anything other than the most superficial levels. It was like a large chunk of his personality was missing, or was at least very stunted. It was as if that part of us that empathises with people, and demonstrates and expresses compassion, was missing in him; then again, I could say that about many of the people that I have known in my life (especially those that inhabited the punk and post-punk scenes). However, with Sid that aspect was accentuated. Consequently at times he was too one-dimensional for me. However, he was far from being an Antichrist, or from being a terminal bore for that matter. And he did have a sense of humour, which is often a powerful redeemer in my eyes. Sometimes he was like a lost little boy. Predictably, though, as soon as he realised that he had your sympathy, he would try and take advantage of your better nature (normally by attempting to borrow 5p). You could say that he already had a junkie's needy mentality.

It was at that time that he invited me to go and sit in on the weekly sessions that he had with a counsellor. I accompanied him on a couple of occasions. I must admit that it was quite funny; the counsellor was incredibly earnest, and did everything he could to engender a positive attitude in Sid. Of course, Sid would have none of it, and would do his best deadpan voice, and pretend (many a true word said in jest) that life was pointless and that he wanted to kill himself. The counsellor would seek my assistance in making Sid feel better about life. Predictably I was a wicked sod, and would state that 'Well, maybe suicide is a viable option for

John [Sid]. Actually, I think that it may be better for all concerned; after all, he has no reason to go on living.' The counsellor bloke, who was a bit of a Hampstead trendy-type individual, would look totally aghast. What amazes me about that scene is how me and Sid would have no problem keeping very straight faces, we never started giggling, or gave the game away in any other way, we were both young blokes but were already very good performers.

Over the last couple of years I have spoken to a couple of writers researching books or magazine pieces on Sid. I told them that although I had been friendly with Sid, it was hard to say much, because there was an ever-present vacuous aspect (wilfully so) to Sid that made it hard to reminisce with any large degree of affection or indeed interest. One of those writers, a bloke called Pat Gilbert, caught up with me in Tunbridge Wells. I was on tour and that was the only convenient place for me to make a meet. I apologised to Pat for making him travel deep into middle England. Pat told me that it was no problem, because Sid had lived around the corner from the hotel where we were having our conversation, so it had given Pat a chance to walk around the locale and find the actual house Sid had lived in, before coming to meet me. What a coincidence! Out of all the venues I could have chosen to meet and speak about Sid, I select one a couple of hundred yards from where he grew up. I suddenly felt a strong surge of compassion for Sid. My eyes went a bit moist. I mean, imagine the shock of having to leave verdant Tunbridge Wells and move, via Bristol and rented accommodation on Evering Road (the scene of Jack 'The Hat' McVitie's murder by the Kray Twins), to a tower block on Queensbridge Road. It doesn't bear thinking about.

I saw a vision of a lonely little kid moving from place to place with his poor old junkie mum, too afraid to hope that anything good would ever happen in his transient and empty life. A bit of a clichéd vision, I know, but what are clichés other than well-worn truths? I recalled the first time that I ever went to his flat. His mum was banging up heroin and he was banging up speed. I was only sixteen, but I knew full well that your mum shouldn't be getting you on to needles. Even then I knew that it probably wouldn't be long before he followed her example and went on the smack.

Is it any wonder that Sid wanted fame (or notoriety) at any price? He would do anything to get attention. And let's face it, he cracked it; in terms of twentieth-century iconography, Sid's cartoon-like image is right up there, almost on a par with Marilyn Monroe's up-skirt shot. Sid's narcissistic attitude foreshadowed the postmodern *zeitgeist* of our age that is epitomised by the kitsch, dumbed-down attitude that pervades much of contemporary culture. The subtext that lies beneath the sarcastic presentation of a Graham Norton or a Jonathan Ross is that everything is crap and that nothing is sacred. Nothing is of substance, and nothing is worthy of being revered or discussed deeply, or indeed taken seriously ('apart from the Ramones', I can hear Sid say, in his best deadpan voice).

*Of course, I have to thank Sid for my stage name, which is basically a spoonerism of my real name. He was drunk and slurred my name into 'Jah Wobble'. The 'Jah' part was perfect, of course, because I was such a big reggae aficionado. As soon as he said it I said, 'I'm keeping that!' I thought that it was perfect, it stood out and I knew that people would never forget it.*

## 10 RILLINGTON PLACE

By the spring of 1976 Margaux and I had left Kingsway and moved over to Kilburn. We found a cheap bedsit. We would have stayed in East London but you just didn't really have anything other than council accommodation there in those days. Of course, we could have stayed in squats, I had already had a few nights in squats, but I knew that Margaux was really not the squat type. The place in Kilburn was gloomy and dingy; it had what I would describe as a '10 Rillington Place' sort of vibe. Instead of a Dickie Attenboroughstyle character, we had to suffer a nosy old landlady who lived on the ground floor. She would be out of her room on the slightest pretext. I remember that she complained that Margaux and I sometimes went into the bathroom together. I think she thought that was an outrage against common decency. That Kilburn bedsit used to have an ever-present over-boiled cabbage smell in the hall, an unpleasant phenomenon that could be found in most B&Bs and cheap hotels in those days.

An album by Big Youth called *Natty Cultural Dread* and a tune called 'King Tubby Meets The Rockers Uptown' by Augustus Pablo were my favourite records at that time. We had a nice sound system. In order to pay the rent Margaux worked as a waitress, while I did various labouring jobs. I worked for an agency up Kilburn High Road. One of those jobs was at Wembley Stadium, where I worked alongside a Sufi who came from what they then called Persia. He was a tall and noble-looking individual. He had a pretty calm vibe. We both used to spend time with a plane and sandpaper smoothing the wooden seats that people sat on in those days, so as to prevent them from getting splinters in their backsides, putting out the traps for the greyhound meetings, doing a bit of painting, as well as tending the grounds (a few patchy bits of grass with some bushes) around the arena part of the complex.

The summer of that year was one of the hottest on record. By the time July came things were sluggish at the employment agency and there was no work, so I went and signed on as unemployed. The Oberführer of the bedsit (a blue-rinsed woman from Hendon, or somewhere similar) was informed by the Gruppenführer housekeeper that I had signed on as unemployed and so that was it, our marching orders were received (the housekeeper had spotted the buff-coloured DHSS envelope). The owner and the housekeeper thought it would become a DHSS hostel overnight. To be honest I was happy to get out of Kilburn as it just wasn't my manor. I felt like a fish out of water.

It was around that time that we went up to Manchester for a

week or so. Marg's grandmother lived there. My first memory of Manchester is of walking through Moss Side in the middle of a heat wave (rather than in the pouring rain). Upon returning to London me and Marg went over to the Notting Hill Carnival; that was the year it all kicked off and there was a riot. We found ourselves slap bang right in the middle of it. None of the locals were bothered with us as they were too concerned about getting stuck into the Old Bill. That was the first time that I ever saw a petrol bomb thrown.

## THE *ZEITGEIST*

All the people I knew had a lot in common. They had all grown up in poky council flats, were brighter than average, and had a certain *je ne sais quoi*. There was a sense with all of us that we somehow wanted to escape the rather sedate destiny that had already been mapped out for us by square society. We were also far too sussed and bright to believe anything that trendy Hampstead intellectuals or hippies had to say. There was a 'quotient x' present among us all that was among other things wilful, angry, narcissistic, courageous and bold.

Some might comment that this sounds like any group of teenagers. However, there was something different about the particular group of young people that I knew. They were the complete antithesis of today's 'Big Brother' generation, where everyone fights and connives to be popular. In a way the punk phenomenon allowed for a sort of misfits' charter. Unknown to me there were a lot of youngsters feeling exactly the same as us in Salford, Manchester, Glasgow, Edinburgh, Liverpool – indeed, all over the country.

*I think of us as the 'end of the line' generation; the last lot to grow up in a society still relatively untarnished by free-market economics and monetarism. We had our adolescence at a particularly turbulent time, politically speaking, in this nation's post-war history.*

*The ruling classes were very concerned at the growing power of the unions. They also feared and suspected many in the Labour Party.*

*However, rather than do the crude 'tanks around Parliament' thing, the landed gentry took their bankers' advice, and got a lady from Middle England and readied her to tend shop. The atmosphere in the UK was, generally speaking, moribund and gloomy (while having an underlying feeling of anxiety). It was the antithesis of the bright optimistic vibe that predominated in the sixties. Much of 1970s London was dark and gloomy. You only have to look at reruns of old shows like The Sweeney; mile after mile of corrugated-iron fencing, dilapidated houses and run-down council estates. It was a similar situation in every major post-industrial city of the UK.*

So that was the background scene as John Lydon auditioned at the jukebox in Sex. Some say that by mistake he got the 'wrong John', that Vivienne Westwood had recommended Sid. I don't know about that, but when McLaren chose John Lydon he hit pay dirt, because he got more than a charismatic frontman. John was full of venom, came from somewhere (i.e. not the suburbs), and was able to represent something that lay deep in the heart of disaffected British working-class youth, in a way other lead singers in UK punk bands could only dream about. It took a little while for the Pistols to build their reputation, but by that scorching summer of 1976 it was really beginning to happen. The Pistols were a great band, the best of the punk groups by a country mile. Unfortunately they spawned a multitude of very poor imitators. To be honest I was bored witless by most of the bands on the punk scene. They were generally pretty unimaginative in their approach, whereas the Pistols really had something about them. Once they had been going for a few weeks John invited me, along with John Gray, to see them rehearse at their premises in Tin Pan Alley. I don't think he realised how excited I was. I had never been in a rehearsal room before. Steve Jones really was a very powerful guitarist. I have seen quite a few proficient guitarists with reputations try and do that (seemingly) simple power chord thing that Steve does. Not many can do it with the same panache.

*I recently had a jam with him in LA, on the radio show that he hosts there. He effortlessly picked up the tune that I was performing with my band. He can play; make no mistake. He generously offered me the opportunity to partake in pie and mash after the show was finished. He had arranged for a box of it to be flown in from London. Lo and behold! The geezer who turned up with it was an old pal of mine from the East End called Kevin, who is an ardent Millwall fan. To be honest it was the concept (pie and mash in LA) more than the actuality that I enjoyed, because pie and mash doesn't really lend itself to being frozen, flown a few thousand miles and reheated.*

I always liked the cut of Steve's jib. Nowadays Steve looks like, and comes across as, a relaxed bloke who likes young birds and doughnuts. Good luck to him, he's a nice bloke.

Paul Cook was straightforward and did the job. He really hit them, which is what you want from a rock drummer, and I think that he was lot steadier, in regard to timing, than the great majority of drummers on that scene. In his style he wasn't dissimilar to Kenny Jones (another Stepney geezer). Glen Matlock was very much in the British tradition of melodic rock bass players. Ronnie Lane and McCartney both come to mind. I think that in the eighties Peter Hook of New Order took the bass even farther down the road as a melodic instrument in a rock(ish) setting.

Most of the people around the Pistols seemed to be a bit nervous about me being about, which was silly really, because I would never have attempted to do them any harm. To be honest I think they were probably a bit nervy with all John's mates. Whatever, there was definitely a standoffish vibe with them, but then again we could all be a bit of a handful.

Not all the people around the Pistols were uptight. For instance, Sophie, the secretary of Glitterbest (McLaren's company), always struck me as a genuine person. She was very easygoing, and didn't seem to take it all terribly seriously. Jordan, who worked in the shop, was another good person. She was very bright and never had a problem with us. She was totally happy to come down the pub, and was very down to earth. I thought that McLaren seemed a bit slippery, albeit in an entertaining way. Basically he was a sharp rag-trade Jew, full of wind and bluster. He was very engaging in conversation, adaptable to whatever company he was in. I rather liked him.

He didn't hold his drink very well (although he didn't get ugly, just a bit messy), and he had absolutely no taste in regard to music; in fact, he seemed to have no real interest in music (bar a few old rock and roll records/artists). Nothing too unusual in regard to that last remark – most music business managers, in my experience, are not really that bothered about the actual music. They will often feign an interest, knowing that it is expected of them, but, if you can be bothered, it's easy to expose their lack of knowledge and genuine enthusiasm. To McLaren's credit he never pretended to care about the actual music, which is probably why the stuff he made in the early eighties with Trevor Horn was actually quite good. I was in McLaren's company on a few occasions. I remember thinking at the time, Why is this older bloke happy to hang out with all these youngsters; doesn't he find it a bit boring? Of course, the answer is probably the obvious one, i.e. it was a control issue. It was a pretty unchallenging scene for McLaren. Essentially he was dealing with impressionable teenagers. He could push all the pieces around the board to his heart's content without anybody ever really questioning him, let alone challenging him, in regard to financial and other matters. I'm not saying that there was an unbelievably Machiavellian aspect or anything, although I would admit that it has a rather sinister overtone; indeed, it was one that Malcolm played up to after the Pistols split up. He adopted a Shylock persona, in order to make light of the situation. However, that doesn't make the reality of what's gone on less real. Many a true word said in jest and all that.

I think that to start with John Lydon thought the world of

McLaren. More than he ever admitted. It's understandable that he would have been mightily impressed and influenced by the West London shopkeeper. It was clearly apparent that John modified his appearance and attitudes based largely on Malcolm's influence. I'm not sure how much the respect and admiration were reciprocated by McLaren because I didn't see him that much, but I suspect that the feelings of high esteem were mutual. However, John Lydon is not slow on the uptake, particularly in regard to money matters. Even after the Pistols had signed major deals, John was still short of money and living in either squats or pretty grotty low-rent flats on short-term leases, around King's Cross and other equally dingy areas. He wasn't happy with that and became increasingly frustrated with McLaren. John began to voice his disapproval, and started to get a bit bolshie (or at least a bit more bolshie than usual).

When it became clear that he could not control John to the nth degree, I think that McLaren's emotional reaction was to wreck the party. He waited until the furore was at its height and then abandoned John to his fate. In purely monetary and business terms it was a bad decision to alienate John in such a fashion, and reveals McLaren as a deeply flawed individual, and far from the brilliant businessman persona that he invented for himself on the back of the EMI debacle.

However, I would have to concede he was a very good salesman. The free publicity that he conjured up was incredible, and his modus operandi has spawned a multitude of imitators. His weakness was that he didn't know how to run with that publicity, and make the Pistols truly fulfil their potential, because he still had the limited ambition of a high-street shopkeeper. But in the cosmic scheme of things, so what? It probably makes the story even better.

Anyway, similar to Sid, he's another one with a sense of humour, and that is a significant redeeming factor in my eyes. I think that he can probably be filed along with many others of his ilk under 'likeable rogue' ('lovable rogue' would probably be going too far). It's ironic that John Lydon, although highly critical of McLaren, went on to behave in a fashion very similar to Malcolm during my time with PiL. In fact, in some respects his modus operandi was a carbon copy of McLaren's. I sometimes wondered, after I left PiL, if John realised and acknowledged that, or if it was completely unconscious behaviour.

I saw the Pistols quite a few times. The three Pistols gigs that I remember best probably weren't their best performances; however, the locations were really memorable. The first was at the most incongruous of locations; a Soho strip club. There were some deeply weird, nutty, underground people at that gig that I never saw again at a Pistols show, or anywhere else for that matter.

The second show was of course the infamous pleasure-boat trip up the Thames, which ended with the boat being boarded by the river police, and loads of people being nicked. It was funny that night, there were quite a few yobs about, and yet they nearly all managed to slip away scot-free after the boat docked, whereas a lot of the arty mob felt the long (and forceful) arm of the law. I must say I do remember being a bit involved with all that. I recall standing at the door of the wheelhouse with Malcolm trying to get in and talk to the crew, who had locked themselves in. I wanted to convince them to take the boat down the Thames and out into the North Sea. Lastly there was a gig in Falmouth. I travelled down with the band. I remember it was a fun couple of days, getting mad drunk and all that. It was like a sort of extended jolly up to the seaside.

## PUNK

I won't bang on too much about the (so-called) punk scene; it has been discussed more than enough over the last thirty years. It has got a bit absurd now in my view, with people studying it at universities on media studies courses. It's discussed in the same way as the Impressionist movement or the Russian Revolution is, and to be honest I just don't think it's worthy of that. *(I mean, don't get me wrong, but I think I'm far more interesting; don't you?)* Make no mistake, I owe punk a large debt; without punk PiL would not have happened, and I doubt very much if I would have gone on to play bass professionally. But to be honest I was absolutely bored with the whole punk thing by the summer of 1977. Furthermore, everyone I knew was. For that first year or so it was fresh and it was a laugh. I remember that big night down the 100 Club when the Pistols, Siouxsie and the Banshees, The Clash and Subway Sect played. I was standing on a chair at the back when The Clash came on. I remember that they played a cassette of a political debate at the start of their set; I hadn't ever seen anything like that before, it had great dramatic effect. (I subsequently saw them a couple more times but they didn't do that again.) However, to be honest I didn't really like what they did, it wasn't to my taste. I found them a bit lightweight.

We used to give The Clash a little bit of a hard time, we couldn't take them seriously, all those silly songs like 'Bank Robber'. I thought that they were a manufactured band as compared to the Pistols. I also thought that they took themselves very seriously. However, I ended up drinking on a couple of occasions with Joe Strummer and found him to be a good bloke. In 2000 I saw Joe again; we were both on the same bill at a benefit gig for the Poetry Olympics in London. It was great to chat to him; he was still genuinely enthusiastic about music. To be fair the individuals in that band seemed to mature better than many of their contemporaries.

When the punk thing was at its zenith we all went to the Roxy Club in Covent Garden. Don Letts was the DJ at the Roxy, which was great because it meant we could groove to reggae when the bands weren't on, rather than put up with an unremitting diet of prototype punk music.The atmosphere in there, at least to start with, was electric. I remember me, Vince and Ronnie mucking about one night jumping up punching the ceiling; it was a pretty flimsy false-ceiling-type structure and the panels started falling out. Suddenly everyone in the room followed suit, jumping up and down smashing the gaff up, and in a few minutes the ceiling was stripped bare.

## VIOLENCE

It could really get a bit hairy in the punk era (of course, we never used the term 'punk', we hated it). You had to be prepared to stand up for yourself. If you were from a working-class environment, and you made yourself sufficiently different from the lumpen mass, you would encounter hostility, often accompanied by violence, sooner rather than later. In particular, a lot of the beer boys and teds assumed that it was fine to try to assault you, often with impunity from the law. Well, with me (and my mates) that was a mistaken assumption. This was around the time of the Queen's Jubilee, and that only made it worse as punks were seen as anti-monarchists. We had one or two serious run-ins. However, there were one or two incidents that had a humorous aspect. I can, for instance, remember an occasion when me and Vince faced a very large mob of teddy boys in the subway area below Hyde Park and Marble Arch in 1977. We had been drinking down King's Road, and closing time had arrived, so we got a carry-out, and made our way, while sipping Special Brew, up Sloane Street and across Hyde Park. A large mob of punks had approached us as we left the pub and said that the teddy boys were rumoured to be on the warpath. I knew a few of the punks, they were football hooligans; they asked me and Vince to join forces with them, but we thought that striding up and down King's Road as part of a gang was childish nonsense, so we just laughed it off.

We were both half cut and were aiming to saunter through Hyde Park finishing our beers before strolling through the West End. We would then get on a bus and go to one of the various pubs that we knew, anywhere between Stepney and Stoke Newington. Once there we would torment and wind up the bar staff and regulars. So basically we were bowling along having a bit of fun, winding each other up.

Suddenly we sensed people standing around us; we looked up and saw that we were surrounded by fifty or so teds, all looking at us with their beady little eyes. They were all ages and all shapes and sizes. Oh dear. Before they could attack us, as they were definitely about to do (as officers from the Met stood around laughing, by the way), we got into them. I got a good punch in on the biggest one. Luckily they were so astonished that it caused them to freeze momentarily. That gave us time to leg it like mad up the stairs and into the park. I ran across the road at Marble Arch with the teds in hot pursuit. I just managed to avoid being hit by a cab, but it sent one of the teds flying. I managed to jump on to a bus, getting away by the skin of my teeth. Thank God the traffic was flowing that day. Vince had taken off through the park. I was convinced he was done for, but apparently they had all gone after me.

Me and Vince, both unaware of the other's fate, phoned John Lydon from telephone boxes. 'Fucking hell, are you all right?' John Lydon asked me. 'Yes,' I said, 'but I think Vince has been done.' 'No, he's all right,' he reassured me, 'he just called, he thinks that you've been done, come and have a beer.' I got a phone call from Vince the following Monday. 'Look in tonight's paper, man, we're in it.' It turned out that there'd been an *Evening Standard* reporter following the teds around along with the Old Bill. Apparently the geezer I punched was 'the leader'. The reporter said it was the 'best punch of the day'. I was quite proud of that.

*Against all the odds a writer of my acquaintance recently located (God knows how) a copy of that edition of the* Standard, *while doing some research on a related matter. He gave me it as a surprise present. I left it on the floor by the bed. A few days later my wife was tidying up and assumed that it was an old paper (well, it was; thirty years old), and binned it.*

It was around that time I got into a few rucks with a bunch of white racists who lived near me in Stepney, who loved to give the Bangladeshis (and everyone else) a hard time. On a couple of occasions I interceded when they were giving the newly arrived immigrants a hard time. It culminated in them daubing 'white nigger' on my motor one night, and giving it a few dents. The next day a police patrol went slowly past as I attempted to clear up the mess. 'Oh dear, what a shame' was their sarcastic comment. With the aid of Ronnie B I dealt with it once and for all a few days later. I never had any more trouble with that gang again. One of the things that got me about that little firm was the tatty old state of the flag of St George that they used to fly on their balcony. I thought to myself. 'If you're going to be a fascist, at least take a real pride in your appearance. I mean, OK, you don't have to walk about like Il Duce, with flamboyant epaulettes and all that, but at least keep your flag starched and ironed.

*Ironically I ended up having a run-in with a large Bangladeshi gang in Whitechapel in 1999. By that time they had become the new fascists in the area. My crime was to be white and walk through their patch after dark.*

I must say that when I started the process of looking back at these years, I was surprised to recall the number of fights (actually, most of them could be labelled skirmishes) that I was involved in, they took far longer to tally up than I had expected. However, I think that the era, as well as the environment that I was living in, was a massive factor in that. If you asked any of the chaps I knocked about with then (and I am still good pals with a lot of them), they would make it abundantly clear that I was not really one of the tough guys.

I can remember a handful of occasions when the level and proliferation of the violence were really quite shocking, especially by the time that I was in my early twenties. Those scenarios will not be included in this book. I find it a dark and ugly thing to meditate upon. With the wisdom of age I can see that acts of violence and aggression have a distinctive tendency to simply produce more acts of violence and aggression in the future. Violence never actually solves anything. I think that violent men tend to be fearful men. Although, let's be honest, violence, a product of fear and anger, resides in most men and women. It is part of the human condition. It simply manifests itself in different ways. For instance, some of the passive–aggressive people that I have encountered in life are, in their own way, terribly violent and aggressive. They assault people's psyches rather than their bodies.

Anyway, I have never as yet (he said, touching wood) been sentenced to a term in prison for violence, or anything else for that matter. I must admit that at that time (the mid to late seventies) I spent a small number of nights in police custody. I would not pretend that my mum and dad were never disturbed by the police in the middle of night, checking that I had given them the correct address. Then again just about everyone that I knew had run-ins with the police, most of them more frequently than me.

I was outstandingly lucky on a few occasions with the Met. I took hidings from them in the cells on a couple of occasions. However, there were a few sensible desk sergeants about in those days, who had the good sense to realise that a night's reflection in the cells, nursing a few bruises courtesy of their colleagues, was adequate enough punishment. There was one famous occasion when, after crashing Ronnie B's car over Sloane Square and into a wall (of the public toilets, I think), I vociferously (and stupidly) tried to resist arrest. Ronnie was there with me. I had been drinking, and had stupidly downed a Mandy as well.

Well, did I pay a price for that or what? I took a few hits that night. But surprisingly at about seven in the morning the police let me go. They did me for a whole list of motoring offences, but didn't charge me with assaulting the police, or drink-driving. They didn't even do me for obstruction. To be honest I deserved a few good kicks and punches. In effect I was behaving like a joyrider (even though I hadn't actually stolen the car), utterly stupid and dangerous behaviour that needed to be remedied. At Horseferry Road Magistrates' Court a few weeks later two of the younger Old Bill who were there on the night of the offence came and shook my hand about it and we had a chat and a laugh.

So anyway, that last incident aside, I should make it clear that I did not start fights. I always tried to get away from violent confrontations as quickly and as efficiently as possible. I have never been one of those blokes who relish having a ruck. There have been loads of occasions in life when I made myself scarce when I thought that violence was likely to break out. I may be guilty of all sorts of bad behaviour; however, I genuinely have never been a punch-up merchant. I have never in my life gone out hoping for a punch-up.

## THE SOCIAL

At that time I alternated between various dead-end jobs, which would normally only last for a couple of weeks or so, and signing on as unemployed. There were always a lot of dossers hanging around the Settles Street unemployment office because of the large number of homeless hostels in the area. Generally the dossers would all go and queue up on the same day and be given their giro directly because they were of no fixed abode and therefore had no address for a giro payment to be sent to. But the place was like a magnet to them so they'd sit around there drinking all day every day. I have to be honest, I couldn't even manage to sign on once a week on time (even when they made it once a fortnight I still couldn't manage it). As I said earlier, I tend to be a late bird, and also I was often out with mates drinking and drugging to the early hours, so I tended to turn up there in the afternoon. I used to have to go to the merchant seaman section around the corner to 'bang on'. (That facility also catered for 'late signers' as well as seamen.) My mum and dad quite justifiably thought that I was a useless lazy good-for-nothing, and told me to sling my hook (again). I was regularly bedding down in mates' squats, and I thought that I had better find my own pronto; however, as luck would have it, Ronnie Britton managed to get hold of a house in Edmonton Green in North London. He was supposed to be getting married to a girl that he was going out with over that way. He had already been going out with her for a while. She and her mates were suburban soul girls. She always seemed OK to me, to be fair. I knew Ronnie would only ever bring chaos and despair to her life, of course.

## THE HAUNTED HOUSE

Ronnie had already moved in; he also had a nice car at that time. Same as me, he was still seventeen. Ronnie was very streetwise, and would make the most of any opportunity that came along in life. Consequently he lived in relatively comfortable circumstances for one so young. I had introduced him to the punk scene and almost immediately he had blagged himself a job working as a tour manager for Johnny Thunders and the Heartbreakers. He got me a job as a roadie for a package tour that they did along with Cherry Vanilla and The Police. We were the most useless road crew in the world. I remember on one occasion we had to drive all the bands on a coach from the Adelphi Hotel in Liverpool to Eric's, the famous Liverpool nightclub, which was basically around the corner from the hotel. Well, somehow we ended up deep in North Wales after going through the Wallasey Tunnel. The amazing thing is that no one pulled us up on that tour for being useless, we got away with murder. I remember that Ronnie had a row with the drummer – Nolan was his name, I think – from the Heartbreakers. He threw him to the floor, which did the bloke's back in, so that night's show was cancelled. I must admit that I didn't really like the vibe around the Heartbreakers; there was lot of heroin use going on. And of course, typical of many heroin users, they liked to draw others into their murky little world. I didn't like what I saw in my short stint with them, but I will give them this: when they weren't too stoned they could play, but to be honest I was contemptuous of them. I thought that the American side of punk was generally full of mutton-dressed-as-lamb degenerates, most of whom were smack heads, who could do with acquainting themselves with a bit of soap and some hot water.

On that tour I remember that Sting from The Police was actually OK, he seemed a decent enough bloke. I remember he took a lot of interest in the reggae tapes that I played on the coach. I'm pretty sure that judging from his reaction he had never heard stuff like that before. The job was easy money, but I warned Ronnie about staying on too long with the Heartbreakers because I could see where it was all going to lead. To be honest I said something like 'Ron, they're cunts, rob 'em and fuck off'. But he didn't listen and before too long he had a smack habit.

*It's funny, whenever I used to watch junkies 'jacking up', I would be reminded of the Catholic mass. To them the taking of heroin was like a sacrament; the spoon, the tourniquet, the flame – it really was akin to a religious ceremony. Up to that point I viewed heroin use as something boys and girls from privileged backgrounds did, as some sort of misguided bohemian statement. Heroin addiction was something that was still relatively uncommon in society. Now, of course, along with crack, it's everywhere.*

Tellingly, it was only after Ronnie got into heroin that the ante got upped in regard to his criminal activities. At heart Ron was a very likeable bloke. When he eventually featured on the BBC's *Crime Watch* the presenters talked about him (so I was told) as a bit of a 'cheeky chappie'. Apparently he dressed as a postman as he brandished a sawn off shotgun at the staff of a building society. A scary scenario to be sure, but there was obviously something in his demeanour that revealed him as a fundamentally OK bloke. I can imagine him having a giggle as he got dressed for the part.

Anyway, all that was in the future, and as soon as Ronnie knew that I needed somewhere to stay he asked me to move into the house at Edmonton Green. I happily agreed. However, something wasn't right about the place. I didn't feel comfortable in any of the rooms. For some inexplicable reason I chose a small room without windows to be my bedroom. I found that I would get the terrors in there, especially when I was in the house on my own. I sensed a malignant presence there, specifically in the upstairs corridor right by the stairs. I could sense it waiting just the other side of my bedroom door. I used to feel a terrible chill there at times. I would go for a walk around the area just to avoid being there (what a grim and morose place most of Edmonton is).

I was out on the piss with John Lydon around that time and he told me that he had severe and urgent need of accommodation, so I suggested that he should also take up residence at Edmonton Green. He agreed, as I think he quite liked Ronnie. I remember coming back there with John one night. I was hanging up my coat, and as I did so I thought I saw him going up the stairs out of the corner of my eye, sort of looking back at me. 'Do you want a cup of tea?' I shouted up the stairs. 'I'm just putting the kettle on,' he said from the kitchen. I went into the kitchen with an incredulous look on my face. 'I just saw you go upstairs,' I said. He gave me a funny look like I was having a laugh or something.

That was the first sighting that I made of whatever it was. The second sighting came when I was sitting downstairs in the living room. There was a door with a frosted-glass window that opened on to the little hall. There were other people there. We heard the front door open and saw a large black-clad figure go past the frosted-glass door. We then heard smashing and banging from upstairs. I wasn't disturbed because Dave Crowe had been staying at the house, and he always wore a long black leather coat, and he sometimes borrowed a key, so I thought that it must be him. However, he was a guest and I thought that he was pushing it a bit by coming in and smashing the place up. I was also puzzled as to what could have upset him so much because it seemed a bit out of character, he was normally a fairly quiet bloke. So I went upstairs to remonstrate with him. Lo and behold! When I got upstairs there was no sign of anybody. All the drawers were pulled out and clothes had been chucked about. All the windows were locked from the inside. There were quite a few other incidents. A girl got chucked down the stairs when there was no one around to push her, and a really rank smell would appear at times at the top of the stairs.

We had a few mental parties at that place and the police were called on a couple of occasions. On one occasion when they turned up we were all covered in flour (we had been doing a seance to try and get the spirit to appear, and somehow that had entailed chucking flour on each other). We invited the police in, but they wouldn't come. When they had first turned up and hammered on the door someone had chucked flour down on them, not realising who it was. Technically an offence had been committed and you would normally have expected the police to storm the house. I don't think they were afraid of us; rather I think that something about that house freaked them out. They gave us a severe warning and left. Apparently later that night when I was busy doing something else, John and Dave Crowe and some others swore that they heard the front door slam. When they looked out of a bedroom window, they saw the spirit leaving the house. It was like we had won in a way. Even the ghost thought that we were insufferable. We eventually found out that the house had been bombed in the war and a family killed there. I don't know if that is of relevance in regard to the ghost.

*Predictably it wasn't too long before Ronnie had the place taken away from him. He had split up from his fiancée by then; in fact, I don't think the poor girl ever came to the house. No rent had been paid on the house for months. The only place I can recall that rivalled that house for such a strong haunted vibe was a venue in Michigan that I played during a US tour in 2001. It was a slightly unusual building as compared to most venues, more like an old hotel, with a large ballroom and lots of interconnecting rooms. I don't know what was upstairs but downstairs in the basement was a bar area; no longer in use as a bar, it had been put to use as the dressing room for the headline act. That place was humming with energy. I was transfixed. Somehow it wasn't just a dark vibe, there was a sense of light there as well, and it wasn't cold and clammy. There was a fireplace there; it was like all the light in the room was being drawn into that disused fireplace. The band's meal would be served in that bar area, after being cooked and prepared upstairs. I just sat in the same position in meditation for ages in that room before the food was brought down. The woman who brought the food down said, 'You've noticed it, then?' (She was of course referring to the haunted presence that permeated the room.) She said that the lady who cooked the food refused to go down into that basement area, as did many others. She said that things 'had happened' when they were down there 'that had freaked them out'. I didn't*

All posing away like good 'uns at the Roxy: Ronnie with Debbie and a girl called Tracy O'Keefe (who sadly passed away not long after this photo was taken). I'm the idiotic-looking bloke doing a silly face at the back

©Peter Kodick Gravelle

68

*push her to give details about those incidents; there was no need to really. However, she did tell me that the venue had formerly been a Croatian social club.*

## MANCIPLE STREET AND THE FIREWOOD INCIDENT

After Edmonton Green I lived in a squat in a council flat in Manciple Street in Borough, with a geezer called Anthony English and a girl called Debbie, who was a very well-known (pretty) face on the punk scene. Anthony came from the same estate as John Lydon. His brother Steve was a very well-known face in the security industry and looked after venues and celebrities. For a while I had stayed at a flat in King's Cross with John Lydon; indeed, that is where I met both Anthony and Steve. I liked both brothers enormously and had some very good laughs with both of them. I got on well with all the mob from John Lydon's estate, especially his brother Jimmy, who had a sense of humour similar to my own.

Tony and Debbie were both very nice people, and generally I got on fine with them. However, on occasion I really wound them up. Both of them worked; Debbie in McLaren's shop, whereas Tony was a labourer on building sites. I also worked, but unlike them my approach to work was erratic, hence if I started a bender on a Friday night then that would probably be that, and I would be out of commission for a few days recuperating, so it was unlikely that I would manage to get up for work on the following Monday. Subsequently, as usual I resorted to a nocturnal existence, which meant that I tended to disturb them when they were trying to sleep.

They were made of sterner stuff than me when it came to facing grey, cold Monday mornings. I really upset them when on a very cold evening, after drinking with Vince and a bloke of our acquaintance called Brian the Ted, I chopped up the few bits and pieces of furniture that we had to make a fire. It was a very thoughtless and selfish thing to do. They came back to a flat that had no furniture. I think that was the final straw for Tony. We both found ourselves drinking at the same pub in North London a couple of days after 'the firewood incident'. Tony had a few drinks in him and really went for me; I remember at one point he had a broken pint glass about an inch from my face as we wrestled on the floor of the pub. Of course, no one tried to break it up. He was a strong bloke, and all I could do was fight a desperate rearguard battle. I ended up rolling over a pool table, grabbing the pool cue that was lying on the floor and whacking him. The unbelievable thing is he never went down, just gave me a look of disgust as he swayed a bit, and then he stormed off. I stood there giving it the alpha-male bit (vaguely similar to the victorious ape in 2001, I suppose, waggling the pool cue about), but really I was praying that the mad fucker didn't come back for more. Happily, though, that was the end of it; the fight had cleared the air and we were the best of mates again. I bumped into Tony a few years ago in West London. He is still, I'm happy to say, a very sound bloke. And God bless Debbie, wherever she is, I haven't seen her for well over twenty years. Shortly after that incident the two of them left the squat and I can't say that I blame them; the place was a dump and I was a nuisance.

I ended up there living alone in that squat on a diet of soup and bread while doing lots of speed and cider. (To this day Vince goes on about my diet of bread and soup; that's all I ever ate there.) I had been doing large doses of speed for year or so before that time. I was still only seventeen. In retrospect I think that's a very young age to be living a life like that. Speed in the form of amphetamine sulphate powder was the popular street drug of the time. On a couple of occasions I took crystal meth. My God, that was very potent stuff. Sometimes we would be awake for two or three days at a time. (You would end up hallucinating more than you would on hallucinogenic drugs owing to the sheer lack of sleep.) Of course, I loved the highs, but absolutely dreaded and abhorred the 'comedowns', which I swear used to do me in more than anybody else I knew. We used to score the 'sulph' on a Friday night at the Brecknock public house on the Camden Road.

By the time the summer of 1977 had come around the quality of the sulph was already declining. Instead a 'pill' form of speed was back in vogue; these were known as 'blues' owing to their colour. There was also a type of blues pill known as 'speckled blues'; they were blues tablets that had little brown patches on them. They were rumoured to be cut with strychnine. How charming. They certainly gave you a bit of a gut ache in the days following their use. When you are on speed you tend to really cane the booze. However, at that time I suffered from restricted funds, so I went for the cheapest option: cider. My normal tipples at that time were Guinness in winter, lager in summer and brandy whenever. (Whisky always got me ugly drunk; later on I got a strong penchant for Bourbon, owing to spending a lot of time in the States.) I lived a completely nocturnal existence. The vibe got a bit like Polanski's *The Tenant* (although I hasten to add that, unlike Roman, I didn't at any time walk around the flat dressed as a lady, plus I never even contemplated chucking myself out the window). I used to go for long speed-induced nocturnal walks across London, sometimes with company, sometimes not. I remember that I could not take my eyes off the moon on a lot of those walks.

# Chapter Four: PiL

## THE BASS

I had a lot of time sitting in that squat on my own. It was around
that time that I got into the works of Stockhausen, Ligeti (which
I got from the library), and some other pretty obscure electronic
stuff. It was that year (1977) that I really got into playing the bass,
which was the only instrument that I was interested in playing. My
first bass guitar was a Music Man copy, a short-scale little beast
with an action that was ridiculously high. It was, to say the least,
'cheap and cheerful'. It was burgundy and white. Getting hold of a
bass was not something I did in order to get into a band. The desire
to get a bass wasn't contingent or dependent on anything other
than I wanted to play the bass. The initial attraction was a sonic
one; primarily I was fascinated and captivated by low frequencies.
However, pure 'weight' and accentuated low-frequency response in
regard to the bass is not, in my estimation, the be all and end all.

Basically you have to groove. When you really groove you
forget yourself. When you forget yourself you are on the right
track. It was masterful players such as Family Man and Robbie
Shakespeare, who really knew how to groove, who played the
heavy bass that I was inpired by. Heavy bass had an effect on me

that was essentially visceral; I felt and perceived it at gut level. It took the emphasis away from my head and 'thinking'. It still works like that for me.

*Increasingly over the years I enjoy starting my cycle 'off the one'. I like coming in on the 'two and' or the three or whatever. Normally the one is 'covered' by the bass drum anyway. Ideally, of course, one 'loses the one'. You could say that in a way you lose the one to find the one (true way).*

Up to that point I'd had a couple of goes on electric guitar and it did nothing for me, all those fiddly cramped chord positions, it just didn't feel right. I've got big hands; in fact they're a bit like a navvy's hands (although they also have a delicate aspect not normally found in rough working-class men such as me). They are somehow well suited to the bass. (I hasten to add that this does not mean that I think all people with large hands should avoid playing guitar, I'm simply pointing out how I felt in relation to my large delicate hands and the bass guitar.)

*It is true that very early on I had a go on Sid's bass, but it's not true that it was the first time. Sid hated me playing his bass. He also hated bass lines, preferring the 'punk pedalling' style of the geezer in the Ramones. Sid at that time was living in a long-established, and now infamous, squat in the Warwick Road area of London. There were a lot of musicians crammed into that place, Keith Levene included. I really got on with Keith in regard to music. However, I never really liked that West London squat scene. Apart from the heroin subculture thing, which I despised, I thought that the majority of the squatters there were boys and girls of the Home Counties playing at 'slumming it'.*

I got a small practice amp as well as the bass. I initially played with a pick, as did nearly everybody on the punk scene. However, that just didn't feel right to me, so over the course of the next couple of years I used to practise playing with my fingers. I wanted to be like the reggae and R&B bassists that I had seen. I was very fortunate that there were so many good reggae bands around on the London live circuit at that time. I wanted to obtain the sort of subtle tonal variation and control that those players seemed to have. My approach was simple; I used a lot of open strings and made geometrical shapes based on where the dots on the fret were. To me that was very simple. I didn't know it at the time but that placed me firmly in a modal context, playing a 'fixed' selection of notes that is reminiscent of medieval forms of music, as opposed to playing in a way based on modern-day major/minor scales or other conventions in regard to contemporary harmonic structures. (I won't bore you as to why, but both Plato and Debussy would have understood.) I can remember the 'shape' of the very first bass line that I made. Within a matter of weeks I flogged the amp for beer money. I wasn't worried because I would hold the bass against the headboard of my bed in order to get resonance. So I had this crappy little bass, with a ridiculously high action, that I had to hold against a bit of furniture in order to get a sound. Well, am I grateful for that or what? When I subsequently joined PiL and got a fantastic new shiny black Fender P and an Ampeg stack it was like going from an old Ford Anglia (my first car, as it happens) with a high, well-worn clutch and crunching gear change to a brand-new Jag.

## BEYOND LOGIC, THOUGHT AND REASON VIA THE BASS

*Aptly enough, as I write this, I am travelling steadily, but at a snail's pace, on a train through the West Midlands, the home of Jaguar cars. Looking out the window of the train at these old industrial heartlands is a rather bleak, lonely and melancholy experience, and yet I find it strangely inspiring. It's so comforting in its post-industrial familiarity. To me it's John the Baptist territory. A wilderness of breakers' yards and derelict factories, interlaced with train tracks and canals. I am reminded of three (scenes from) films. Melville's* Le Doulos *(the fence's house, and surrounding area), Lynch's* Eraserhead *(the long walk at the beginning of the film) and*

Stalker *(the train ride down that strange narrow-gauge single track, a powerful metaphor for the reaching out and journeying to the place that cannot be reached by logic, thought or reason).*

*It's not easy to really talk in a deep meaningful way about music generally, let alone the mystery of bass specifically. It's like trying to talk of God, or Buddha's nature, or the Tao. (Those that speak do not know, and those that know do not speak.) Even thoughts cannot reach, penetrate or comprehend this that I am groping towards, let alone words. But I'm writing a book on my life and I am a bass player, so I have to say something about it.*

*The thought of 'riding' the power that I heard emanating from reggae sound-system bass bins was utterly enthralling. Even today as I sit here, my heart skips a beat at the thought of 'BASS'. I now realise that when you truly accept bass as (essentially) an emanation of God (at gut level), as the 'ground' of existence, let alone music, you make a friend of impermanence, everything vibrates, moves, is in a state of flux, therefore the fear of losing what you have, or of not getting what (you think) you want, diminishes. You will truly ride the rhythm. You will reside in the resonance of Om. To you the open 'E' string becomes spiritually vehicular. You can ride the sonic boom to heaven.*

*I just revisited the preceding section, a day after I wrote it, thinking that it might sound a bit gushing, and that maybe I would/ should rework it. But the thing is I do mean it; about an hour ago I returned from having a swim. On the way back in the car I belted out some of my latest cuts. Well, the system in my car is very loud. It has an absolutely outstanding bottom end. When I pulled into my drive and parked, I sat transfixed; the vibration was utterly unbelievable. I turned the rear-view mirror so that I could view myself in it (I wanted to make sure that I was still there). The mirror was vibrating massively. Any sense of permanent physical form or boundary dissipated. Everything was a blur. Suddenly my wife appeared at the car window. For once she gave me a shock; it would normally be the other way around, me appearing from behind the large green wheelie bin, or some similar hiding place, as*

*she steps from her car. I could not hear her, but I could see that she*
*was trying to communicate with me. I was stunned, for it was as*
*if she was awakening me from another existence. For a moment I*
*genuinely forgot what language was. She was laughing (she generally*
*has a very pleasant disposition). 'I knew you were back,' she said,*
*'the whole house was vibrating.' I was immediately ashamed and*
*wondered what my neighbours would think of me. Normally I only*
*blast the music out when I'm on the motorway. So anyway, basically*
*what I'm saying is, it's heartfelt this 'bass thing'. It still gets me.*

## TRAVERSING MOUNT KAILASH

By December 1977 I had been evicted from the Manciple Street
squat and was back home on the Clichy, very much on sufferance.
There was an estate laying adjacent to the Clichy on the other side
of Jubilee Street; we used to call it the 'Jewish Estate' because of
the large number of Jewish people living there. There was a small
library right in the middle of that estate. Whenever I was walking to
Whitechapel station I would go in a clockwise direction around that
library. Whenever I was heading back from the station, I would also
go clockwise. I had followed that clockwise convention for years.
My life was scattered with those sorts of repetitive actions/rituals.

And then on an early spring day in 1978 on my way back from
Whitechapel when I reached the library I went completely against
nature; I went in an anticlockwise direction around the library. It
was as if something outside of me was pulling me. It felt strangely
liberating, as if I had nothing to lose.

*Apparently the Buddhists pilgrims of Mount Kailash in Tibet*
*circumnavigate the mountain in a clockwise direction, whereas*
*the practitioners of Bon, the ancient religion of Tibet, go in an*
*anticlockwise direction. I can't say that I can recall ever bumping*
*into anybody else on my way around the library, certainly not*
*practitioners of 'early Tibetan religions'.*

As soon as I got in the phone rang; it was John Lydon asking me to join a band that he was in the process of putting together. I was certain that my decision to go anticlockwise around the library was the reason that John Lydon had called me and asked me to join his new band. Some psychiatrists will hate that 'library' story, because it only goes to strengthen and bolster the illogical belief in the 'magical thought' processes that blight and hinder the lives of OCD sufferers. Then again they may feel that it only serves to demonstrate the impotence of such rituals. After all, I broke the ritual and nothing bad happened; indeed, good news came shortly after. In those days the term Obsessive Compulsive Disorder (OCD) didn't exist, of course. People would just think that you were a bit obsessive and intense.

Anyway, I say all that because paradoxically my obsessive thinking, which was my biggest problem, became my greatest ally in respect to developing my own obsessive, repetitive style of bass playing. I was happy to play the same line again and again and again and again and again. I found that if I focused one hundred per cent on the bass line I felt good and time passed in a flash. It just felt so right. It was like a duck taking to water. I have only ever felt that same immediate sense of competence in regard to one other thing: clay pigeon shooting. About twelve years ago I was with my wife in Scotland and we went clay pigeon shooting. I didn't miss one of those clay discs; the geezer teaching it wouldn't have it that it was my first time, he thought I was pulling his leg.

## GOLF AND HEROIN

*At this point I have to mention golf and heroin, in order to make you understand why I never did clay pigeon shooting ever again. I have done heroin and played golf on one occasion each. In regard to heroin use I was with a group of mates in the West End about twenty-seven years ago. One of those chaps was a bit of a career criminal and had recently moved into knocking out smack. He was quite a character, very well known around the East End. He was quite a tough guy. One day me and a couple of other geezers called round for him in order to go for a drink. He lived right up the top of a tower block over Clapton way. His missus really had a go at him, calling him (among other things) 'irresponsible', 'unreliable' and 'selfish'. He picked her up and locked her in the wardrobe and then moved another wardrobe in front of the one that she was in; she was going absolutely nuts. We left his flat and got the (standard) urine-smelling and graffiti-daubed lift down to ground level. As we left the block a large impact immediately adjacent to my left made me jump out of my skin. His missus had managed to escape from the wardrobe, and had thrown an armchair over the balcony. She hurled abuse down at us. Other smaller household items followed; we ran for our lives. We were very fortunate to escape unscathed.*

*Anyway, back to that night up West. We had all had a good drink and a puff, and rather recklessly got stuck into the 'H'. Before long all the chaps, apart from 'the dealer' and me, were spewing up in the toilets (if you are not used to heroin it will cause you to vomit). He turned to me and said those famous words 'You've done this before, haven't you?' But I hadn't; it was my first (and only) time. I felt the illusion of calm and completeness that opiates classically give; a warning bell rang in my head. I had the good sense to leave that evil drug alone. I knew that it would be the end of me. It would have taken me over.*

*In regard to golf, in 1998 I was on holiday in Mauritius with Zi-Lan. We won some soppy competition to get a free course of golf tuition at the hotel complex where we were staying. I didn't have the 'clay pigeon' experience; however, I was very good for a beginner (she wasn't bad either). Yet again I got very scared. I had visions of myself in a patterned V-neck jumper and white slacks, rabbiting on about 'birdies' and 'irons'. I knew without doubt in the deepest core of my being that I would become a fully fledged 'golf tosser' if I ever played again. I knew that, just as on the night that I ran away from heroin, I must leave that golf course immediately, and never return. You only have room for so many obsessions.*

79

EXCITEMENT

I can't convey to you how excited I was to get the call from John
Lydon. At least I could now tell my mum and dad that I would in
a very short time have 'a permanent job' and that I could return
to giving them twenty pounds a week as regular as clockwork. So
I went over to the house that John Lydon had recently moved into
at Gunter Grove in Fulham. Keith Levene was already there with
him. Keith was one of the best and most knowledgeable musicians
on the punk scene. He had a wonderful harmonic sensibility that
many guitarists have since tried to imitate. I think he learnt a lot
working as a guitar roadie for Steve Howe, the guitarist out of the
seventies prog rock band Yes. Also, as a nice middle-class Jewish
boy from North London, I'm pretty sure that he would have been
sent off for piano practice or something similar as a young lad,
because he seemed to me to have a pretty good knowledge of scales
and harmony, as well as musical terminology. (I believe his first
name is really Julian. And I must say the name Julian and piano
lessons do go hand in hand.) He certainly had more knowledge
than you could expect to garner in a casual manner along the way.
I learnt a lot from him in a short period. Not in regard to bass, but
more general technical stuff, about how the drums are set up and
tuned, how a rehearsal room PA works, etc. Apart from being a
guileful guitarist, he knew how the 'jigsaw pieces' of a band should
fit together. At the time I thought it was a judicious move by John
to get him in. Keith thought that I would be ideal to play bass in
the band; he knew what I could do from hearing me play Sid's
bass at the Warwick Road squat. There was a feeling of mutual
admiration in regard to each other's musical talents. We got along
very well with each other.

The first thing that I did with my first month's wages was get
my mum a spin dryer from Rumbelows at Whitechapel. I paid
cash and carried the thing all the way home myself. I thought that
my arms were going to drop off. She was well happy. Obviously I

needed a new bass so I was taken down to the CBS store in Soho Square, by Keith and a member of our road crew, where I chose a brand-new black shiny Fender precision bass. I was as pleased as punch. Soon after that we had our first rehearsals. I opted for an Ampeg head and cabinet in regard to my bass amplification. At that time Ampeg was the only game in town in terms of bass amplification; however, that is not the case any longer. It's good that they have some competition, because their stuff is so expensive.

I think that Keith and John were both confident that I would be able to do a job on the bass. However, I think that even they were surprised at how well it went. Of course, it was ideal (for me) that Keith and John were happy for me to lead the charge and come up with the bass lines first. I'm sure that I would have floundered in a band taking a more 'traditionalist approach', i.e. the bass following the chords and riffs of the guitar. As it was, right from the word go I felt unfettered, and therefore I was fearless. In some respects my playing was limited, you could even call it naive, but because of my limitations I adopted a very direct approach and the result of that was very effective.

*Even after leaving PiL I continued to start all numbers I played on with the bass without a count-in. Believe it or not it wasn't until I worked with the dance music producer François Kervorkian in 1983 (three years after leaving PiL) that I (consciously) learnt to count beats and bars. Up to then I knew (in typical self-centred fashion) what my 'cycles' were and stuck to them. In retrospect my approach was very simple and Zen-like. I stuck to my task. Even when I was struck on the head by a pig's head (during the second performance that I ever did with PiL, in Paris in late 1978), I didn't waver, I held firm. The process is similar in spirit to that undergone in Sanchin training. Sanchin is a famous karate kata (set move). It originated at the Shaolin Temple in China, and in time it was taken up with enthusiasm by Japanese practitioners of karate-do. It is quite slow and the breathing is very deep and powerful. As you go through the*

This Dennis Morris picture captures the feel-good factor prevalent in the early days of PiL

©Dennis Morris

moves the sensei (teacher) will attempt to knock you off balance. It's as much to do with the balance of your mind as it is with your body. It is a fantastic preparation for life, let alone fighting. In regard to the bass, I depended first and foremost on intuition. Indeed I still do. It is necessary to remain innocent. The intuition is directed from our solar plexus. That's where the deep stuff happens right there in the core of your being. I love those two words, solar plexus. To me they mean 'the knowing sun in the guts'.

PiL

It took a little while before we had a suitable name. Calling the band Public Image Limited was John's idea. I favoured a name that I had thought of: the Carnivorous Butterflies. *(Look, it's OK; I'm*

*not bitter; it's enough that I finally see those three words in print.)*
We were all buzzing with ideas in regard to our new band and we
embarked on a few weeks of rehearsals over at Tooley Street, which
lies to the south of London Bridge. Nowadays it is a very well-to-
do area around there, with buildings that have a nautical theme,
and those funny shops that sell scarves and cashmere jumpers at
exorbitant prices.

Back in the seventies it was just another depressed low-rent
area with a 'Sally Ann' (Salvation Army hostel) up the road. Hence
you had music rehearsal rooms, greasy spoons and pubs with lino
floors and paraffin heaters rather than ridiculous designer retail
outlets. Richard Branson's Virgin Records picked up the tab for the
cost of the rehearsals and road crew. That money was eventually
paid back from the first advance that PiL received. Branson was
involved because he had John's signature on the Pistols' contract,
and therefore as far as he was concerned John and any new band
he formed was going to be 'his'.

Virgin also sorted the road crew out. They were from the
Epping area of Essex. They were hippies, but because they came
from Essex they got it completely wrong. Their governor thought
he looked like Dennis Hopper's character in *Easy Rider*, but
really he was a dead ringer for Catweazle, the character from
the seventies kids' show. They were a nice lot of blokes, but not
good roadies; to be honest they were blaggers. I think that they
had interests in other money-making 'schemes'. Those 'schemes'
were enhanced by their music business connections. I remember
on one occasion getting a nasty electric shock off my bass, which
is something that just shouldn't happen, because the standard 13-
amp fuse should blow in the plug, therefore protecting the person
holding the bass. Predictably, upon inspection the plug contained
a tube of rolled-up silver paper sitting where the fuse should be. I
went mental at them.

Our first task as a band was to find a drummer. An ad was
placed in *Melody Maker* and we saw a few aspiring drummers.

None of them seemed right until a Canadian bloke called Jim Walker turned up. He was just right for where we were at. I really gave him a big thumbs-up. He was nice and solid, and had half an idea about how to tune his kit. He was undeniably a rock drummer, but he had a slightly funky, almost African tinge to his playing.

So to begin with everything was tickety-boo in PiL. We were all the best of chums and full of mutual admiration. However, even then it was evident to me that there would be trouble ahead. I can call to mind the day that I journeyed over to London Bridge on the tube, ready for a day of rehearsing. I got on the Northern Line tube at the Bank.

*The train I got on was '1938 stock'. These well-made and reliable workhorses finally went out of service in the early nineties. The last tube line to utilise them was the Bakerloo Line. Incorporated into the design of 1938 stock was the famous 'Westinghouse brake system'.*

So anyway, I got on the train and sitting there, slumped, fast asleep against the window, was Keith Levene. He had a trail of spittle dripping out of the corner of his mouth. He was ashen and dishevelled, smacked out of his nut. I sat directly opposite him. I couldn't be bothered to try to wake him. There was no point as he would be in no fit state to rehearse anyway. I thought it was better to let him kip (probably all the way to Morden, at the end of the line). I expected him to turn up an hour or so late. I sat there and thought to myself, Enjoy this, John (referring to myself), because it ain't gonna last too long. I knew it wouldn't work long term with a junkie on board.

Anyway, he didn't show up that day at all. I didn't say anything, but was interested to see what he would have to say about his absence the next day. I remember he invented some cock-and-bull story about waking up with the flu at somebody else's squat and getting locked in and not being able to get to a phone, etc. Bullshit ad infinitum. There would be plenty of that to come in the next two years in all sorts of ways. Nonetheless, I still liked Keith, enormously at times. He could in typical junkie fashion calm you down and win favour with you, just as you felt you were about to throttle him. He was as bright as a button, and you could really have a laugh with him, and as I have already stated, musically we really had something going on. That musical empathy continued right the way through from when we first met at the squat in Warwick Avenue to about two thirds of the way through the *Metal Box* sessions.

## 1ST EDITION

We cracked on at Tooley Street and before long we had just about enough material for an album. To start the process we began recording our debut single, the eponymous 'Public Image'. Indeed, the first bass line that I ever presented to John and Keith was the bass line that became the bedrock of that tune. In essence the line is very simple; a double-time pulse on the open 'E' string and then down on to 'B', and then an open 'A' string and then down on to 'D'. I liked playing in 'E' simply because it was the lowest note on the bass. Sonically my bass amp was set to the max, with all the treble and very nearly all the mid range taken out.

'Public Image' was very fresh sounding and energetic. It had been the first song that we had worked on in the rehearsals. Keith spent a few days working out the guitar part; the resultant harmonically rich sound complemented my deep bass groove perfectly. Jim Walker just needed to add a classic rock backbeat. John added his vocals and we all instantaneously knew that we had a winner. John utilised the anger that he felt towards Malcolm McLaren to good effect, in regard to both the lyrical content and its delivery. He really set his world to rights when he performed that vocal. 'Public Image' the single became our calling card, I think it really made people sit up and take notice.

Predictably there was trouble on that session, which took place at the renowned Wessex Studios in Highbury. There was an assistant engineer there who was a big bloke (certainly bigger than me at the time) and probably a couple of years or so older than me. We were all over in the pub having finished work but were supposed to return to pick up cassette copies of what we had done that day. I asked the bloke two or three times if we could go back and pick up the cassettes because I wanted to get back over to Stepney. He was very arrogant to me in front of his mates. I think he thought that because I was younger than him it would be all right if he toyed with me a bit, so I insulted him.

He attacked me and it was all very ugly and unpleasant. He ended up covered in blood a few minutes later. He had received blows to his head, nose and mouth, but to be fair he was quite game because he then dived on me and we wrestled about a bit and that's when his blood went all over me, it was even in my eyes. Eventually I gouged his face and managed to kick him off, and that's when we heard police sirens. People at the pub were understandably distressed but it actually looked a lot worse than it was. I was fine and the bloke in question wasn't that badly hurt. I think it was just a 'couple of Band Aids job', and he would have been sorted. (I wish the bloke well, it was just one of those things, I certainly don't harbour any resentment towards him, and I hope that he doesn't towards me.) As the sound of the approaching police sirens got louder, Dennis Morris, the photographer, bundled me into his car with Grace Kelly (really), his girlfriend of the time, and took me over to his flat in Hackney to get me cleaned off.

## DENNIS

Dennis Morris was well known at that time for his photos of Bob Marley and of the Sex Pistols. He was involved right from the beginning with PiL; his presence and input were absolutely crucial to the packaging of PiL, right the way through from the 'basic corporate concept', the logo, the first single and first album and up to and including *Metal Box*. I cannot remember a band or artist having a logo up to that point.

*My favourite use of the logo was the silver buttonhole badges that a bloke called John Stevens made at that time. He is now known as 'Rambo' and accompanies John Lydon as his PA. But in those days he was in the jewellery trade. The buttonholes were very discreet and classy.*

The cover of the first single, 'Public Image', was a pastiche of a tabloid newspaper, whereas the *1st Edition* album cover was a parody of various magazines such as *Time* (me), *Vogue* (John) and *Mad* (Keith). For Jim we did *Him*, a gay magazine. He had to take his shirt off for it, and have fake sweat poured on his torso. It was very hard getting him to do it, he hated it. Jim is a very un-gay bloke, which is precisely why he was given that particular 'pose'. There was a great sense of playfulness about those covers. It was a lot of fun doing the poses. In mine I pretended that I was a louche matinée idol. I felt like a character from a Graham Greene novel. I sported a pencil moustache, which I loved. I tried keeping it in 'real life' but was laughed out of court by everyone. Outside of the photographic studio it made me look like a forties spiv. We did most of *1st Edition* at The Manor studios in Oxfordshire.

The Manor was owned by Virgin. Yet again, just as at Wessex, I wasn't that impressed. It was a very expensive studio. In effect, of course, we were getting our advance from Virgin and then giving it straight back to them by way of studio fees. The process is not dissimilar to the old coal companies' modus operandi, where the miners would spend their hard-earned and paltry wages at the coal company's shop. The Manor had what I would describe as a fake medieval vibe; it had a load of hippy girls there doing the cooking, cleaning and waitress duties. Basically they were playing the part of medieval wenches. A couple of those girls were OK; they would let you know, in a confidential sort of way, that they knew it was all a bit of a nonsense really.

*As we all know, the fake 'Court of King Arthur' (rural) thing is a fairly common syndrome with the English upper classes, as it is with members of the rock aristocracy, not that the two groups are by any means mutually exclusive, of course. Basically it's another take on the 'country pile thing'. As well as serving wenches, there was a swimming pool and a go-kart track there, so that imbecilic musicians with short attention spans could keep themselves amused.*

In short succession we did track after track, and before we knew it we were near to completion. In the process I became completely smitten with being in recording studios. In fact I am as excited by the process today as I was back then. I am very fond of *1st Edition*. It's actually quite poppy and upbeat. I'm especially fond of 'Annalisa', 'Theme' and 'Lowlife'. My funniest memory is of doing 'Fodderstompf'. Keith didn't make it down for the initial recording of that track, so it was just me, John and Jim. We had a good drink, and then we proceeded to muck about doing crazy vocals that clearly stated that we only needed one more track in order to fulfil the contractual obligation to Virgin Records. All done to a disco beat. It was a mickey-take expressly designed to make Virgin feel uneasy, but against all odds it actually turned out to be quite a groovy track. We had virtually run out of recording budget so we did it at Gooseberry, with Mark Lusardi doing the engineering. Now that place I loved, it was the complete and utter antithesis of the Wessex Studios and The Manor. It had a cheap old Soundcraft desk. Gooseberry was especially popular with reggae acts. The house engineers were Mark Lusardi and Dennis Bovell.

To gain access you had to go through a pair of trapdoors and down a short, steep flight of metal stairs. It was underneath a Chinese restaurant (predictably, seeing that it was in Gerrard Street). It was dank and smelled of mould. In summertime it would be infested with fruit flies. But whatever; it had a killer bass sound. Me and Mark Lusardi would spend a bit of time positioning my bass amp to get the best resonance for the particular set of notes that I was playing. For instance, if the root note of a line was 'A' we would find the part of the room that had a good resonance around that note. We would then use two or even three different mike positions as well as a DI input. Gooseberry had low ceilings and the exposed surfaces were mainly stone walls, so basically it was one big bass trap. Although the studio definitely had technical limitations, Lusardi more than compensated for those with his brilliance as an engineer.

Towards the end of 1978 we prepared for our first concerts. Our debut concert was to take place in Brussels, followed by a show in Paris. These shows were to take place in the week leading up to Christmas. I had never been abroad and so I didn't have a passport. So I had to get the train to Peterborough to the passport office there in order to get one issued immediately. The plan was to return home after those shows and defy convention by playing shows on Christmas Day and Boxing Day at the famous Rainbow concert hall in Finsbury Park. We scheduled those shows at that time because we all dreaded the annual boredom of Christmas, when just about everything (even most pubs) closed. Not only was the trip to Belgium and France the first time that I had ever been abroad, it was also the first time that I had ever been on a plane. Not to mention the fact that these would be my first ever gigs.

Predictably there was trouble at the Brussels show. We got into a fracas with a gang of big-looking geezers down the front. Their corny leather-clad leader kept gesticulating, drawing an index finger across his neck and pointing at me. After a fairly short set we left the stage. Again he drew his finger across his neck, so I blew him a kiss; he went mental and tried to get up on stage, but we managed to repel him. I think someone gave him a nasty kick in the head. It was then that we found out that he was the head of security. We ended up barricaded in the dressing room, while a load of security geezers went mad outside trying to smash their way in. We had a security bloke with us on that trip called Colin. He was a black geezer out of North London, if memory serves me well. He was a great aid in helping to repel that attack. Eventually Belgium plods turned up and cleared the area. What a way to end your first gig! Most novice musicians sip a beer or two with their mates backstage after their first show. Whatever, it was great to get the first one under my belt.

*I spent much of that trip speeding out of my nut, while quaffing fine French wines. I was very taken with both Brussels and Paris. Within a few years I had come to the conclusion that Brussels was stupidly underrated as compared to Paris. People perceived it as being boring and staid but that wasn't the case. I ended up spending quite a bit of time there through the eighties and nineties. I quite liked the cultural contrast between the Walloons and the Flems. I remember creating a dance in Brussels circa 1984, when very high on 'diplomatic pouch' cocaine courtesy of my Dutch crew, that I called 'The WalloonFlem'. It alternated between what I described as swirly-twirly esoteric baroque Catholic mannerisms, and a staunch straightforward Reformation march-cum-boogie, based on straight lines and geometrical shapes. I hoped that I could unite these opposing aspects of the Belgium state via my 'creation'. I had plans to perform it live on Belgian TV on a Saturday night. Sadly it never happened.*

When we went to Charles de Gaulle airport to return to Blighty we found that there was some sort of air traffic controllers' dispute back in the UK. The flights back to Heathrow were severely affected. I got the woman from the record company to change my ticket to a flight going to Birmingham. I waved the rest of the band a cheery farewell. I got the last seat on the plane. It was freezing weather and snow lay on the ground.

Anyway, I got to Brum and then got on a train back to London. I was gasping for a drink to settle my nerves so I made my way to the buffet car. When I got there I saw a sight I will never forget: there was a middle-aged bloke sitting at a table perusing a copy of *Mayfair* magazine (a soft porn publication), while tossing off, as bold as brass, with not a care in the world. I recall that I was astounded. I turned away and rubbed my eyes. I had been caning the speed so I had hardly slept and I thought that maybe I was hallucinating. But I wasn't. The bloke looked quite like the noncy little chap on the animations that Terry Gilliam did for Monty Python, and was muttering to himself in similar fashion. Anyway, it turned out that the bloke was mentally ill. Two burly transport police constables got on at the next station and took him off. I don't think that he had ejaculated, so anyway, that was a result for the Old Bill (I can't swear to that because I didn't scrutinise him that closely).

I was very nervous before the Christmas Day gig at the Rainbow. I was even more nervous than I had been at the two Continental 'warm-up shows'. Making its live debut was the dentist chair that I used whenever I played bass with PiL. I can't remember where the chair came from, but I loved it and so did the punters. I felt that I could play a lot more accurately sitting down. This was a very unusual thing for anyone but a drummer to do, of course. The chair had first been used on the video shoot for 'Public Image'. I still like to have a chair onstage. (I play an old Ovation bass and the thing weighs a ton, it must be the heaviest bass ever, and often my sets are well over two hours long, so it's nice to rest your legs a bit.) The atmosphere was charged at the Rainbow that night, but there was a lot of unrest in the crowd. It really was the fag-end of punk and a good proportion of the crowd just didn't get PiL, and they were out to voice their displeasure with John's new direction. However, I don't think that there was any real violence. The gig was promoted by Jock Macdonald, a well-known face around the punk scene. Jock was Glaswegian and a big Celtic fan. We were very friendly with him around that time. I recall a mental trip that we made with him up to Leicester, on a whim, to visit one of his brothers. We caused mayhem all the way from London to Leicester and then back again.

I thought that our performance was slightly perfunctory, but at least there were no terrible mistakes. Quite a few people who saw both shows said that the Boxing Day show was the better of the two shows. That would make sense because first-night nerves had dissipated, although we were all still very nervous. My main memory of that Boxing Day gig is getting to the venue not long before show time. I had not slept until about six in the evening, and then, when I was wakened, it was half an hour to go before show time, so consequently I had to belt across town like the clappers to make it in time. I had no stage pass on me. I kept knocking on the backstage door and telling them that I was in the band. However, the security men kept telling me to fuck off before slamming the door in my face. It took ages to get them to go and get someone to verify me.

I had a massive customised bass rig for those two shows. It consisted of two Ampeg amps 'in series' and two stacks. One stack was an Ampeg 8 × 10 inch, the other was a reflex cab containing an 18-inch Gaust speaker. A 'good hippy' called Tony sorted out the PA. He is still going strong in the West Country apparently. As well as the two PA stacks that you would expect to find on both sides of the stage, we also had a stack at the back of the hall. We wanted an 'all around' sound. I still like that 'all around' thing. I like to be enveloped in sound coming from all directions; to float in an ocean of music.

SPINAL TAP

At that point the band had only been in existence for about nine months but already the cracks were well and truly showing. Some time around the autumn of 1978 a girl called Jeanette Lee was invited to 'join the band' by John and Keith. I knew Jeanette from occasionally going into Acme Attractions on the King's Road where she worked as the shop's co-manager. She was petite and reasonably pretty. She based her look on Cathy McGowan, the sixties TV icon. Acme's other manager was Don Letts, who was also Jeanette's boyfriend. They really appeared to be an item. And then inexplicably, to me at least, she appeared to fall for Keith Levene, and by way of that relationship gained entrance to the inner sanctum of PiL. I didn't trust her; to be honest I thought that she was a player. Like Don, she knew how to 'get in' with the right people; she was very friendly with Joe Strummer, for instance. The feeling of dislike was mutual; she hated the arrogant way that I would walk into Acme and take the piss left, right and centre out of her and Don.

Unfortunately John seemed as taken with Jeanette as Keith was. I'd only ever known John to have one girlfriend, Nora, who was quite a few years John's senior (she's the mum of Ari Up out of the Slits). Nora was the daughter of a West German newspaper baron. She was apparently a very rich woman. I remember when John shyly introduced her to me at a gig we were attending at the ICA in London. I was gobsmacked, firstly because he had a girlfriend and secondly because, apart from being older than us, she was elegant, graceful and sociable (a very good laugh as well). She definitely wasn't from 'our world'. I went around to her house in Shepherd's Bush a few times with John. It was absolutely mental. She was absolutely batty, in a funny and endearing way. Some mad things happened around that house. (I remember laughing so much on one occasion that I could not get up off the floor, and I ended up pulling a muscle in my chest.) And in her own way she obviously cared for John deeply.

Anyway, John and Keith requested a meeting with me to inform me that Jeanette would be joining the band. Jeanette was present at the meeting. I made it clear that I thought it was nonsense. In fact I thought that it was fucking mental. I was absolutely horrified. She couldn't play anything, couldn't sing. I remember asking her (and them) what role she would play. Predictably there was no real answer. I recall that a few weeks later she seemed to adopt the mantle of 'manager'. That lasted for a few months. I was prepared to give that a go, at least she had now been given a job to do, but I remember that nothing changed or improved in regard to the running of the band. It was also mooted that she would make a movie. Yet again zilch, nothing really happened save for a bit of Super 8 footage.

Jeanette would unwind with us. However, she was always careful to stay in control of herself. I never trusted that in a person. She never strayed far from the side of either John or Keith. I suspect that I was the first bloke that she ever met who couldn't be manipulated by her. By the time it came for me to leave the band her face was on the front of PiL record covers! Welcome to Spinal Tap.

*I subsequently met a lot of people like Jeanette in the music business. Indeed, she has gone on to carve out a very successful career in the music business (in management, looking after people like Jarvis Cocker). Her experiences with PiL probably prepared her for the most awkward of artists. I wonder what Jeanette would say if one of the bands that she now manages told her that they wanted a shop manageress of their acquaintance to join their band; even though that person was not actually a singer or a musician or indeed any sort of performer. I wager that she wouldn't think that it was a jolly good idea. I saw Jeanette briefly at a party around 1983. I was pretty drunk. She walked up and said hello. I was a bit scathing to begin with, but she made her apologies and acknowledged that what had happened was out of order. That was good enough for me, I granted her absolution for her sins, and staggered off to another party somewhere. And then in 1992 we were placed on the same table at the first ever Mercury Music awards. She was accompanying her boss Geoff Travis (of Rough Trade). I must admit that the first thing I thought was, Oh dear, Jeanette is still wrapping nerdy geezers around her little finger.*

*But to be fair she was absolutely fine, very good company in fact.
Then again, by now of course I was not any sort of an obstacle to
her, I was just a bloke she knew from the past. Predictably she was
absolutely scathing about the whole PiL experience. She started to
give me the rundown on what had occurred after I had left PiL,
but after a few minutes we both started laughing (at the absurdity
of it all) and agreed that our lives now were what mattered. For
the rest of the long evening we never even mentioned PiL. I've
talked to Jeanette on a couple of other occasions since then and
she was fine. You can actually have a normal conversation with
her, whereas most of the people from that punk scene tend to be
very hard work. I think that Jeanette is one of life's survivors. In
any sort of a dicey or dangerous situation I would not bet against
her coming through unscathed.*

Even apart from the Jeanette issue I had other severe doubts
about how the band was being run. We had no management and
no agent. It is not the end of the world if you do not have typical
bog-standard music industry people fulfilling those roles, but
you must ensure that those roles are undertaken, hopefully
by people with a bit of savvy and know-how in regard to the
music business. John's mate Dave Crowe looked after the money
(much of which was kept in a shoebox under Dave's bed). Dave
was a fairly sensible bloke, at least to start with. He had some
experience of straight office jobs. I had gone drinking with Dave
a few times before PiL and we had got along fine, and when
he got the gig with PiL he was OK with me, i.e. if you asked a
question you got an answer. However, when he saw the way the
wind was blowing in my relationship with the others, he too
closed ranks; after all, he was John's mate. I think Dave was,
at heart, an honourable and decent bloke who was temporarily
'contaminated' by circumstances.

So there was no proper structure in regard to the running of the
band. Furthermore, the lawyer representing John was primarily a
litigation lawyer. His name was Brian Carr. He had worked hard

to cultivate the sort of stern and formidable image that would be expected from a lawyer specialising in litigation. He looked very similar to Abraham Lincoln (minus the top hat). I would imagine that it represented exactly the sort of image that prospective clients were looking for in their lawyer; it gave the impression of an upright puritanical, vaguely Quakerish sort of a man. To give him his due it was a very well worked-out image.

I believe that Nora (via her family's connections) had found Carr to represent John in the fight against McLaren. None of us except John had anybody representing our (individual) interests. Consequently we ended up signing both our publishing and recording rights to Virgin. Quite a few people advised me against doing that. To sign both sets of rights to the same company was, and probably still is, considered to be unwise, unless you are recompensed with a larger advance than you would otherwise get.

*Publishers collect money from the record labels, so it stands to reason that if both entities are under the same ownership, it may transpire that the publishers will possibly not be as aggressive and diligent as they may otherwise be when it comes to chasing the publishing share of record sales income (known as mechanicals).*

Furthermore, the royalty split in regard to publishing that was agreed with Virgin was 50/50. That, in my estimation, is very poor; a band with a name singer should, in my view, have been on at least a 70/30 split in terms of publishing. John's deal was separate with regard to publishing; he had already signed a separate publishing deal with Warner's. I think our deal was a 50/50 split because the lawyer had asked for a slightly higher advance than we otherwise might have got, therefore Virgin insisted on a lower royalty rate. I think that it was all about getting an advance as quickly as possible. I think that John was desperately in need of money at that time to pay his legal bills in his fight against McLaren and Glitterbest. At the end of the day it was a fabulous bit of business by Virgin.

I was only eighteen when all this bullshit was happening, and it's a lot for a young bloke to deal with. To be honest the money aspect was never an issue until I felt certain that I was being treated unfairly. In fact, in those early days I wanted us to be independent; I remember asking John, 'Do we really have to sign with Virgin?' Apart from anything else they had no credibility or 'hipness quotient'. Even then I knew that the independent route was viable. Labels such as Factory in Manchester were already up and running and demonstrating that it was far from impossible to operate as an independent. I felt that politically it would have been such a hip thing for us to do. But to be honest no one else in PiL ever demonstrated the slightest inclination to go down that path.

Supposedly all income (including publishing) was to be split four ways between the four members of the band. The only problem was that all this income, including publishing income, would be paid into a company, Public Image Ltd. We were to all become directors of Public Image Ltd.

But what worried me at that time was the issue of the accountability of directors. I had heard stories about blokes who were made directors of companies and were then left holding the baby (in the form of a big debt) when everyone else had done a runner. Those blokes were known as 'patsies'. As time went on I got more and more uneasy about the directorship thing. I mean, for starters, one of my co-directors was a junkie, that's a bit of a worry to begin with. What was I to gain from being a director? I really just wanted to get paid properly. It wasn't like the company was going to amass assets and be worth anything. There weren't likely to be any dividend payments, so what was the benefit to me? I was not happy with the publishing contract in any way, but especially insofar as Public Image Ltd would receive the money and not us as individuals. Every musician knows that the only substantial money you are ever likely to see over the long haul tends to be publishing (writer's) income.

People like Wayne Jobson and Dennis had explained how publishing worked to me. Both of those blokes were Jamaicans (of course, Den is first and foremost a Londoner), and they both knew the awful liberties that had been taken with the rights of many Jamaican artists, especially the publishing rights. Why could I not be paid my share of the publishing advance directly? I was beginning to smell a rat.

Our drummer, Jim Walker, smelled one as well and he did a runner without signing the publishing contract and that was that; his time with PiL was up, because if you didn't sign the publishing over to Public Image Ltd then it was pretty obvious that you would be out. Because the first album and single had already been released, and had sold well, he was able to walk into a lucrative publishing contract. I don't think that was much consolation to Jim. He did not come from a poor background, so it wasn't really a money thing. He had been so excited when he first joined, he had been beside himself, in fact, but now he realised that it was basically a joke. I was desperate to get Jim back, but there was no way that was going to happen. I knew that he would not be easily replaced, especially in regard to live shows. Jim had to put up with a fair bit of teasing in PiL, and I can't say that I was entirely blameless there. I remember finding out (from his passport) that his middle name was Donat. Predictably, in true juvenile fashion, I changed it to 'Doughnut'. However, Jim was not without a sense of humour.

I mainly felt guilty about Jim's departure because he had expressed his fears about the financial management of PiL very early on, and I had severely admonished him. I felt a tremendous loyalty to John at that point. I had felt that it wasn't Jim's right to come in and criticise the situation. I was absolutely sure at that time that John would not let us down. Jim and I hooked up again after I left PiL, and I was able to apologise to him. The misgivings that he had in regard to the finances of PiL were totally valid.

In regard to the financial side of things, if John had said to me at the outset, 'Look, I'm the name here, you ain't, so I ain't gonna cut you in on the deal but I'll pay you a hundred pounds a week, and if you do good… then I'll then cut you in,' I would have been happy. I just wanted to be playing, and would have preferred a more 'straightforward' situation where I knew exactly where I stood, as well as enjoying a more realistic wage. Instead we had this convoluted arrangement where we all became directors of Public Image Ltd.

I was a few years younger than the rest, and admittedly could be a bit hyperactive, and a bit prone to mickey-taking and jolly japes. I could be a wear-out; however, I was behaving better than I had done in the past, simply because I now had something to focus on. I wanted to put all my nutty energy into playing bass with the band, and as young as I was even I understood that if there truly was to be a band, business had to be taken care of in every sense. I knew that running a band was not rocket science. You make records and do shows. You need an effective management structure and for somebody to act as your agent. We had neither. In the two years that I was with PiL I think that we did less than twenty shows. We should have been doing twenty a month for at least part of every year. I also knew that you could not, for any length of time, carry passengers or hangers-on, because you need, in your early days at least, to be a close-knit unit and stick together.

We had already received the entire first recording advance, which I think was around £75,000. All I was getting was a weekly wage (still £60 per week, which to my mind was derisory). I did not worry unduly about not receiving a big lump sum out of that recording advance, because I knew that studios and road crew needed to be paid for, as did our large drug tab, let alone John's legal bills, I wasn't even too concerned about not getting a penny from PiL merchandise, or from gig fees, but as I say, my wages were insultingly low. Additionally I strongly suspected that Levene was putting a good part of that advance up his arm, along with one or two of his pals, and I must say that did annoy me. I couldn't see any other way that he could be supporting his habit, or how one or two of his mates could be supporting theirs.

Public Image Ltd eventually received the publishing advance, which was, if memory serves me well, thirty grand (that's probably getting on for about £90,000 in today's terms), by which time John Lydon had purchased the flat downstairs from the one he already owned. (This was in the days when a flat in Fulham could be purchased for £30,000.) Can you imagine how I felt? I hadn't received my share of a sizeable publishing advance and John had bought a new flat to add to the one that he already owned; I felt that was very naughty. The irony that all this was going on at the same time as John's dispute with McLaren was not lost on me.

Of course, ultimately it was a bad long-term business move for John to do what he did in regard to money. If he had managed the thing better he could have paid the likes of me fairly and still, in the medium to long term, made an absolute fortune for Public Image Ltd (and essentially that was his company, ultimately he controlled the finances). Actually I don't think that anybody came out of the Public Image of that time with anything material to show for it apart from John.

I don't think that John can help himself in regard to money. I suspect that at the beginning of PiL he actually had some egalitarian motives (which were possibly fuelled by speed for some of the time). It was announced in a very grandiose way that PiL was going to be run along egalitarian lines. A new way of doing things was the order of the day; it was going to be a democracy. It was all going to be very different to McLaren's way of running the Pistols. However, as soon as the money started coming in he was like a little boy with sweets; he did not share them out in a way that we thought was fair. Admittedly you could often get a beer and a couple of lines at Gunter Grove, and that was nice, appreciated and all that, but to be perfectly honest a couple of free beers and a bit of sulph doesn't pay the rent, does it? And anyway, unlike a lot of visitors there, I was happy to 'buy my round' in life.

Jeanette and Keith eventually took up residence in the new flat. I was still desperate to get out of my mum and dad's council flat, but I needed more than sixty quid a week to do that, what with the deposit that would be required by a landlord. I was absolutely gutted with the way things were turning out. Remember, by this point we had enjoyed a Top Ten single and a Top Twenty album. To still be on sixty quid a week was an insult. Even when the advances for *Metal Box* started to come in the situation did not change; in fact, it began to get worse, and I even had to chase them for my wages. Additionally nobody had advised me to join PRS. When you are a member of PRS, any song that you are a writer or co-writer of will earn you money when it is played on the radio. No one told me about it! It is one of the first things that young musicians whose compositions are getting airplay are advised to do. When I left PiL I finally became a member of PRS, but at that time membership was not retrospective. So consequently I lost out on a few thousand pounds.

## THINGS GO FROM BAD TO WORSE

By the late spring of 1979 the vibe was getting pretty grim in and around the band. I wasn't as frequent a visitor to Gunter Grove as I had been in 1978. The feel-good factor that existed then had really diminished. John had thrown some good parties at that time. It wasn't unusual to have people like Dr Alimantado, Althea and Donna and I-Roy (top bloke) rubbing shoulders with football hooligans and even the odd toff. It was very West London; in the sixties and seventies the hedonists of the various social strata tended to intermingle around Chelsea and Notting Hill in a way that wouldn't have happened elsewhere in London, let alone in the rest of the UK.

However, by 1979 there were a few others apart from Keith who were now doing smack. An atmosphere of secrecy and furtiveness was evident at Gunter Grove (certainly whenever I was around), as well as a general mood of torpor. Like the abodes and power bases of many a big artist it tended towards being a dark and desperate place, full of people jostling for position. I suspect that it wasn't too different from the vibe around the Rolling Stones in the decadent druggie Chelsea scene of the sixties. The Stones' base was in Edith Grove, which is the next street along from Gunter Grove. I sometimes wondered if that was merely a coincidence, or if John Lydon had chosen that location deliberately. I think that, owing to the influence of Jeanette, he was very taken with the whole Donald Cammell Chelsea Set thing. Lydon was fascinated by the Chas and Turner characters from *Performance*. Both John and Jeanette and to a lesser extent Keith were very taken with the idea of being mysterious, dark and decadent, in the way that members of rock bands traditionally tend to be. Unfortunately, when you become immersed in all that, compassion, empathy and humour tend to go by the wayside. Humour really is the only antidote. The devil would much rather you stone him than make fun of him.

I didn't cling desperately to the scene at Gunter Grove the way so many others did; in fact I increasingly avoided Gunter Grove, because as much as anything it was a drag. I thought that it was all a bit silly really. I'm sitting here thinking that I'm painting a very black picture of PiL and the year 1979; there must have been a few good times outside of the studio, but I'm struggling to think of any, to be honest. On the occasions that I was around at Gunter Grove I would tend to 'cut out early' and make my way back to the East End. That journey along Chelsea Embankment and up past the Tower of London became very familiar to me.

I can't pretend that the problems of PiL were with me 24/7. I did have another life. It was not too bad being at home; my mum and dad now saw that I was sort of 'employed' and so eased up on me a bit. I was still 'going steady' (as people used to say) with Margaux, and the two of us would often go down to the coast for the weekend, in order to spend time alone. I would knock about

Another feel-
good moment
from early PiL

©Dennis Morris

with Ronnie and Vince, and other geezers like Dave Lynch, Westo
and Terry Penton. I never used to take them around to Gunter
Grove with me, simply because there was no point. PiL had
become completely separate from all the other areas of my life.

So by now I was really thinking that PiL was fucked; however,
I decided to make the best of it, because I also knew that I was
absolutely inspired to make music. It was like a physical force
inside of me. I had to play, I felt compelled. I got my head down and
continued the process of composing bass lines, and drumbeats. I
planned on doing one more album with PiL, if I could manage
to stomach the vibe around the band, and see it through to its
conclusion. In addition there was talk of going to the States; that
was a big deal in those days, and I fancied a bit of that before the
inevitable 'parting of the ways'. I also decided to plough on with my
own solo stuff. I had already done a solo single ('Dreadlock Don't
Deal In Wedlock') in 1978 with the Jamaican reggae producer
Wayne Jobson. It was a tongue-in-cheek record that featured me
chatting on the mike. Dennis Morris did a fantastic cover shot for

that record of me with a fake one-foot-long spliff and top hat. It was a lot of fun doing the shots for it.

And guess what? I got well paid for it too. So I figured that if I did do some more solo stuff, as well as having fun, I might be able to generate some more much-needed income for myself. If things had been better with PiL financially I definitely would not have looked to kick off doing lots of solo stuff so early in the game. (I'm sure that would have come but probably not for a couple of years.) If John had let me have my publishing money, or put me on a decent wage, things would have been different. If we had done more shows and been a bit more active I wouldn't have had either the time or the inclination for solo stuff.

By the time I left PiL I had completed one album, *Betrayal*, and one extra-long extended-player, 'VIEP'. That extended EP format came to be known as the 'mini-album' and typically would be about thirty minutes long, which I think is a nice length for a bit of recorded music. Both those records are a bit patchy but the high points of both are very good and still stand up to scrutiny today. Indeed, they have both remained available and 'in print' to the present day, so I must have done something right.

The *Betrayal* cover was quite striking, I was done up like a cross between Tommy Cooper and Lawrence of Arabia. We had a painted backdrop just like they used to have in old B-movies. As well as the backdrop we dumped a ton of sand in the studio. I also went for a walk out of the photographic studio and down Portobello Road dressed like that. I can't remember the name of the photographer or the art director that I used, but they were really good. They both really delivered. I steered clear of using Dennis Morris for the art direction in case it put him in a difficult position. I also kept the solo stuff, generally speaking, fairly light (in spirit, not acoustically). I didn't want to 'muddy the waters' of PiL in any way. I also made an off-the-wall single with Keith, 'Steel Leg Versus The Electric Dread' (Don Letts was the Electric Dread and Vince was Steel Leg). Keith played drums on that. The extra money came in really handy. To be honest it was a piss-take record, in the same way that 'Fodderstompf' was a piss-take track. You only have to listen to Vince's side ('Lonely At Christmas') to realise that. I saw that Don was bitching recently about his part in that EP. He complained that no one on the session, myself included, appreciated that the lyrics that he wrote for 'Haille Unlikely' were really going out on a limb in regard to the prevailing attitude of the Rasta movement of the time. Well, we did appreciate them (not so much their delivery, more the sentiments behind them), that's why we used them. I felt that black separatists were just as mistaken in their views as white separatists.

Don used to remind me of Dustin Hoffman's Ratzo character from the movie *Midnight Cowboy*. (I really don't mean that in an entirely derogatory way. I had a certain sneaking regard for Ratzo too.) Don is certainly 'streetwise' smart and can weigh people up in an instant. His eyes dart around continuously behind his tinted glasses, as he talks fast. He has played his hand of cards extremely well. He has worked himself into a position whereby all the 'mug punters' see him as the man in the know in regard to the punk era.

Don was a hustler who flogged dope, and played up to his role as 'Rasta friend to the stars'. When I first came across him I gave him a hard time. I thought that he was all mouth and trousers. After a while I stopped that, when, at least when talking to me, he had the sense to stop the fast-talk bullshit. When the bullshit is taken out of the equation you have a much better chance of getting on with people. We actually had some nice, sensible conversations. I remember him telling me that as far as he was concerned everyone was a hustler, but that the cake was big enough for everyone to get a slice. He frowned on people getting completely taken to the cleaners and being denied their slice. I thought that was an eminently reasonable point of view. He has done one thing (that I know of) in his career as a director that I thought was very good. It was a documentary on Gil Scott-Heron for BBC 4. It made for compelling viewing. I couldn't believe it when I saw his name as director on the end credits, so fair play to him there.

## FILM TREATMENT IDEA

*The one bit of power that I had left in the PiL situation, apart from putting down good B-lines, was that I was still able to book studio time at Gooseberry without anyone interfering. There was a bit of muttering about pulling the plug on my Gooseberry visits from Jeanette, but I made it clear that if that happened I was 'up the road'. It really would be game over. It was at The Manor, in the garden, that she tested my resolve. Behind her stood Keith and the rest of the PiL entourage, minus John. I was very firm in the way that I told her 'no'. Not histrionic or flamboyant in the way a Latin might be. I was quietly forthright; a bit similar to Gary Cooper in High Noon, even if I do say so myself. There was a stand-off. I stood facing Jeanette and the others. I had the sun behind me; they were all squinting their eyes. But my gaze was unwavering. A bead of perspiration ran down Levene's face; he knew that he was double-dealing, the low-down, yellow-bellied sidewinder. Everything was silent except for the sound of a door banging fitfully in the distance, and the high-pitched whine of the wind as it rushed over the rolling Chilterns. We stood there for what seemed an age. Suddenly there was the sound of somebody hawking phlegm from an upstairs window. It was John Lydon; he spat his brown-stained spit into the bird bath that stood on the lawn. There was resonant sound, almost metallic in nature, as the thick liquid hit the side of the ornate bird bath. With the minutest jerk of his head he summoned Jeanette and the others back into the TV lounge. I reholstered my bass in its case and set off for Chinatown; I'd be there by sundown.*

# Chapter Five: The Metal Box

## THE METAL BOX

So I continued to go down to Chinatown to visit Gooseberry. In fits and starts, we also continued to work at both The Manor and the Townhouse Studios. I considered Townhouse to be the lesser of two evils because we were more productive there than at The Manor, where John and Jeanette would sit like couch potatoes watching videos for hours on end, while Keith would be off scoring. Plus The Manor was out in the sticks, and at that time I hated the countryside, especially Oxfordshire. It was Middle England to the power of ten. One bright spot was the fact that I had passed my driving test. I was able to use the advance money from my solo stuff to get a car. Of course, as soon as I got the car I was bombing about all over London. It meant that when there was nothing happening at The Manor I could slip off no matter what the time was to go and see some pals, or else go and do some work at Gooseberry.

By now I had a funny little Roland analogue rhythm box, a little 'wasp' analogue synth, my short-wave radio, a Godwin String Synth and some other bits and pieces, such as hand percussion and a melodica, in my bedroom at Paymal, as well as my bass and little practice amp. I would play and develop lines for hours at a time. I used to feel engulfed by the music. It was as if I was being pushed along by a force from outside of myself; I felt exhilarated for long periods while playing. I still feel like that most of the time that I play (excluding band rehearsals, they nearly always feel like 'work'). Playing to the rhythm box for long periods of time was very good for my timing, and for my stamina (mental and physical) and ability to stay focused. I built up a whole catalogue of lines. I would nearly always start the process with no preconceptions, as if it was the first line that I had ever done. I still take that approach. It's like always being a beginner. Shunryu Suzuki said, 'In the beginner's mind there are many possibilities, but in the expert's there are few.'

However, there are bass lines that come in that 'unknowing way' which then need to be honed and refined. Among them was 'Poptones'. I still see that tune as the jewel in the PiL crown. It was actually influenced by the octave runs that you can hear bass players doing on disco records in that era. ('Swanlake/Death Disco' is also quite disco inspired.) 'Poptones' has a funny little chromatic 'B' part in it that matches the octave-based 'A' part perfectly. I wanted a modulated (moving) line that was spread over the full three octaves of the bass and yet was also a fixed regular groove, with a specific pulse. I had noticed that with 'Theme' from *1st Edition*, when I modulated a line over three octaves, and kept the tempo down, it made the most of Levene's tonally rich guitar sound. I felt that we could 'go one better' and do something really unique; simple and modal with the PiL 'primitive vibe' and yet at the same time very musical. That line is as symmetrical as a snowflake. To give him his due Levene went mental for it. We were at The Manor. We had a drummer with us who was pretty good, he played on one of my solo tracks, but the bloke just couldn't get the right feel for 'Poptones'. He kept going double time, when it was patently obvious that the track needed more of a laid-back, half-time sort of a groove on the drums. In the end Levene put the drums down on that track; his drums are a bit loose, but that is actually a good thing. I sometimes prefer the vibe of a capable musician playing the drums rather than a 'proper' drummer. I love Stevie Wonder's drumming, for instance, and I once saw a video of the singer Chaka Khan drumming, which was really very good indeed.

It took him a day or so but eventually Levene put down that killer guitar part. John fell in love with the track and got busy putting the lyrics together. It was always exciting waiting for John to put down his vocals, and in my view there isn't a duff vocal performance on *Metal Box*. That is just about how every PiL track came together: bass, drumbeat, guitar (or in the latter stages synth tones) and then John's vocal. Being a three-piece-cum-four-piece band, who did not do harmony vocals (thank God), once his vocal was down that was it, that was the track, bar the mixing, done. I think the lyrics to 'Poptones', in part at least, refer to a journey we took in Joe the roadie's 'Japanese car', out around the country lanes of Oxfordshire. As usual the sulph had been caned in the days previous and the comedown beckoned, so no one was saying much, and Joe had one of his dodgy cassettes playing. I think that Nora was there. The lines about 'foliage and peat' and 'losing my body heat' apparently referred to a kidnapping/murder case that John had read about. I may have all that completely wrong, but I would wager not. Whatever, it is a haunting track. We all really gelled together on it.

By now that was just about the only time that I got along with John or Keith; when we were actually in the studio working. In fact I can't even remember one major bust-up or big disagreement in the studio. It is often said that it was because of the darkness and confusion around PiL that *Metal Box* was such a classic recording. However, I now think that the reverse is true: *Metal Box* was an artistic success in spite of the massive problems in and around the band.

Outside of the studio the atmosphere between me and the

others was, by and large, increasingly poisonous. I have vivid memories of Thatcher's victory in the general election that year. We were in the studio on the night/day that she won. It was on the telly in the corner with the sound turned down. (There stood Thatcher, as bold as brass, misappropriating St Francis of Assisi's prayer, looking for all the world like a madwoman.) I was banging on about what bad news it was. But everybody in the studio, including the engineers, was absolutely unconcerned (in fact a bit into it possibly; there were a lot of closet Thatcher fans around in the music business). Keith especially was completely apolitical.

*Anyway, I tell you that because I desperately want you to be convinced of my left-wing humanitarian values. Whereas some of the others (I'm not naming names here), whenever a 'take' went well, would run about the studio with their 'I love General Franco' T-shirts pulled up over their heads, in the fashion of Premiership footballers when they score a goal.*

It was at Townhouse that we did 'Careering', which is my second-favourite track from *Metal Box* – 'Poptones' is my favourite – and probably my favourite John Lydon vocal performance. Yet again it's not a 'proper drummer' on 'Careering'; I put the drums down on that track. If you listen to the drum rhythm it is very similar to the sort of rhythm a drum-and-fife band would create, especially the Turkish military version of that (such a thing exists). It is probably the most 'dubby' thing that is on *Metal Box*. The B-line is all on the E string, but it is melodic nevertheless, with one half of the line ascending and the other half descending. By now Keith had got hold of a Prophet synth. He used that on 'Careering'.

*By that time Levene was virtually a spent force as a guitarist. His mind was scattered; it wasn't focused on the job at hand; most of the time his mind was on getting down the Grove, so that he could make his connection. Make no mistake, junk was his primary concern. So towards the end of the* Metal Box *sessions he was riddled with insecurity, far more interested in feeding his habit and manipulating the situation to his advantage than in developing or refining his guitar style. If you doubt what I say, think of one guitar part that he has done since then that would stand up to comparison with his guitar parts on 'Public Image', 'Theme' or 'Poptones'. Those tracks contain my three favourite Levene PiL guitar parts. They are the three tunes that he really got it together on, and they are now very nearly thirty years old.*

The drums on 'The Suit' are actually an analogue loop that I made at Gooseberry with Mark Lusardi. I played the drums and we mixed it down to quarter-inch tape, cutting it to length and then using editing tape to connect the ends (loop it). I then stood with a pencil held at a fixed point until the 'take' (back on to multi-track) was completed. I played the bass like a 'sample'. I made it lurch slightly, like a loop regenerating; it's pretty hip stuff that was way ahead of its time. In fact the bass and drums had originally been used on my solo track 'Blueberry Hill'. As soon as I had finished my own mix I nipped up to The Manor with the multi-track. I remember cajoling John out of the 'telly and video' room at The Manor to check it out. I suspect that he hated using stuff that I was originating elsewhere, but when the stuff was as good as 'The Suit' what could he say? Any bad feeling temporarily diminished and we got on with it.

Apart from me and Keith we used three other drummers on *Metal Box*: Dave Humphreys, Richard Dudanski and lastly Martin Atkins, who played on one track, 'Bad Baby'. I love his vocal melody line on that track. Augustus Pablo would have loved that melody. Anyway, Martin Atkins had checked a lot of disco out and that resulted in him having a good 'high hat technique', and OK timekeeping. (My bass playing on 'Bad Baby' was inspired by the style of a bass player called Cecil McBee.) I found that Richard Dudanski tended to gain time a bit (which to be fair can be a good thing to do sometimes); however, his overall style was very good. He made extensive and imaginative use of the toms, which really suited compositions like 'No Birds' and 'Socialist'. Dave Humphreys was a good all-round drummer with a good steady backbeat. It is sometimes said that the drummers on the PiL sessions were given a hard time and that they were bullied. However, that isn't true. I certainly don't remember it that way. I got on with all of them better than anyone did. To be honest it worked out well having so many different sorts of drummers contribute to the album. Their differences of style helped to give it rhythmical variation.

There were one or two drummers who came down to audition around the time of *Metal Box* but for one reason or another it didn't work out. I remember one of those blokes doing a bit of speed and getting straight on to the (at the time ubiquitous) Space Invaders machine. He also did a couple of tabs of acid. It was apparent after two or three days that he was now seeing Space Invaders everywhere he looked. He ended up propped up in his four-poster bed (in his super-large bedroom) while we kept him amused by doing a 'Space Invaders live' routine. I'm pretty sure that it was me, John and Keith and a couple of others; we set fire to some newspaper that we had spread out on his floor (we wanted the fire and smoke to make an atmosphere). We then shuffled from wall to wall with completely blank faces, slowly at first, and then faster and faster as we gradually got nearer to him. We would drop out one by one (much like in the video game) until there was only one of us moving frantically. Meanwhile the drummer had some sort of mock console in his hands and had the illusion that he was controlling the game and shooting us. It was great fun; the bloke had eyes like saucers and was laughing manically. The newspaper fires that we had lit caused a bit of damage. Virgin were very concerned that we would burn the place down and complained. It was of course a stupid thing to have done; we just hadn't thought it through. We were stupid young blokes letting off steam, albeit in an irresponsible and dangerous fashion.

## UMBRELLAS

There was a lot of talk in interviews at that time of PiL being not so much a band as an umbrella organisation. I once quipped, after hearing that bullshit term for the hundredth time, 'Yeah, what we mean is we're going to sell brollies down the market when all this goes tits up.' That didn't go down too well with the others (who, following John's lead, were all especially po-faced that day). I was one hundred per cent convinced that nothing would ever come of the oft-quoted 'umbrella organisation'. I think that Keith saw the term on a financial page of a newspaper and thought that it looked impressive. It certainly inspired a lot of megalomaniac fantasies in the band, concerning making films and 'er, making videos'. I knew that nothing would ever come of this 'umbrella organisation' thing, I thought that it was complete and utter bullshit. It turned out that I was right. It amazed me at the time how journalists would never pin them down; I started to realise that you could get away with saying any old bollocks. Most music journalists are even tamer nowadays.

## DECONSTRUCTION

*I could see where they were, albeit in a very muddled fashion, trying to go; into the conceptual realms so revered by 'modern artists', where you break down hierarchies as well as the borders and divisions between entities. At the time I intuitively recoiled from it. (I didn't know then about all the ins and outs of modern art or the situationalists, but I had seen Hancock's The Rebel.) Looking back, my instincts were sound. I now know that the non-direction that PiL were beginning to take is indicative of the sort of woolly-minded thinking that lay at the root of deconstructionist theories (of course, the deconstructionists would say that there is no root). That sort of thinking infects so much of the postmodern world that we inhabit, and paradoxically results in the sort of static unimaginative thought patterns that produce the worst excesses of (stiff and unyielding) political correctness, as well as cold, brutal, inhumane modern art. Ultimately it's a lazy and self-deluded way of dealing with the world which is nihilistic and detached. And of course you don't get rid of hierarchies, you just form new ones. Legions of hippies have been led sheep-like into thinking that way since the sixties. Unfortunately some of them now work within governments and in other powerful positions. They will be the death of us if we're not careful. A fifth column is what they are.*

*Well, they say that even a stopped clock is right twice a day, and I can think of at least one successful example of deconstructionist theories in action. It just so happens that it's in sport rather than literature or art. Renus Michel's Dutch football team of 1974 was a thrilling example of the dissolution of structure and hierarchy. You may be thinking, Well, that's big of you to allow just one example. However, please don't go thinking that I'm a 'set in stone' traditionalist, who is probably still trying to come to terms with the Reformation, let alone Darwinism. I know full well that ultimately there is no hierarchy, indeed that there is no 'centre'. But I do know that there is a process to follow, parts to be played, responsibilities to be fulfilled, and that it is indeed good to be good.*

## THE METAL CONTAINER

The recording of *Metal Box* took about nine months or so to complete. The time came for discussions on the album sleeve. I was surprised to be included in the discussions, because by now there was a feeling of antipathy lying just under the surface between me and Lydon. To begin with it was John, Dennis Morris and myself discussing it, and the idea of a cardboard sleeve was kicked into touch very quickly, as was the bog-standard 33 rpm album. We were unanimous that it had to be a completely different sort of presentation. One of the main reasons that we went for three 45s (although I seem to remember that the last side was 33⅓ rpm) was because we wanted to get the best bass response possible. The combination of wider groove space on the discs plus the increased rpm helps to give a good bass response.

Various materials were discussed, as was the potential cost of getting vinyl-sized containers made up. For reasons of an aesthetical, practical and financial nature, wood, plastic, glass and cloth were rejected. We kept coming back to metal. I'm pretty sure it was John who said that it should be called *Metal Box*. Dennis Morris kicked into gear. He had actually gone to school near one of the Metal Box Company's sites in Clapton. What really clinched the final decision in favour of metal was the fact that the Metal Box Company already manufactured round metal canisters; mainly for use as cinefilm containers. Dennis knew that, and so he helped broker a deal.

## CHRIS DROPS BY AND DENNIS DEPARTS

It was around that time that we had a meeting with Chris Blackwell, the boss of Island Records. Dennis Morris set it up. As I recall there was a distinct possibility that the American rights for PiL would be available, and Chris was very interested in that. I remember that Chris had a glamour model in tow. Her name was Minah Bird; I think that she was the first black page-three girl. I must admit that she was a hell of a looker. We all had a beer and then we clambered into Chris's Bentley and went to a restaurant in Notting Hill (when it was still Notting Hill). I was absolutely thrilled to meet Chris Blackwell; after all, this was the bloke who had 'discovered' Bob Marley. I was very excited that night because even I, the silly kid that I was, knew that to link up with Chris would be a very smart move. I was very impressed with the steadfast and intelligent way that he had worked on breaking Bob Marley to a wide audience without compromising him as an artist. He and his Island Records label were everything that Richard Branson and Virgin were not. At that point, and for the next few years, just about every release on Island made sense. It already had by that time a great back catalogue. I didn't by any means like it all, but I could see why, with the odd exception, everything on it had been given a release.

My pessimism about PiL's future temporarily dissipated. I thought that if Chris Blackwell was going to be involved then surely it would work out OK. I think that my feelings were similar to the feelings that fans of ailing football clubs have when a go-ahead, progressive (and rich) chairman gets involved: they suddenly believe that the Messiah has turned up and all is saved. I probably did Chris's (and everybody else's) head in rabbiting on about production and all that. I'd had a drink and a snort and was totally overexcited. I was very taken with the John Martyn album *One World* at that time. Chris had a production credit on that along with Lee Scratch Perry and I wanted to discuss it with him. I have to say that to this day he is the only record business tycoon that I have ever met who I liked. He is far more down to earth than most of those types. You certainly don't feel that he's secretly looking down his nose at you.

Of course at the end of the day he's a businessman like all the rest, as well as being a toff (with colonial overtones to boot, I might add); however, the bloke genuinely loves music, and in those days he relished a challenge like the one that PiL represented. After the restaurant we went back to Basing Street Studios to 'hang out and chill', as all you hipsters would now put it. We went up to the little apartment that Chris had lent Dennis on the top floor of the studio complex. There was a good feeling in the air, everybody seemed happy, and from what I remember a schedule was planned in regard to how we would proceed with the marketing of *Metal Box* in the States. Apparently Chris Blackwell got Tommy Motola, the famous American music business magnate, interested in the venture. Dennis had drawn up plans for a large *Metal Box* installation to be set up in Times Square that people could actually walk into. There were plans to make a massive promotion fund available. (Dennis told me that 5 million dollars was being set aside.) It was around that time that we were putting together the cover for *2nd Edition*, the double-album version of *Metal Box*; Dennis Morris, as well as hooking us up with Chris, continued to act as our art director. Yet again he came up with a truly winning idea: we had plates of very reflective foil spread out on an uneven service; we then put our faces (one at a time) against this foil. A photograph was then taken of our distorted reflections. It gave a very striking effect. (It was a bit like a Francis Bacon painting.) Nowadays, of course, you would probably use a computer software program to get the desired effect. Dennis did a layout of the cover, which was to be a gatefold design. However, Keith had a big problem being on the inside of the gatefold. He wanted to be on the outside; on the front cover no less! It was pretty obvious that Keith had a big problem with Dennis. I think the problem was that Dennis couldn't be manipulated.

There was another meeting with Chris Blackwell a few days later at the Island headquarters at St Peter's Square. I left once the essential points had been discussed. I'm told that Keith then raised the subject of Dennis's involvement in the project. He raised concerns about Dennis having too much power in the situation. He was also critical of Dennis being cut into the deal, and threatened to leave the band if indeed that happened. I'm told that Dennis told John that he had to make a decision over who he would back: either himself (Dennis) or Keith. John backed Keith and in so doing he backed the wrong horse. That as well as the shenanigans involving the *2nd Edition* cover was more than enough for Dennis, and he walked, and from what I remember somebody else had to complete the cover's layout. I thought that Dennis going was a crying shame. It was my first real taste of music business callousness. Just about everybody in and around the band had appeared to be Dennis's pal, but of course when he was gone that was that; he was never referred to again.

Funnily enough me and Dennis had clashed when we had first

met, just as PiL was forming; we were virtually at each other's throats. However, we quickly came to respect each other and became friendly. There were similarities between us: we were both from East London and the two of us were quite independently minded. We had both started doing our respective 'jobs' at a young age (Dennis was only fourteen when, as a fledgling photographer, he had gone on the road with Bob Marley). Both of us are typically proud Leos. When we both chose (individually) to walk away from PiL it was with our heads up. There was no whinging or public recriminations from either of us. We were geezers. I have a lot of respect for the bloke. We still occasionally talk nowadays.

Chris Blackwell considered Dennis to be the 'key man' in any possible deal, so now that Dennis was gone he dropped us like a hot potato. Keith got his way and got on the front cover. Funnily enough I wasn't even bothered about that. For all Keith's confident, often arrogant, veneer, I could tell that just under the surface he had all sorts of insecurities and doubts, and if putting him on the front cover shut him up (temporarily), and was cool with John, then fine, whatever. But what did upset me was losing a possible deal with Chris Blackwell. The same dark shitty vibe descended.

*As fate would have it I ended up signed to Island as a solo artist within a couple of years. I went on to have five different periods of being signed to Island. As recently as 2002 I made a peach of a record with Bill Laswell called 'Radio Axiom A Dub Transmission' for Palm Pictures, the label that Chris started after he sold Island, so the connection is still there, even in this century.*

*In one of my earlier sojourns with Island in the early eighties, we sometimes used Basing Street Studios. Lucky Gordon (of the 'Profumo affair') was the cook at Basing Street at that time. He was a good cook (of Jamaican stuff), but was a pretty glum and taciturn bloke most of the time. Then again I've found quite a few cooks to be like that. Once they get to know you, and you let them know that you appreciate their food, they are OK. They don't come on all friendly, but they will tend towards giving you a little*

*half-smile and a larger portion than everyone else, and that's OK
by me.*

*Metal Box* was released in the UK towards the end of 1979. I
think it was around that time that we did *The Old Grey Whistle
Test*. During 1979 we only did three shows, two in Manchester and
one in Leeds. The second of the Manchester shows was booked by
Factory Records boss Tony Wilson. I got on well with Tony and
his partners Alan Erasmus and Rob Gretton. Tony was a great
help to me when the time came to extricate myself legally from
the shambles that PiL was fast becoming. I was very impressed
by the Factory set-up. It was everything that we should have been
doing with PiL, in terms of setting up our own label, and having
our own power base; they had a great spirit. I felt very 'at home'
with them. Could you imagine that other possible world? PiL run
with a Factory Records ethos. Now that would have been good.

### MILES, OM KALSOUM AND *APOCALYSE NOW*

I can recall doing a promotional video for the track 'Death Disco'.
Acklam Hall in West London was hired for the day. I think that
it was a straightforward 'live performance' video; there was
no storyboard or anything, at least not that I remember. It was
pretty poor, very amateurish, even for those early days of promo
videos. When I finally saw the finished cut I remember thinking
Well, come on, can't our umbrella organisation do better than
this? I also recall a *Top of the Pops* appearance. I couldn't wait to
go to 'make-up' so I could get a tooth blacked out. The make-up
department was a bit flummoxed with my request. I then sat in the
dentist's chair grinning like a man possessed. Our handful of TV
appearances were far more impressive than the videos, because
when appearing on TV far more opportunity was afforded for the
personalities of the band to be spontaneous. There was certainly
more exuberance demonstrated when we did TV performances.

However, 1979 wasn't all bad. We did an interview with a bloke called Angus MacKinnon, for the *NME*. Angus was one of the very few journalists who gave *Metal Box* a good review. He really 'got' it. Angus became a good friend of mine from the day of the interview onwards. He told me about a new film that was about to come out called *Apocalypse Now*. Angus had seen a preview of it in his role as a film reviewer. As he had *Metal Box*, I think that he was just about the only journalist in the UK to give the movie a rave review. Coppola held up Angus's review at his UK press conference and cited Angus as the only British journalist who had the brains to understand the film. I went to see it a week or two later. My world was absolutely rocked. It is still my favourite movie of all time.

Angus introduced me, over the course of time, to Miles Davis's entire back catalogue. Angus felt that there were some aesthetic similarities between *Metal Box* and Miles's late sixties/early seventies period. It was a connection that a bloke called Kenny MacDonald, who was to all intents and purposes the PiL tailor, had made a few weeks previously. Kenny was into a lot of very far-out left-field jazz stuff, and when he heard tracks from *Metal Box* he insisted on sitting us all down to listen to the first side of *Dark Magus* (which became my favourite Miles Davis album). Like Angus, Kenny reckoned that *Metal Box* was not a million miles away from *Dark Magus* in spirit and I think that he was correct. It sounded fantastic on John's big system. To be honest the others were pretty underwhelmed, and we only got through one of the four sides before the others in the room, apart from me and Kenny, deemed it 'unlistenable' and took it off. However, I was absolutely captivated, it was really wild and primal. Similar to my introduction to dub, it was a cathartic moment. It really got me thinking. Kenny is presently serving a very long prison sentence. I wish him well.

Within a week or two of that first blast of Miles I was fed a huge amount of the Miles Davis back catalogue by Angus. In fact Angus turned me on to some great music over the next few years.

Most of it jazz. People like Arthur Blythe, John Coltrane, Charlie Mingus, Pharoah Sanders (who I had already heard by way of Lonnie Liston-Smith), Lester Young and all the usual suspects. However, it was the electric-period Miles that had the biggest impact on my imagination.

I was continuing to check out my short-wave radio. I would tune into, among others, Radio Cairo and Radio Tehran. The singer I kept hearing via Radio Cairo was Om Kalsoum. They used to play her non-stop. I suppose that was because she had passed away only a few years before. Her state funeral was even bigger than Nasser's. It was attended by several million mourners. It took me ages to find out who the singer was, because the programmes were in Arabic and I couldn't understand what the announcers were saying. I got used to hearing Om Kalsoum with a continuous slow oscillation (similar to phasing), as the short-wave signal bounced up into the stratosphere and then back down again. Most of those broadcasts featured recordings of live performances, so the first sound that you would hear was those wonderful yearning Egyptian string parts. That would go on for a few minutes and a little bit of a groove would develop with the rest of the orchestra and then it would die down, and there would be a flurry of furious clapping and I knew that this great diva had entered the stage. You could sense the tingling anticipation running through the audience. A hush descended that was charged with electricity; and suddenly there was her voice, immediately full of warmth and yearning. I eventually found out the name of her main composer, Mohamed Abdel Wahab. I avidly collected cassette-only releases of his solo stuff. It was pretty hard to find, but if you scoured around Edgware Road you could get lucky. It was highly innovative stuff that would utilise Western styles and instruments with traditional Egyptian ones. So you would for instance hear a Fender electric bassist swapping rhythmic patterns with a darbuka player. It is some of the most playful and innovative music that you could ever hear. It was very ahead of its time.

# Chapter Six: America

In the spring of 1980 we went off to tour America. It was to be my first time in the States so I was very excited. Martin Atkins had joined the band by that point and to be honest he was the only person on that tour that I got on with. At that time Martin was a young, ambitious drummer on the make, but he was OK. I auditioned him for the band and within a few minutes it was obvious that he could handle the gig. He was a dependable drummer, and someone to have a beer with. We started out in Boston (well, Cambridge, Massachusetts, to be exact), and then flew down to New York. It was there that we got picked up by two limos at the airport. Yet again, in those days that was a big deal, it had a telly and a bar and all that, but I remember just sitting there in the back of that limo thinking, Is this it then? I just felt empty, but I remember laughing and thinking, Well, that gets that out of the way, then, I know that this is bollocks. I think that the general vibe in the band contributed to me feeling that way. I would rather have been picked up in a Morris Minor and been with people that I was getting on with.

The first of our two New York shows was a big deal. We were

playing a place called the Palladium, which was considered a prestigious venue. I seem to remember that James Blood Ulmer supported us. I think that John and/or Keith had sorted that, and credit where it's due, that was a good call. All the New York faces such as Iggy Pop and Martin Scorsese were out in force and there was a great atmosphere. We went on and got on with the set. It was going really well, I vaguely remember John crouching down behind the bass amp, we had eye contact and he looked absolutely terrified, more than just stage fright, he looked like he'd seen a ghost. I think that I went and crouched down near him and I think we briefly exchanged smiles. I believe I even lay down on the floor while playing (I may have all that confused with another gig on that tour, it's a long time ago, but I do think that all that happened in New York). After about twenty-five minutes John walked off. Keith looked a bit hesitant and then he scuttled

Martin Atkins, John Lydon and me, pictured at Gunter Grove circa 1980

©Janette Beckman/Redferns/Getty Images

after him. There was a big audience, all seated; I can remember looking out at them all gazing up at the stage. I can't remember what tune we were playing at the time. I remember Martin looking at me quizzically; I think I looked back at him and sort of shrugged and we just carried on. I started improvising bass lines, quite funky ones, yet they still had 'weight'. Martin kept the groove going with a hip (for the time) disco groove. I recall me and Martin smiling at each other; it was quite a moment for a rookie rhythm section, to play as a duo to such a large crowd. All the punters piled down the front going mental, there was a great vibe and we rocked them for another twenty minutes or so. I remember thinking, Let's not push our luck, so I gave Martin a nod to say 'come on, let's finish' and we left the stage. I can remember people calling out and chanting my name, but was I happy? No, not in the slightest; I wanted to murder John and Keith, I thought that what they had done was tantamount to going AWOL in the middle of a battle. I thought that they were a complete and utter pair of bottle jobs. When I got in the dressing room I found out that they had gone back to the hotel already. I couldn't believe that! I was enraged; however, Jeanette displayed her ability to read both people and situations, and so she had stayed in the dressing room. For the first time that I could ever remember she wasn't umbilically attached to John or Keith. She knew that I would go mental, and that it might possibly be a deal breaker, and that I would want to return to Albion forthwith. And she was right. Within a few seconds I was demanding my passport. She worked on placating me (I don't think that I had even talked to her up to that point on the tour), and all the time people were coming in the dressing room to congratulate us on a great show. It was mental. I vaguely remember Martin sitting in the corner with a towel wrapped around his head looking shell shocked. In only his second gig with the band he had been left alone with just the bass player for company and no script, and he had stood his ground without hesitation.

## STRONG PRIMAL UNDERCURRENTS

*There was another weirder aspect in regard to this incident. As I describe this other aspect I have two requests. Firstly, forget dialogue, language or indeed speech of any kind; in fact forget civilised refined behaviour as we would understand it; think primitive societies. Secondly, I ask you to picture it in slow motion; imagine it as an intense action scene from a movie where the director feels that he has no other option but to resort to slow motion in order both to accentuate the speed and intensity of 'the moment' and to convey the sheer primal horror of the particular scene that he is dealing with. Even Spielberg and Scorsese have on occasion resorted (effectively) to this clichéd procedure (the graphic opening scenes in* Saving Private Ryan, *and the fight scenes in* Raging Bull, *for example, use this technique).*

*So here we go: I came offstage (wild eyed and high on adrenalin) with Martin Atkins following me. The coterie of people standing side-stage parted before me. As soon as they caught my eye they looked away; it was as if they were trying to make themselves smaller before me. It was as if I had become, to them, a deity. When I got into the dressing room Jeanette moved in very close to me, she maintained eye contact, while keeping her head lowered, she became smaller and 'fluffier' and for the first (and last) time, I almost hate to admit this, attractive to me. She was making shy and tender touching movements to my hands and arms. It was the next best thing to 'grooming me'; I was the king baboon. There were other girls around, they too seemed small and 'fluffy', it was as if they were displaying their privates, parading up and down like female baboons. I was the young lion surveying my pride. I was the woad-painted Celtic chieftain. I was the man. (It was all a bit like Captain Willard, when he appears at the entrance to Colonel Kurtz's lair, after having topped the great man.) Suddenly that perspective disappeared; speech and thought and reason were back and I could hear myself howling and whining and effing and blinding. However, it reaffirmed something that I had already realised at a deeper level; PiL was a wolf pack, and I was beginning to be perceived as an 'alpha male wolf' rather than a maverick outsider lone wolf (albeit a lone wolf you would be ill advised to directly challenge). Essentially that was the problem.*

## AMERICA 2

The Sex Pistols were in the past and I was very keen to leave the whole punk thing behind, including the 'auto-response' sneers and hostile, confrontational attitude. It seemed so teenage to me. I was now twenty-one and I didn't want to be a member of a 'teenage gang'. That's why I really hated the walking offstage coupled with John's seemingly non-stop bolshie sulky attitude. I thought it was stupid; he was no longer Johnny Rotten and it was no longer the Sex Pistols. He was now John Lydon and this was Public Image, and those crowds in America were by and large very open and receptive. They were not really 'punk audiences'. They certainly were nothing like the audiences back home in the UK. They really understood that *Metal Box* contained light as well as dark. Over the years *Metal Box* has come to be referred to, largely by your bog-standard dim-witted thirty-something music journalists, as a dark and morbid impenetrable classic. You always get the impression that most of these people who spout on about *Metal Box* have never really listened to it. (In a way it reminds me of James Joyce's *Ulysses*, insofar as it's discussed far more than it is actually read.) Those Yanks, because of their wider musical vocabulary (especially in regard to modal jazz), really got PiL. I think that John, through his stupid stubborn obstinacy, missed a great opportunity with PiL.

At the time of my departure I felt sure that there was something deeply wrong with him. The number of 'bad calls' and decisions that he made just did not make sense. It was cutting off your nose to spite your face on a gargantuan level. Unlike every other person around him I couldn't sit back and pretend that it was OK. I seem to remember that in the early days of PiL and before, all that negative stuff would be tempered with a degree of humour and self-deprecation. However, by the time of the US tour he seemed to be utterly unbearable nearly all the time and I had to get away. Of course, this sort of behaviour is by no means unusual in big stars (or even successful business tycoons).

Brian Clough and Margaret Thatcher are the two other strong characters that John reminded me of the most. I honestly think that in terms of personality John and 'Cloughie' are doppelgängers. I think that in essence their strengths and weaknesses were very similar. Examine how they both conduct themselves in interviews; their body language, coupled with their flamboyant and confrontational styles. If an interviewer points out an apparent inconsistency or failing in either of them, the offending questioner will ruthlessly be cut down to size for daring to step out of line. Both had/have an intense charisma and they both have/had an absolute strength of will. Both are/were determined to win at all costs. When they put their mind to it they could engender tremendous and fierce loyalty in those around them. Both of them really liked a pound note, to the extent that it had a detrimental effect on their work relationships. Richard E. Grant's Withnail character also comes strongly to mind when I think of John, especially pre-PiL. These comparisons to Clough and Withnail are ultimately a compliment. I love both those characters.

## NARCISSISTIC TENDENCIES

*It's very easy when writing an autobiography to lay the law down and point the finger at everybody else, but please don't think that I am painting myself as Mr Normal and Well Adjusted at that time, because I most certainly was not. I was the proverbial 'loose cannon'. I too had more than a degree of the old narcissistic tendencies. Indeed, I can still have flashes of them. I understand*

*that 'arrogant high' when everyone around you seems so feeble,
inconsistent, untrustworthy and unreliable. I also know the other
side to that coin, the low depths of self-hatred and depression, and
the absolute absence of self-esteem. Of course, both aspects are
an unrealistic nonsense. They are to be gently laughed at. I think
that it is a good idea to get these narcissistic tendencies out in the
open, where they are revealed as absurd. They then tend to wither
and die. They don't like it in the light. They like the dark, they hide
behind lies and untruth and self-deception. Anyway, I must go; I
am sitting writing this in a five-star hotel (five? I wouldn't give it
two). I called room service and ordered the Caesar salad, but they
have brought me the Greek salad. I'm furious. I'm going to have to
call the duty manager. To be honest I feel like jumping in a taxi and
going straight to the airport. I feel like going home. I can't take this,
I'm cracking up. None of you know what it's like in this business.
The shit I have to put up with. None of you understand. You're all
little people.*

## AMERICA 3

The day after the Palladium show John and Keith acted like
nothing had happened but I knew that there was a lot going on
under the surface. The people from the record company showed
us the reviews of the show that had been published in the press.
As I recall they were all stunning. This was a very different
situation as compared to the UK, where PiL hardly ever got a
decent review.

The *New York Times* in particular went to town on it. They gave
it the same sort of respect that you would expect them to give to
an Ornette Coleman concert. I thought that was fantastic, because
we would not have got that sort of respect in the UK. Most UK
journalists didn't know what to make of PiL. I came up 'smelling
of roses' in the *New York Times* review. Everyone was very happy
for me; I know that, because they told me they were.

Funnily enough, the next couple of days were probably the best on that tour. Martin Scorsese was making a film, *Raging Bull*, and he wanted to have a meet in regard to us doing the soundtrack. I went to meet him with John. We ended up sitting in a penthouse apartment with Scorsese; because of the combination of my first-ever jet lag, speed comedown, booze and general tour weirdness, I was very spaced out (I think I must have had a puff as well). My memory is a bit hazy, but I seem to remember that John left soon after we arrived with some biggish geezer who worked for Scorsese. I don't know where they went. They may well have explained where they were going, but in the state I was in I probably just grinned inanely at them. So anyway, I was left in the apartment with Scorsese. I was very happy because the bloke was an absolute hero to me. *Taxi Driver*, as far as I was concerned, was a masterpiece. Paul Schrader wrote the incredible screenplay. Apparently, Schrader was brought up in a strictly Calvinist household, and didn't see a movie until he was eighteen; he's a very interesting bloke. The soundtrack by Bernard Herrmann is also something I never tire of.

Scorsese was like a cat on a hot tin roof, just couldn't sit still. He was jabbering away like crazy. I recall him beckoning me to the window. He pointed down at the people milling around on Broadway. (We were several floors up in a skyscraper.) He asked me if I would care if 'one of those little "dots" suddenly stopped moving'. I immediately knew what he was on about; he was reciting Orson Welles's speech from Carol Reed's adaptation of Graham Greene's *The Third Man*, the one where Orson is on the Ferris wheel and goes on about 'the Renaissance', 'cuckoo clocks', 'the Borgias' and 'Switzerland'. Basically Scorsese did a performance. He was very wired and his delivery was far more urgent and imploring than Orson's. His face was no more than two feet from mine.

*I certainly wasn't disappointed with Scorsese, he more than lived up to any expectations that I had. To tell the truth I don't like all his films but when I do I love them;* Taxi Driver, GoodFellas, Casino, Last Temptation *and* Kundun *are the ones for me.*

I can't remember how the encounter ended, but eventually John came back. I dimly remember *Raging Bull* being discussed, the storyline and all that. I don't think they showed us scenes from the film or anything. I vaguely remember thinking that they weren't really serious. Anyway, we never did the soundtrack for *Raging Bull.*

The next day we played another gig in New York, this time an ad hoc affair at a club called Gildersleeves. I think that the purpose of the gig was twofold, to raise extra revenue for the tour, and to keep Warner's, the record label, sweet. It's not unusual to do an 'extra show' at a small venue when touring so that all the people from the record company and retailers can come and meet you. So you get introduced to 'Bud from Midwest Radio Promotions'. You are supposed to pump Bud's hand enthusiastically, and when he bellows 'Are you having a great time in the USA?' you are supposed to bellow back, 'Hell, yes!' Everyone tells you that 'your album is amazing!' and 'we all love you here!'

*When you get taken around the record company offices these same bullshit mantras are repeated endlessly and enthusiastically by all concerned. You get taken into offices where fat vice-president blokes are in the process of practising their golf putting, while talking on hands-free telephone receivers that are attached to their heads. This has been one of the many 'Groundhog Day' aspects of my life in the music industry. Of course, it never does turn out that 'everything's great!' You normally end up dropped by the American label a few months later. (Don't get me wrong, I'm not complaining; I think it's bloody amazing that I still get these US deals. After all, it's not as if I sell a million albums there.) About a year ago I went through that same familiar scenario again. We were sitting in a preposterous fake French restaurant in New York. I started to fantasise about impaling the Midwest*

*Radio Promotion guy's hand with my fork. So I feigned tiredness and hastily left.*

The show at Gildersleeves was, I think, the best of that tour. No one left the stage early, and the vibe was OK. The evening got off to a good start when the bloke doing the 'MCing' got 'pied' courtesy of the famous 'Pieman' of the late sixties 'Yippie movement'. It was all my doing. I had heard a lot about the Yippies, and wanted to meet them while I was in New York. They were to me what hippies should have been, they were lively and humorous, and decidedly to the left. It was Joe Stevens, *NME*'s resident photographer in New York, who introduced me to them.

I was desperate for the Yippies to introduce me to the legendary 'Pieman'. The Pieman was known for publicly 'pieing' establishment figures such as Edward Teller and Andy Warhol. The Yippies set the meeting up. The whole thing was conducted as if we were organising a gangland hit. I was told to return to my hotel and I would be contacted. A woman called and told me to go alone to such-and-such a diner and to sit at a certain booth and to have thirty dollars (or however much it was) in an envelope as well as a photograph of 'the hit'. So off I went and I was sitting there having a hot dog when a bloke sat down behind me. 'Have you got the money?' he says to me in hushed tones, so I pass him the envelope, I says to him, 'The photo and name of the bloke you have to hit is in there as well.' 'When and where?' he says. 'Gildersleeves tonight,' I say, 'just before Public Image go on stage.' 'OK,' he says, 'what flavour?' 'What?' I say. 'What flavour?' he repeats. 'Blueberry, strawberry, chocolate, cherry, custard, what do you want?' 'Strawberry,' I says, thinking that's the end of it. 'What size?' he asks. I took the biggest. So that night the poor old MC (I think he was a DJ), who Martin had befriended after the Boston show, got pied. He came on stage to announce us and just as he opened his mouth he got 'whacked'. He was an OK bloke and did see the funny side. I must admit that it made the stage a bit slippery.

Anyway, like I said, it was a great show. Just as at the Palladium, there were a lot of celebrities present. I remember that towards the end of the show a load of punters got up on stage, dancing. They weren't bad dancers either from what I can recall. I saw some of that show on YouTube recently. It was the first time I had ever seen live PiL footage. I thought that it was pretty good. The sound, as we all know, is normally crap on 'bootleg'-type footage, owing to it not having gone 'through the sound desk', but whatever, it is still pretty good. To look at it you wouldn't think I was so pissed off; I just look very impatient in between numbers. Anyway, the band sounds, bar a little bit of dodgy tuning, nice and tight. I remember being very happy with that show at the time.

We played Atlanta a couple of days later and things really took a dip again. John walked off stage again early on in proceedings. I told him he was out of order. I had chatted to some of the punters outside the venue earlier in the day and it turned out that some of them had driven all the way from Florida, which probably entailed a ten-hour drive. As we left the stage he made some disparaging remark about me 'wanting to play to the kids, man', taking the piss basically, making it sound like I was being a 'fake rock reactionary' or something. Well, I wasn't like Steve Jones, Paul Cook, Glen Matlock or Sid. I wasn't going to tamely put up with that crap. I knocked off the nutty-looking safari hat that he was wearing as soon as we got off stage and effed and blinded a bit. I felt like knocking his block off, to be honest. I think that he knew that he had overstepped the mark. I think that we hardly talked again after that, not properly in the way that mates would, but to be honest the friendship was on its last legs by then anyway. But at least we went back out there and finished the set.

However, the whole walking on and off thing caused some bad feeling in some sectors of the crowd and some of them were still lurking around well after the show finished. Some of these punters had a vaguely hillbilly sort of vibe, battered cowboy hats and tatty denims, they were 'ugly drunk'. Two of these 'hillbillies' approached me at the rear of the venue as I left. There were two blokes from Warner Bros there as I left; I think that they were keeping an eye on me because they sensed I was on a bit of a hair trigger after the events of the evening. The two hillbillies said to me, in a very aggressive manner (and to get the full benefit of this you have to imagine them speaking with Southern accents), 'Y'all [referring to PiL] didn't even bleed man… at least Iggy [Iggy Pop] bled.' I swear that those are the exact words that they used. I remember them because I thought that the language they used was marvellously evocative, and for months afterwards, whenever I had a drink in me, I addressed people in exactly those words, using the same Southern drawl that those good ol' boys had used.

Don't get me wrong, though, they were a nasty pair of cunts who wished me ill. I must admit that following the earlier events of the evening I was feeling rather belligerent, so I assumed the character of an Edwardian gentleman and said to the one who had admonished me, 'Sir! Sir! I put it to you that you are a homosexual, and that this tough macho attitude that you are displaying is simply an act. Sir! Sir! I put it to you that you have a crush on Iggy Pop, sir! I accuse you of being a faggot!' Well, talk about light the blue touch paper and stand well back, those two geezers went mental. The blokes from Warner's went mad at me because I had made a bad situation considerably worse, they flung themselves in front of the good ol' boys, and screamed for back-up from the venue's security, which duly arrived, but to be honest I wouldn't have worried if the Warner's blokes had pissed off and left me with the two good ol' boys; those hillbillies didn't realise that I also contained a high degree of pent-up aggression and would happily have set about them with maximum speed and vindictiveness.

Of course, being on tour with a band brings all sorts of underlying tensions to the fore. Even so, in spite of my inexperience, I knew that that tour was really pretty exceptionally shitty. I saw one or two things on that tour (not connected directly to the band but concerning the crew and 'general entourage') that made me very uncomfortable indeed, to the point that I spoke out loudly against them. When you are as uncomfortable with a situation as I was, and you have tried, without avail, to communicate your misgivings, you have no option but to bail out. If you don't there will be a price to pay, and I was starting to pay that price; I was suffering from stomach/abdominal cramps. A chronic ache deep down in my (knowing) guts; it had begun some time towards the end of 1979. That's what can happen when you try to 'swallow' your anger and unease; you can get physically sick.

I can't remember too much about the rest of the tour, but I do recall Levene having heroin withdrawals on two or three occasions. Once we left New York it became a problem for him to find suppliers. I remember that, unfortunately for him, a couple of those occasions of withdrawing coincided with him having to fly. To be honest, by this time I had no sympathy for him. Jeanette and John would fuss around him, along with the cabin crew. I remember them helping him down the aisle of a jet plane; he was almost doubled up and covered in sweat. Jeanette was telling everyone that 'it's OK, he's got flu'. I recall that, rather wickedly, I was in my element. I stood up and in my best John Cleese voice made an announcement. 'It's OK, everybody, he's going through cold turkey, nothing to worry about, he's a heroin addict, you know.' I remember Jeanette looking daggers at me and I remember looking back at her with a big broad smile on my face. I thought, That's right, love, all bets are off. I couldn't give a fuck any more. They wrapped Levene in a blanket and he shivered like a leaf for the rest of the flight. He heaved a couple times into the sick bag. I couldn't work out why it wasn't possible for someone to bring some smack from New York to give to him. Maybe he didn't trust the quality of the stuff in New York. Instead some people were dispatched urgently to fly from London to New York on Concorde, who then flew on to hook up with the tour. I was surprised at that; it must have cost an absolute fortune, and even if the band didn't pay for it directly at the time, eventually the tab would have been picked up, I'm sure. It made me wonder if it was just Keith who needed sorting, because that is some drastic measure. Those airfares for the couriers would probably have been more than I earned in wages from PiL in all my time with them, a fact that did not escape me at the time.

The rest of my memories of the tour are pretty sketchy. I think that we got chucked out of some famous hotel that we were staying at in LA, owing to our bad behaviour. I also recall being in the minibus with Jeanette and Keith and the tour manager and a driver, going from the hotel to the venue, of whatever city we were in. They were playing some loud rock music that I didn't like, plus I didn't feel great, I had a gut-ache. I had asked them to turn it down, but they blanked me. It was a 'pecking order thing'. They were both really starting to 'strong it' at that stage. So I went down the front of the bus and kicked out the dashboard. 'That's better, don't you think? A nice bit of silence,' I said.

We did the *American Bandstand* show, which was an institution in the States. However, I had never heard of it. By the time we went to do the show I was pretty wasted, and had to go to the medical room to have a lie-down. It was nice and quiet in there and I really needed to catch a bit of sleep. Well, the next thing I know I wake up and there is a geezer stooped down over me saying hello. Well, for a start I was very pissed off at being woken up, and then I was disturbed by the geezer; he looked deeply weird; he had a deep suntan and bright white 'too perfect' teeth. The bloke said, 'Hi! I'm Dick Clark.' Well, to be honest, that didn't mean anything to me and I said something like 'Why did you fucking wake me up, mate? I was well away.' I was quite annoyed with him. I really didn't know that he was a famous bloke on the telly in America. I wasn't trying to be clever or smart or anything. To be fair the bloke was probably just trying to be a good host and be welcoming. Most 'big presenters' of shows now wouldn't have that sort of personal touch. Once I realised that he was just trying to be friendly I shook his hand and he seemed OK. A myth developed about that little scene, people say that he was very offended by my attitude, but he seemed all right to me. We really messed about during our 'live' mimed performance. John ran around like a demented border collie disturbing the sheep-like dancers in the studio, and I got on the drums and gave Martin the bass.

I also remember on a night off in Detroit going with Martin to see the Crusaders (featuring Randy Crawford singing 'Streetlife'). We were warned most severely not to go, because the theatre was in an exclusively black neighbourhood and had a bad reputation; however, I just could not resist it. It was a fantastic concert, much better than the one I had seen them give in London a few months previous to that. Unlike in London there were no preposterous solos; the Detroit crowd wouldn't have swallowed that because they wanted to groove. We had got to the large seated venue a bit late, and as we went to our seats the black people around us seemed amazed to see a pair of white geezers sneaking in. When the house lights went up at the end it seemed like the whole auditorium was staring at us. I couldn't believe it, we were the only white people in the place that I could see. I wasn't used to that sort of racial segregation.

*Anyway, the tour finished in San Francisco. Happily, in the twenty-seven years that have elapsed since then, I have never done a tour that made me as unhappy as that 1980 sojourn to America with PiL. Oh yes, I nearly forgot. The tune that went around and around my nut in the States in 1980 was 'Funky Town' by Lipps Inc. You heard that tune everywhere that you went. That song is sometimes referred to as 'the last hit of the disco era'.*

## KNOCK KNOCK (WHO'S THERE?)

As soon as I got back to London after the tour I wanted my wages. This proved difficult, as typically no one would pick up the phone at Gunter Grove, so eventually I went around there and knocked (and knocked) on the door until Dave Crowe answered. I went in and told him I was really sick of being fucked around in regard to getting paid, and I wanted a big hit of money. He just nodded and gave me a 'help yourself' sort of gesture. I think he knew that I had the high moral ground; so I went to his room and got the shoebox full of cash from under his bed and left. I immediately took Marg back to America with me, because I wanted her to see some of the sights that I had seen. I recall that just before we flew out from Gatwick the Old Bill pulled us out from the departure lounge and searched us. As we flew in to Miami we could see fires burning. It turned out that a 'mini-riot' was going on. We went coast to coast. I recollect that we went to see a Solar Records package tour concert somewhere in Florida state (miles away from the nearest town). The Whispers were playing along with Shalamar. I think that there was a third group on the bill but I can't remember who they were. We got caught in a torrential downpour on our way back to Miami after the show as we drove back through a massive thunderstorm. The engine got flooded and nearly conked out in the middle of nowhere. I remember that I had a dull ache in my gut that whole trip.

When I got back I got straight to it and phoned Gunter Grove. Surprisingly Lydon answered. I told him that I was going to leave, and said that I wanted to do it as nicely as possible. I told him that I would phone Brian Carr (John's lawyer) to sort a meeting out. He acted as though he had company and didn't want them to know who he was talking to, or what it was about. We talked very briefly. He answered me quietly; he just said stuff along the lines of 'yes, OK, thanks for telling me' and 'yes, no problem, I'll see you there'. His manner seemed conciliatory. I actually hoped that even at this late stage he might belatedly 'do the right thing', turn up at the meeting, shake hands, and get Brian Carr to sort out the paperwork pertaining to me getting my publishing royalties paid directly.

I was hoping to dispel the bad feeling that existed between us. However, I had seen enough examples of how John dealt with people, Dennis for instance, to know that was unlikely. I also hoped that a bit of extra money could be sorted out. I would not have expected a fortune because, as I said earlier, even then I was quite realistic in regard to how quickly money can be spent by out-of-control bands (and when the sulph and booze were forthcoming I had never complained). More than anything I was hoping that John would 'do the right thing' and salvage himself in my eyes. You know… just turn up… be a geezer.

*I knew that Levene would not try and help. He had the typical junkie's capacity for treacherous double-dealing, so he would certainly say one thing to your face and another behind your back. Only after he departed PiL a couple of years later did he cry crocodile tears in regard to me leaving. However, at the time of the event he knew where his bread was buttered in regard to servicing his habit, so he had to stay on the right side of John. But apart from that he was happy to see me leave PiL; he knows it and I know it. He was beginning to get blown away by me. He couldn't keep up. It scared him, and made him insecure. It wasn't deliberate on my part (to leave him behind) and I did not rub his nose in it. It's just that in regard to playing I was getting stronger and stronger by the day, and he was getting weaker and weaker as a creative force.*

In regard to John, I was thinking, Come on, it's the parting of the ways, but let's be big about it. The money side of it was just that, a 'side of it'. I'd actually liked to have sat down and had a cup of tea with him, shook his hand, looked him in the eye and said, 'Thanks, mate, all the best,' because as rough as it had got I wouldn't have swapped it for the world. After all, what else would I have been doing?

He had got me 'started' in regard to playing music properly. It was a massive thing to me. Two years before that I had been on the dole going nowhere. I also fully appreciated I had personally benefited from the effectiveness of the Virgin and Warner press and publicity machines. I now had 'a bit of a name'. More importantly I had learnt the basics of how the process of 'putting records together' worked. So all in all I was grateful for all that; however, I felt that I had repaid the debt with interest. In fact, I now felt that I was owed.

I set up the meeting with Brian Carr. He told me that he knew all about me leaving, and that there shouldn't be any problems, and asked me how such-and-such a date was for me to come to the office. He told me that he had talked to John and Keith and that they would both be there. Of course when I turned up at the lawyer's office on the chosen day neither of them turned up. I wasn't that surprised. Brian Carr was apologetic. Nothing got sorted out in regard to me leaving the band. Typically John was behaving like a callow youth, an awkward teenager. He decided to stay in his bedroom and let the lawyer deal with it. Anarchy in the UK, anyone?


## IT'S JUST BUSINESS

Like *The Sopranos* or the Stock Exchange, it was just business. A dirty stinking business, but business nonetheless. I had to wise up to that quickly, and I did; in fact I was already a good part of the way there. The music was everything to me, but I had to realise that to most people around the business it was just that: a business. I had to learn to keep my guard up and protect myself. And learn I did.

A couple of days after that meeting with Brian Carr I got a call from the Virgin press office, asking if I wanted to give a quote in regard to my departure from PiL. I said something along the lines of 'tell them that there are more important things in the world than the trials and tribulations of a rock band'. I was determined to have dignity. I had seen a few of the bands from the punk era split up by then, with all the accompanying press-release bullshit about 'musical and personal differences'. Normally within a week

MEMOIRS OF A GEEZER

or two of that statement the various factions of the bands would be in the music press slagging each other off. I thought that was kids' stuff. I really wanted to avoid that. That same afternoon I received a call from a tabloid newspaper journalist wanting to do a story. He offered a lot of money but I turned him down. He got a woman journalist to call later on but the answer was still no. It was never going to happen. I mean, can you imagine the photos accompanying the piece, me looking all forlorn and hangdog with my face cupped in my hands? No way! It wasn't out of loyalty to Lydon. It was out of self-respect. I always said that if I ever told the story I would do it my own way. In a calm and considered fashion; and that's what I've now done.

As soon as I left PiL in 1980 I resigned as a director. This was just as well because a few months later the Inland Revenue came knocking (literally). They were chasing a large tax debt that was owed by Public Image Ltd. It was handy that I had proof of my resignation as a director of Public Image Ltd to hand. If I hadn't already resigned as a director things would have got quite awkward for me. A company that had been appointed as accountants to Public Image Ltd also contacted me. They knew that I was no longer involved but were looking for the whereabouts of any remaining directors, because they (the accountants) were also owed money. Eventually Public Image Ltd went into receivership.


## PiL THE POSTSCRIPT

*About ten years after I walked out of Brian Carr's office, I was beginning to go through another of my little commercial 'purple patches'. I seem to have one or two every decade or so. I had just finished a show at the New Marquee Club on Charing Cross Road, with my band the Invaders of the Heart. Lo and behold, who turns up in my dressing room afterwards, but John Lydon and John Gray. I was happy to see them both, and greeted them both warmly. Unfortunately it's always impossible to talk to people after*

141

*shows, because there are always twenty other people trying to talk to you at once. I think the two Johns stayed for no more than ten minutes or so. I took the visit from Lydon as a sign of respect and conciliation and that was good enough for me. (In a way it was like he had turned up ten years late for that meeting at the lawyer's.) And anyway, I had absolutely no axe to grind in regard to PiL. In the ten years that had elapsed much had happened in my life. It had at times been extremely turbulent. Certainly I had been through a lot of changes. The importance of (and the drama of) PiL had faded enormously. (That's not to say that I hadn't always honoured it as the 'beginning' for me. Indeed, I still do.) In fact at that time, the early nineties, people were not that interested in either punk or PiL. It was quite common for me to do interviews without PiL being mentioned. It was very much the time of 'world music', and the 'rave scene' was still going very strong. I had a foot in both those camps at that time.*

*In 1994 Lydon released his autobiography. There was a reception at the Trocadero at Piccadilly in London. I was working in Berwick Street Studios that night. It would have been churlish not to have returned the compliment. That was the last I saw of John Lydon, until two years ago, when I met up with both him and John Gray again. Ostensibly we were supposed to meet to discuss a PiL bootleg that had been issued. To be honest we never even really discussed that matter. I think for both of us, as well as for John Gray, it was simply a chance to sit and have a conversation for the first time in twenty-seven years. We sat at a table for four people. The empty seat was taken, I'm sure, by the spirit of the fourth and missing John; Mr Beverley. I feel sure that Satan would have been happy to give him the night off from stoking furnaces. It really was like stepping back thirty years. The curry house that we were in had decor that was of a late seventies vintage, so that doubled the effect of stepping back in time. We didn't discuss anything to do with PiL; negative aspects or otherwise. We just chewed the fat. We went back to his gaff after the restaurant and John blasted out 'Faith Healer' by Alex Harvey, a perfect choice. I wasn't in any rush to leave and had a good time. It was a nice way to say goodbye properly.*

*I hope that my comments on PiL don't upset anybody in or around the band too much, or for too long. It was a long time ago, and we were all young. (I was the youngest of all, of course.) And for John Lydon especially, it was a goldfish-bowl existence. We all make mistakes and I don't think that any 'hanging offences' were committed by any of us. In our own ways we were all deeply flawed individuals. The important thing is that the music was good. And ultimately that means that all's well that ends well.*

*In fact against all odds, even the issue of the publishing royalties got sorted out – nearly seventeen years after the event. Thanks to the heroic efforts of my lawyer of the time, a bloke called Robert Horsefall. Robert managed to get Keith Levene's sorted out as well, though predictably Levene called me and was reluctant to contribute to Robert's not unreasonable fees. (I don't know if that situation was ever sorted out.) Around that time Levene had also turned up at my publishers claiming that he had co-written a single with me and wanted an advance. It was, of course, junkie bullshit.*

# Chapter Seven: Going Solo

When the news broke in the music press PiL were quoted as saying that I had been dismissed for stealing backing tracks! But I wasn't too surprised and I didn't rise to the bait. I was very keen to put PiL behind me as soon as I could, so I focused on the future. I was obviously very aware that I had been treated unfairly, but I also knew that I was far from being the first person that had experienced this in the music business. The important question was, how would I deal with it?

I discussed the situation with Angus MacKinnon and he got on to Tony Wilson. Tony came over for a meeting at Angus's flat in Westbourne Park and proffered advice as well as some practical help. He not only sorted a lawyer out, he paid for the first consultation. Needless to say he thought that it was a shameful situation. I think that he was genuinely surprised at what a mess PiL was. Within a matter of weeks I was free from the Virgin recording and publishing contract and Warner's contracts. I received no cash settlement of any kind.

As ever I needed to raise some ready cash so I got a job as a courier for Express Couriers, which at that time had offices on the south side of London Bridge. I wasn't at all certain that I would be able to get another band together. I thought that it was eminently possible that I might have had my time in the music game, and that was that. To be honest I still regularly have that same thought. However, before I had time to sit and fret Angus MacKinnon suggested that I did a record with Jaki Liebezeit and Holger Czukay from the German band Can. Angus was good friends with all the Can people, and so contacting them would not be a problem. Angus contacted Hildegard Schmidt, the Can manager, and fortuitously it turned out that she was visiting London with Holger the following week. We met them at a restaurant in Westbourne Park. I was very happy to meet Holger; I really liked his solo album *Movies*, which had just been released. It made extensive use of sampling techniques way before the advent of digital technology. I remember him telling me that there were over five thousand edits on that album. He later said that he was concerned when he first met me because I was drinking pints of beer and he was fearful of beer drinkers. However, later in the evening he was relieved to see me switch to wine. Really, if he had any sense, he would have been disturbed to see me 'mix the grape and the grain'.

I think that Holger must have been about forty-two when I met him. He was dressed in a jacket and trousers that had obviously been purchased from a West German army surplus store. In a former life they had constituted the major part of a Luftwaffe officer's uniform. The uniform was a dazzling white. Apparently he had encountered problems clearing immigration at Heathrow owing to the way he was dressed. I don't think they got too many geezers dressed like Hermann Goering strolling through passport control. He was exactly what I hoped he would be. Dogmatic and passionate in regard to music and how it is approached, and yet full of fun and mischief. He had something of the medieval alchemist about him. I also think that his persona was strongly influenced by Salvador Dali.

Me and Holger

We agreed to do a four-track EP (a format that was really back in vogue at that time thanks largely to punk). The first track was recorded and mixed at Gooseberry. The session was engineered by Mark Lusardi. I had prepared some simple 'parts' for the session: a funky 'on the beat' B-line, with a cute little ascending and descending bridge part. By now I had a Godwin String Synth, which I used as a 'pad' over the main B-line and as a 'double-up' to the bass on the bridge. I used simple triad chords. I brought along the Roland analogue beatbox. I put my parts down and then Holger added some sweet arpeggiated piano. He then added French horn. That was a first for me to behold. It gave the track a real Wagnerian feel. He played as if it was a Teutonic hunting horn. It made me yearn to hunt wild boar while dressed in lederhosen. All in all, 'How Much Are They' had a wonderfully simple yet most unusual blend of instruments and styles.

A pair of junkie girls wandered down the stairs and into the studio. It was summer and we had the doors open and they must have heard the music coming up from the studio. (It wasn't unusual for that to happen at Gooseberry.) I had put down a smattering of vocals, and the mike lines were still 'open'. There was an assistant engineer there called Lester, he was sort of chatting the girls up. At one point they were asking in stoned fashion, as they pointed at various mikes and amps, 'what does that do?' and 'what does this do?' We were making up bullshit explanations, saying stuff like 'we wire ourselves into this equipment and it gives us an incredible high, better than any drug... do you want to buy some of it?' One of the girls said, 'How much are they?' And that was it; we 'sampled' her. And 'How Much Are They' was our title. That tune turned out to be a minor hit. It's been licensed more times than I've had hot dinners. Typically, Mark Lusardi was the unsung hero on that recording. He gave it a tough 'disco' sound, and some nice dub touches.

Within a week or two I went over to Cologne to complete the tracks for the *How Much Are They* EP. I met the master drummer Jaki Liebezeit. His surname translates as 'love time', which is of course a perfect moniker for him. My favourite Can pieces were the long atmospheric groove pieces like 'Hallelujah' where Jaki's hypnotic pulse is to the fore. What can I say about that bloke? He's the ultimate drummer. Playing with him was a revelation. I have been lucky enough to play with Jaki many times over the years. The man is amazing. He continuously updates his style. A few years ago he dispensed with his bass drum pedal. He plays the bass drum with his sticks. He hits his cymbals on the 'upper cut'. It is a very economical style. His reductionism is typically German. (It's no wonder that homeopathy was a German development; it's also worth noting that the Germans' Axis allies, the Japanese, are avid reductionists too.) Jaki's style gets emptier and emptier with every passing year. Every drum is hit perfectly, not too heavy, not too light, with full awareness. He's never sloppy. His attitude is reminiscent of Eastern martial artists. You don't do 100 punches when training. You do 100 lots of 'one punch'. Do you see the difference? The drums are never hit in a sloppy or unfocused way. Jaki's 'DNA pulse' is an exact match to mine. It's hand in glove, so to speak.

After I saw the 1988 movie that stars Dustin Hoffman and Tom Cruise I started to call Jaki 'Rainman'. I felt that Jaki had striking similarities to Dustin Hoffman's character. I am certainly not saying that he is autistic. However, he seems to live quite alone in a world of beats, and he strongly seems to relate that world to mathematics. He has his own theory of beats. It is pretty deep, but it is not some form of hippy-dippy New Age nonsense. It appeared to me to be a truly logical system that would have been practical to implement. It would be good if a musicologist was to spend time with him and learn his system.

Sometimes I refer to him as 'The King of Saxony'. Whenever he came to London through the eighties and nineties he was happy as long as my road crew lined him up with a bit of puff and we left him alone to watch telly in his room. I always adopted the same routine on those occasions. I knew full well that Jaki just wanted his puff and a bit of telly, nothing else. But I used to come on like the gun salesman that Travis Bickle encounters in a hotel room in *Taxi Driver*. So I would begin by saying, 'Have you got your puff? And you have a TV in your room? OK. Do you want a woman? Shall I send a girl to your room?' 'No!' Jaki would reply. I would then spend several minutes going through a long list of various drugs (such as quinine and laudanum) and weapons ('Do you want a tank? I can get you a Chieftain tank with all the proper paperwork'). I would go on and on and on. I did this every single time I worked with Jaki.

Sometimes I would wait in reception for a few minutes and then go back and knock on his door and continue with even more questions (Do you want a toaster? How about a raccoon? What about a fragment of the Turin shroud?). I don't think that Jaki took it that seriously; however, he never smiled, not once during these long exchanges. He would simply keep answering 'no'. He would maintain a grave facial expression throughout. In a way it was an extension of my bass playing. I was being rhythmic and repetitious; I took great comfort in that routine. I think that he knew that. So maybe he was playing along with me to keep me happy. He did have a sense of humour and was a big Buster Keaton fan. In fact when Buster made an appearance at Berlin station not long after the end of the war Jaki queued up to see his hero. He would sometimes talk to me, explaining the differing approaches of Keaton and Chaplin. On the cover of 1994's 'Take Me To God' I got Jaki to dress up as Buster Keaton.

Most drummers are a bit weird. But Jaki takes the biscuit. He is a very deep bloke, who tends to make light of his enormous talent. When you praise his playing he will say things like (imagine a heavy German accent) 'it's normal... I just do the typical things a drummer would do...' (Yeah, right.) And yet he once admitted to me that as a young man he seriously contemplated throwing himself into the sea (at Ibiza) when playing with a jazz band, because he wasn't meeting the high standards that he had set himself. He has an incredible work ethic in regard to his drumming. He refers to his daily long drum practices, sometimes with other drummers and sometimes alone, as 'drum sport'. Indeed, his approach seems more reminiscent of a sportsman than a musician, so the term 'drum sport' seems fitting.

Whenever we set up and soundcheck for shows that Jaki is drumming in, I and everyone else in the touring party will click our heels and shout 'Heil Hitler!' intermittently. We will adopt the attitudes and demeanour of a platoon of Wehrmacht infantrymen. Every action performed by the band and crew is performed 'on the double'. On these occasions members of the band don't politely request the use of a tuner, they will demand it (in loud guttural tones). I will then bellow, 'Achtung! For the Führer!' just as we go on stage. All the band and crew will then bellow back, 'For the Führer!' Jaki hates all this; it's the one thing that makes him go mental. I never tire of doing it. Obviously if he didn't react then I would stop all that. Actually, I think that a band should behave like a detachment of soldiers. That goes for the women as well; believe me, I have nothing against women in uniform.

Both Jaki and Holger are from the East. Holger comes from Danzig, which was then in Germany (now of course it is called Gdansk and is part of Poland). Jaki is from eastern Saxony. I believe that they both crossed over to the West immediately following the end of the war. Holger claimed to have helped blow up a Russian ammunition dump as a young boy. I drove Holger potty on a couple of occasions. I remember we would eat and drink at a place called Café Fleur very near to his apartment in the middle of Cologne. Holger had a strict routine in regard to working at the Can studio. He would begin around lunchtime and finish about 7 p.m. One night at Le Fleur at around midnight I (typically) felt the muse descend. I insisted that Holger drive us out to the Can studio. It was a fair old drive, about forty-five minutes to an hour or so. He was well pissed off. I remember him saying (in all earnestness), 'You have made two mistakes: the first was being born and the second was coming here!' I remember that I nearly wet myself with laughter, it was such a Teutonic and 'final' insult; I thought that it was the funniest thing that I had ever heard.

Now I'm older I can really understand him being pissed off. If it was me now I would simply tell the mad drunken twenty-one year old to fuck off. Anyway, we got Jaki out of the little flat above the studio. He was not fazed at all. There was a lot of screaming and shouting going on. Within half an hour Holger was laughing his head off, having a great time. The result was the track 'Trench Warfare'.

I remember another day, when seemingly out of nowhere Holger erupted and accused Jaki, in English, 'You do not understand! You understand nothing!' Jaki replied, 'No, you are the one that doesn't understand!' They then continued the argument in German. It was a typically Teutonic argument, insofar as it didn't seem to be based on a 'point of principle' (which would be a bit wishy-washy and typically Anglo-Saxon) but rather a difference of ideology (of course, points of principle and ideologies are hardly mutually exclusive, but I'm sure that you get my drift). I was very happy to listen to them go at it 'hammer and tongs' for ten minutes or so. In the end Holger turned to me and said, 'Don't be fooled by Jaki, he is a hippy, he has short hair but he is still a hippy.' To me at that point Holger's attitude represented a dictator's perspective versus an anarchist's (Jaki). I have a foot in both camps. True Germans would probably see my attitude as impossible to maintain. They would perceive it as a weak and untenable situation. They would point out that 'ordered chaos' is a contradiction in terms, a self-negating position (when both are present you can have neither). Anyway, it was a fun argument to behold. Neither of them bore a grudge at its conclusion. It was not an unusual occurrence for them to steam into each other verbally; Holger would always 'start' it by provoking Jaki.

Holger had a great harmonic sensibility. He would build 'little scenes' into the compositions that would build tension and then release it. His main instruments were guitar, piano and the French horn. But he also used 'music concrète' techniques in regard to composition. He had worked with the genius Stockhausen, and absorbed much, especially in regard to tape manipulation (juxtaposition of mood and meaning via editing and collage techniques, etc.).

*Not too long after this I was lucky enough to see Stockhausen perform with his son Marcus (playing trumpet) at the Barbican. There were not that many people there and I sat right in the front row. I felt like it was a 'private show'. Around that time I read a great book which featured Stockhausen in conversation with an American journalist. For a while that book was like my musical Bible. Sometimes the Germanic tendency to superimpose invented cosmologies on to the world does my head in but on the whole I feel pretty comfortable with Deutsch volk. Pina Bausch is another of the German geniuses who I think is worthy of a huge amount of respect. I saw her and the Dance Company of Wuppertal a couple of years ago at Sadler's Wells. My God; one hour forty minutes (no interval) passed like nothing. I was reminded of Stockhausen's tour de force*

*Momente, when one is introduced to eternity; not the eternity of limitless time but the eternal infinity that exists right now in this very moment. Sometimes German art blows all other European art out of the water.*

Holger was the first person that I worked with to use tape vari-speed techniques to such dazzling effect. He would slow the tape right down and detune the guitar to match the tuning of the track. When it was played back the guitars would be really trebly and clear. They would be half an octave up from the normal range of a guitar. They would 'chime' in almost bell-like fashion. He would layer up the guitar parts like that. It would help to give the compositions the poignancy that they yearned to express. They no longer sounded like guitars but more like a cross between a mandolin and a balalaika. It was on those occasions that I realised that it was likely that Holger was genetically a Slav (his facial features strongly suggested that). Much of what he expressed musically was tinged with tragedy. Holger's approach was quite complex compared to what I had been used to with PiL; it was a real eye- (and ear-)opener. Holger was the first person I knew to call tunes 'pieces'. That is more of a classical musician's terminology but I liked it because it helped give the whole process the respect it deserves. He taught me the basics of compositional theory. He probably didn't realise that but he did. If I asked him a question he was happy to answer. I hung on his every word.

*Recently I called him a senile old git and told him to fuck off. It was no big deal, just an argument over money. (I felt that he was attempting to take the piss in regard to a proposed new deal for this old stuff.) Anyway, this kind of falling out makes no difference to how I feel about that time. I have good memories.*

Working at the Can studio was an experience. It had formerly been a small cinema. It was the first studio that I ever went to that didn't have a control room, divided by glass from the rest of the studio. There probably wasn't any grand design behind that, it was probably lack of funds that dictated the studio layout. However,

I was very taken by the 'open plan' feeling. I felt that it aided spontaneity as well as helping the sessions to move along more swiftly than they otherwise would have done. Sometimes you get the feeling in music studios that the people in the control room are in one world, and the people in the 'live' room are in another. The monitoring problems encountered when working in an open-plan space are not a big deal in my opinion. You can solve them.

We also did a bit of mixing at the producer Conny Plank's studio just outside Cologne. Conny and Holger were good friends. Karl Lippagaus, the German national radio DJ, was also hanging out on those sessions. In a way Karl is the German John Peel. To this day he is a good mate of mine. Conny looked like a big Viking. He was the archetypal gentle giant. He died tragically after ingesting some carcenogenic fibres from insulating material that he was moving around when refurbishing his studio. On the night that Holger was mixing there I came back after popping out to a see a Killing Joke gig. Conny was producing them at that time. When I got back to Conny's studio I was a bit underwhelmed by what I heard. I thought that it was a bit tame. Holger was a bit put out by my attitude. However, he was happy to let me tweak it a bit. He joked later that he thought I was going to blow the studio up. Basically I would have accentuated the bottom and top, and hollowed out the middle a bit. A limited approach to mixing, admittedly, but to this day, in regard to my own stuff, it is still an effective one. I like to get 'movement' in a mix (or certainly the illusion of movement). If I were a painter I would use broad vivid brushstrokes, the movement of the brush against the canvas would be clearly visible.

The *How Much Are They* EP came out on Island Records. Eventually we added two more tracks and we had an album, which we called *Mystery*. I insisted that Jaki was cut into the deal and had his name on the front cover. I thought that the bloke was immense. I still do. Both the EP and the album were artistically and commercially successful. Hildegard, the Can manager, handled the business on those recordings. I learnt a lot from her. She had learnt the art, as she good-humouredly liked to point out, of making the 'maximum from the minimum'. She had needed to learn that skill, because managing Can wasn't the easiest gig in the world. From watching her operate I learnt the basics of deals (especially in regard to licensing) and what you are essentially 'selling' ('rights' in 'territories' for a 'period of time'). That's where the term 'the maximum from the minimum' comes in; you attempt to get the maximum amount of advance monies and royalty rates for the fewest rights in the fewest territories for the least amount of time. That's the theory anyway. (In reality most record companies in my experience didn't account properly in regard to sales, so the onus was always on grabbing the most money you could up front because that was probably all you would see anyway.) People may assume that Can always had it easy but that is far from true. I remember them telling me stories of playing Wolverhampton to forty people back in the early seventies. Hildegard had learnt what a difficult and fickle world the music business could be, especially when managing an art band.

Angus MacKinnon did a great cover for *How Much Are They*. It is an atmospheric picture that he had taken in New Orleans, literally 'on the wrong side of the tracks'. We dedicated the record to Ian Curtis, who had died not long before that. The record's quality surprised a few people. So all in all I did very well out of that project. I got to work with two super musicians and got a crash course in 'how to do the business'. How lucky had I been going straight from PiL into that?

PUBS AND CLUBS

At that time there was still a pretty lively pub scene around the East End. It was a common thing for younger people to do a pub crawl all the way from one end of Hackney Road to the other, for instance. I seem to remember that The Queens was the most popular pub on that Hackney Road strip, along with the Sebright. The Bethnal Green area also had some lively pubs. I was very fond of The Birdcage at Columbia Road, for instance. That pub used to have an older clientele. There was a crooner who worked there who would sing Tony Bennett songs. Like all pub crooners he fancied himself a bit, looking into the eyes of the ladies as he sang and all that, it used to crack us up. It was a good laugh. I would often start a Friday evening off there with what I used to refer to as the 'O' gang, Pento, Gibbo, Westo and Robbo, as well as other geezers like Willie Connors, 'Shrew' and Vince. Like most of my mates all these geezers are Spurs fans. I still see them when I go to games. Those blokes were, in fact still are, all 'kicksters'; i.e. they still love a beer and a dirty great big spliff, apart from Glen (Westo) Westerman, who is now a born-again Christian. 'Westo' used to whizz about everywhere in a gleaming Mercedes. I remember that he once ran the car into a tree in Epping Forest. He's a jeweller. A lot of the 'proper chaps' would go to see him for gold rings and medallions and the like. He used to sort out a lot of the West Indian geezers around Hackney and Tottenham. Sometimes I would accompany Glen when he went to deliver their jewellery to them. We would often sit and have a puff and a chat with them, while listening to music. Westo was like me insofar as he could move easily between what you could call the 'black' and the 'white' worlds. Of course, those worlds are not as polarised now as they were then.

I used to run around a lot with Westo. He was good company because he wasn't a yob, you could have a good night out without violence taking place. I remember one afternoon when we ended up partying with some proper old-school villains up in Hackney Road. By eleven o'clock we were pretty far gone, and everyone had left, but the landlord of the pub insisted that Westo and I accompany him over to the establishment of a very well-known face to have some more fun there. However, Westo was pretty wasted so we left him to have a kip in the pub. Anyway, I returned to that pub at about 7 a.m. with the landlord. When we got in the pub we found Westo sitting bolt upright with the governor's two Dobermans growling at him. After we had left they had automatically come downstairs to guard the premises, just as they did every night once closing time arrived. They had found Westo asleep and no governor. They were well puzzled. Luckily they didn't attack Westo. However, he was bursting for a leak because every time he had gone to get up to go to the toilet the dogs had got distressed and started growling at him. He was very relieved to see us. He had been sitting there for hours.

I would often be around the West End during the day. Most of the record companies and publishers were around there, so I would pop in to see them, trying to hustle deals and all that. I would also do a bit of shopping up the West End, around Bond Street mainly. I quite liked Hugo Boss suits at that time. I would often pop in to see my mate Lynchy and have a drink in the afternoon with him. He worked at the Virgin Megastore as the assistant manager. He was a big music nut, who lived up at the Angel. I met him through Vince. He ran the football team at the Megastore, and got me into the team as a ringer. I scored quite a few goals for that team. We even played up in Glasgow once; on the way back I kicked the windscreen of the bus out. For some reason we could not get a replacement windscreen. Unfortunately it was winter and so the whole team had to sit there for hours, as the freezing air hit them full in the face. I really don't remember why I did that.

Once the pubs closed he had memberships for one or two drinking clubs in the West End. It would probably seem strange to people (now that pubs can stay open through the day) to have to go to a strictly members-only club to get a drink between 3 p.m. and 5 p.m. Lynchy would play the fruit machines all day at those drinking clubs. The payouts were quite large. You used to get a very interesting crowd of people in those West End drinking dens. You really would meet all sorts: glamour models, footballers, barristers and of course the odd criminal.

Lynchy was essentially, especially when dealing with 'his own', an honest bloke. However, how can I put this... there were no flies on Lynchy. He used to remind me, and quite a few others, of a young Arthur Daley. He often had a big cigar on the go, and was always doing deals and placing bets. I got him to do my merchandise on the road. He also ran the bar for me on a couple of occasions when I promoted my own shows. He was another massive Spurs fan. When we went to games we would often get in the ground closer to half-time than the first whistle. We just couldn't drag ourselves away from the pub.

On most Friday nights in the early eighties you would find me at the Globe in Mile End Road. The Globe was run by a family called Gerrish. There was John senior and his sons Johnny and Tony. I remember that Tony was an enthusiastic bodybuilder. Tony had a good sense of humour. When the humour got a bit 'out there' and surreal he had no problem keeping up to speed, which, in my experience, is quite unusual for a weightlifting geezer. The Globe was far and away the most popular watering hole for all the trendy young people in East London. At the weekends it would be packed, people would spill out on to the street. The DJs played soul music at high volume. (I recall that Maceo and the Macks' 'Across The Tracks' was a particularly popular tune there.) The girls who frequented the place were by and large very good looking and dressed very fashionably. The barmaids were also the prettiest around. Those East End girls really knew how to turn the style on.

Sometimes we would be invited to parties farther out in East London or Essex. We would always be a bit snobby about that and take the mickey a bit. I would refer to places like Manor Park and Wanstead as Inner Mongolia and to Essex generally as Outer Mongolia. Sometimes we would leave there (not Mongolia, the Globe) and go up West to The Embassy club or even occasionally places like Tramps, but none of those places had punters anywhere near as stylish as the Globe. (It's like the journalist Julie Burchill says, the chavs have always got more style than the rest.) The 'Blitz scene' or New Romantic movement was just kicking off so most of the punters from the Globe would go up to Le Beat Route club in Soho after kicking-out time. But I must say that I wasn't too keen on the music there, and I found a lot of people on that scene ridiculously pretentious. They would come on like haughty Parisians when really they had just got the Northern Line down from Colindale. I remember going up to the Blitz club with Westo and Vince on the opening night. We didn't like the music or the punters much; it was all a bit kitsch for our taste.

Another bloke who was in that East End is a geezer called 'Shrew'. He is a good mate of mine. I don't include him with the others because whereas they are a jolly mob of geezers, Shrew is permanently disappointed. Even when things were going well he would be disappointed. His philosophy was that because eventually things would always go wrong, you might as well bypass hope and happiness and be disappointed now. A very talented local artist called 'Mangray' did a fantastic set of T-shirts based on Shrew. They had Shrew's face on them, and underneath in bold typeface it said 'A Very Disappointed Man'.

I once said to Shrew, 'Shrew, have you ever considered topping yourself?' 'Yes,' he said, 'but I know that they would all be down the pub gloating, saying, oh well, it was always on the cards… well, I ain't gonna give them the pleasure.' Of course, when I say Mangray is a local (self-taught) artist I'm not talking about one of the new flux of artists into the area. Mangray has been doing his murals and stuff for years, in between running a large pallet yard. His large 'I am the voice in your head' mural which he placed in his pallet yard (which backs on to the busy commuter lines into Liverpool Street) was featured a few years ago in an art magazine, directly adjacent to an article on Bill Laswell. That made me happy; two unconnected mates of mine on different sides of the Atlantic getting their due respect.

Among all the trendies down at the Globe there was a hard

core of proper East End types. I used to like to pop in there during the week, when it would revert to being a 'West Ham pub'. It had a totally different vibe as compared to the weekend. Consequently there was no deafening soul blaring out and a cast of thousands clogging up the route to the bar. Instead there was a typically intimate British pub atmosphere, with a dozen or so geezers standing around winding each other up. People like Shrew and David Knibbs, who I had known since nursery school. It was through them that I met the Maltby Brothers, John and Dave (Animal). A lot of people thought that Dave was nicknamed Animal because he liked, when he was pissed, to bite and chew beer glasses (the straight glasses, not the mugs), but in fact his brother called him that because as a kid he refused to use a knife and fork. Apparently it was the act of putting metal cutlery in his mouth that freaked him out. (Actually thinking about it has just freaked me out; I can now taste metal in my mouth.) Animal preferred to use his hands. However, upon being presented with plastic cutlery he was happy. In a working-class household of that time, Dave's attitude would of course have been seen as deliberate and wilfully awkward behaviour. John, his elder brother, played a bit of bass and was a fine footballer, a good creative midfielder. I played football with him a few times. Dave was also a very capable (and brave) goalkeeper.

When I heard about his guitar playing my ears pricked up. I was determined that any band that I put together would have people in it that I could trust. I wanted 'my own' around me.

So I got together with Dave and had a bash with him, and it went well. He was very raw, with a rocky style, but had a nice sense of melody. He could really sound quite folksy at times. He was a big Jimi Hendrix fan, which was a big plus point in his favour. I definitely felt that we could work together. I had tracked Jim Walker down to a squat in Bonnington Square, Vauxhall. I drove over to see him with Dave. Jim didn't take a lot of convincing, so we got some rehearsals lined up. Things went well and we all enjoyed playing together. Jim liked Dave; he thought he was an OK down-to-earth sort of bloke. The Miles Davis electric-period stuff, that I was listening to, had really got me going. I wanted to adopt a similar approach to playing. I wanted the band to be instrumental and I also wanted to avoid having a set list of tunes. I wanted us to improvise and 'feel it' when we went on stage, in the way that Miles's musicians did. So we had ourselves an avant-garde power trio.

## DELLOW HOUSE

Tower Hamlets finally offered me a council flat. I had been on the council waiting list for years. The offer was a 'hard to let' tenancy at Dellow House in Shadwell. It was part of the Solander Gardens Estate. It was a classic old tenement block. It had been built in the late 1800s to house the workers who worked on the construction of nearby Tower Bridge. Dellow House lay just off Cable Street, not far from where the famous riot took place; indeed, just around the corner from the flat there was a giant mural commemorating the riot. My flat was on the top floor, several flights up with no lift. I had a shared balcony that enjoyed views on to the adjacent block, as well as across Wapping and into South London. I went to check the flat out. The deal from the council was a straightforward one. If I turned the flat down I wouldn't get offered another one. Well, there was no way I was going to turn it down.

Shadwell had a pie-and-mash shop and a chippie, and a number of good boozers. The Old House at Home soon became my local. The Old House was a tiny little pub, it was run by a good governor called Paul. I had some great days and nights in there. The local newsagent was run by an Asian family. They were terrific people and ahead of their time in regard to being integrated. The mum and dad were an example to other immigrants; they had retained their original culture but at the same time were really of 'the manor'. They were friendly and outgoing. Their sons and

JAH WOBBLE

daughter were proper cockneys. Bobby, who I think was the eldest son, was an avid Spurs fan. I remember the dad telling me that he had worked on the East London Line as a motorman before starting his business. Shadwell was, I believe, the poorest ward in the country at that time. It was a rough and tough place even when compared to the rest of the East End generally, but I loved it. It was like a little village. I went on to have that flat for fourteen years. My tenancy even outlived the brothel that was located a few floors below.

So anyway, I was made up; I had a flat, even though it was just one big room with a bathroom and a kitchen. I began to calculate how much money I would need to kit the flat out with a new carpet, furniture, cooker, fridge, telly and all the rest, when out of the blue I got a phone call from a club in Berlin. They wanted me to come and do a PA, for a very nice fee (I think about the equivalent of £5,000 now) plus hotel and flights and all exes for two people. They wanted me to mime to three of my solo tracks, 'Betrayal', 'Blueberry Hill' and 'Tales From Outer Space'. I thought, Oh dear, that's going to be really embarrassing, but Berlin is a long way away and no one will ever know. I told the club-owners that they had to send all the money up front (I later found out that it was standard to get half up front and half prior to performance). They wired the money over. In those days you could wire cash via the post office. I think that you could only do something like £100 at a time. So the same telegraph boy had to go backwards and forwards from the post office with the money. My old man was at home at the time, as he had been laid off work and was waiting to start his new job, at the post office. His eyes were like saucers watching me count that money at the kitchen table. He went upstairs for his normal afternoon kip shaking his head in disbelief. (All the Wardle men grab a kip in the afternoon if they can. I do the same now when I'm touring.) It made absolutely no sense to him as to why somebody I didn't know from Germany would send me a large amount of cash simply to show up and prance about miming, certainly not

162

Me with Mingus
the cat on the
balcony at
Dellow House

for that sort of money. Actually it made no sense to me either but I wasn't complaining; after all, I had to kit my flat out, and that could now be done (the rent, by the way, was about £11 a week)! So I had the Berlin money plus the 'How Much' advance, and an advance on a Japanese deal for 'Betrayal'. And I had a new band. Bloody hell! Happy days!

Around that time Ronnie showed up after being away for a few weeks, so I took him over to Berlin with me. What a madhouse that city was at that time. The Berlin Wall was still up all the way around the city. I recall standing up on one of the observation towers that overlooked the wall. From that vantage point I could see the East German border guards scrutinising us with their binoculars. I also remember the Alsatian dogs that were attached via their collars to long sections of wire; they must have been bored out of their minds going backwards and forwards along that wire all day long. There were bullet holes in the buildings that lay adjacent to the wall, where would-be escapees had been fired on as they attempted to make good their escape from the East. Berlin at that time was like a sort of mass transit lounge cum terminal zone.

There were all sorts of marginal people there who were 'passing through'. Berlin had a hysterical undertow. It really was as if many people subconsciously felt that an invasion was imminent. They partied on down, literally as if there was no tomorrow. It was as if they expected to emerge from their nightclubs at six in the morning to be faced by Russian tanks. It was rumoured that there were a lot of people there with no paperwork, and consequently no way out. I don't know how true that was. The club scene there was world renowned at that time. To this day I have never heard DJing as radical as I heard on that trip. They even mixed calypso in with the Sex Pistols. It was the first place I went to that had clubs going twenty-four hours a day. You could easily lose your sense of time there. Anyway, the 'gig' went OK and me and Ronnie had a laugh. On the downside, Berlin was a bit like the movie *Cabaret*. The po-faced decadent thing was pretty evident. There were quite a few rich kids from the suburbs of Sydney, LA and other major cities in attendance. I remember a bird with a monocle, a jet-black wig and a long cigarette holder offering me deadly nightshade. I told her that I was 'all right, thanks, love' but that I'd ask my mate. 'Oi, Ron!' I shouted over the loud music. 'She says do you fancy some deadly nightshade?' 'No,' he said, 'but has she got any arsenic?' Humour is such a wonderful antidote to decadence.

*I found out later that deadly nightshade in a certain form can be taken as a hallucinogenic drug. I knew it then as no more than a deadly poison, of course. I thought that the girl was a nutcase. German folklore has it that 'belladonna' (as deadly nightshade is sometimes called) can be used to evoke werewolves. Well, I didn't need deadly nightshade to become a werewolf. A bottle of Scotch normally did the trick for me.*

Within a few weeks of moving in I was still pretty flush with money so I went and got some pretty expensive Italian chrome-and-glass shelving units from a shop in Holborn. A day or two after that I was with Animal, drinking up the Roman (the Roman

Road, in Bow). There was an aquarium shop that also sold fish there at that time. I decided on the spur of the moment that I should get a big top-of-the-range aquarium, with the biggest and most colourful tropical fish that the shop stocked. I continued drinking with Animal and a couple of others. The bloke in the shop suggested, wisely, that it would be best to leave the fish with him until their 'home' was ready for them. I got a cab back over to Shadwell, with the big tank, the gravel, plants, pump and other accoutrements. I played a bit of music and dossed around a bit. I then remembered the tank. By now it was the early hours of the morning. I wondered what the perfect setting for the tank would be. I decided that my new flash and bloody expensive Italian shelf units would be the ideal setting for my tank. So I placed the tank on the shelf unit and filled it with the gravel. I then started to fill the tank with buckets of water. It took bloody ages. Suddenly there was a groaning sound and the shelf unit started to give way. The whole thing buckled and toppled forward on to me. I tried stupidly to hold it up, but to no avail. I then tried to get away from it but it knocked me over and the whole shebang fell on me and pinned me, face down, to the floor. The water cascaded everywhere. I was stunned and momentarily lost consciousness.

It took a while to extricate myself from the mess. I suddenly felt relatively sober. I realised that the flat below was going to get flooded. I had not yet met the tenants of the flat below me. It wasn't the best of circumstances to make someone's acquaintance. I went downstairs and knocked on the door. It took ages before anybody answered. Eventually I heard a woman's voice asking, nervously, 'Who is it?' I explained that it was the upstairs neighbour and that I'd 'had an accident'. She hesitated and then slid back the bolts and opened the door while keeping the chain on. A woman in her late twenties to early thirties appeared, she was still half asleep. I must have looked a sight, as I had blood running down my head from a nasty gash sustained when the tank smashed. I explained what had happened. As I did so I saw water dripping down behind her. What a way to meet your new neighbour.

Anyway, the shelf units were damaged beyond repair and the brand-new carpet was absolutely sodden. There was broken glass and gravel everywhere. I had to get a big fan to help dry it out (as a thank-you to the fan I gave her my autograph and a bunch of flowers). Mind you, it got very hot in the summer, in that little flat, so the fan came in handy. Conversely it was freezing in winter; it was up high and it didn't have double-glazing or central heating. Sometimes I would find ice in the sink and on the inside of the windows. No wonder it was a hard-to-let flat. It didn't bother me, though, because when you got the fire on it soon warmed up. It was a nice cosy little flat.

## THE HUMAN CONDITION

Eventually, after many weeks' debate, I thought up a name for our avant-garde power trio. I dubbed us the Human Condition. Luckily Jim and Dave both liked the name. I also sorted out a place for us to rehearse. I had come to hate bog-standard, musky-smelling rehearsal rooms (which were normally situated under railway arches). So I had a word with the vicar of St Paul's Church on The Highway. He agreed to let us store our amps and drum kit up in the belfry and to rehearse in the church on weekday afternoons. He was a very nice bloke. (Of course, I made a contribution to church funds.) I remember that on one afternoon that we were scheduled to rehearse, I arrived a lot earlier than I needed to. I went and hid up in the belfry. It was a very bright and sunny day outside so it took a little bit of time for my eyes to adapt to the gloom. I took up an elevated position up in a corner of the belfry. I had hold of the bell rope. I heard somebody gingerly making their way up the narrow and rickety wooden staircase. It was Animal; he was the first to arrive. As he made his way to the top of the staircase I could see him peering into the gloom. Just as he got up the stairs and into the belfry I swung towards him on the bell rope yelling for all I was worth. A second or so later the bell reverberated and he froze in terror and confusion. Within a few seconds he realised that it was me swinging backwards and forwards over his head and he started laughing. We then both waited for Jim to come and did a double-whammy on him, with both of us hanging on to the rope.

One of the first gigs that the Human Condition performed was at the Screen on the Green cinema, which is on Upper Street at the Angel in Islington. I was friendly with the manager there, and he was happy to let us do a show. I seem to remember that we had a terrific-looking poster done up to promote the night, which Margaux made up at the art college that she was attending.

There were a lot of faces at the Angel on the night of the gig. I made sure it was a good night. The evening began with a comedian followed by the Human Condition. We came on and did the business. The combination of Jim and me made for a pretty heavy yet supple rhythm section. I really got into some juicy forward-moving modulated B-lines with that band. We were a bit bluesy on occasion. Animal started to build a bit of a reputation as a guitarist. He was thrilled when Siouxsie Sioux said that he was her guitarist of the year in the *NME*. The evening was capped off by a showing of Clint Eastwood's *The Gauntlet*. Dave Lynch did the bar. It was a great night in every way. We got some excellent reviews, which was a thrill for Animal especially, plus we made a few quid.

The Human Condition went on to perform about twenty or so shows, and we released two live cassettes. I think that the better of the two releases is the *Live In Europe* tape. My best memories of the Human Condition were of touring through Holland, Belgium and Germany. The offer to tour there came out of the blue from an agent called Willem Venema. He had a little company called W Concerts. We did the deal over the phone and he sent over cash to secure the deal. He met us at Schiphol airport. He wasn't what I expected at all. From the way he spoke on the phone I expected somebody who was very square and looked like a businessman. Instead we were greeted by an outrageously dressed Dutch hippy. Willem was the first ever (proper) Dutch hippy that I ever set eyes upon. He had snakeskin boots, with his jeans tucked into them, hair down to his arse and a massive tash. Me, Jim and Dave Maltby rolled up with laughter. But Willem was nothing compared to his mate, Hein Fokker. Hein was the driver for that tour but he soon became our tour manager. He was a real 'Cheech and Chong' sort of a bloke. He looked and behaved a bit like Otto Man in *The Simpsons*. He came from Nijmegen, which is in the north. Like many people in Nijmegen Hein was a Catholic. Like many people from my sort of background he had 'crazy-looking eyes' that often had a humorous glint to them. What a pair of geezers Hein and Willem were. (In fact they are the only hippies that I have ever known that I would use the word geezer in conjunction with.) They seemed to breeze through everything without a care in the world. W Concerts was based in Utrecht. Before starting the tour Willem (who became my agent) and Hein took us to Utrecht to get our backline and drum kit sorted. The company doing that was newly formed. It was a two-man outfit. The business brains was a geezer called Fred Hoovis and the man doing the PAs and out-front sound was called Johnny 'Cable' (everyone called him 'Cable'). At that time Fred and Cable had one van, one PA, some amps and a drum kit. Now their company (which is called Ampco) have umpteen PAs and articulated lorries plus a large number of staff. They are a pan-European company.

Willem went on to become the best-known agent in Holland. To me Willem was the original 'Guilder Boy'. That was the name I gave to all Dutch blokes in the music business. They loved a guilder. However, unlike so many in the music game, once the deal was done they would scrupulously stick to their side of the bargain. I used to see them, in my mind's eye, as fifteenth-century

Me and Willem Venema, a proper Dutch hippy, and one of the few agents who I ever took a shine to

Dutch merchants. You could easily imagine them weighing gold and silver. Their long hippy hairstyles definitely helped to provoke that image.

*They were a funny mix of the old and new. Like many working-class British blokes I fell in love with Holland. I loved their easygoing nature. However, I came to realise that there was more to Holland then meets the eye. It's a funny old country. For all its veneer of easygoing liberalism there is a noticeable puritanical Calvinist undertow, which is at its most evident in the more rural areas.*

Willem was a stickler for tax forms. I would be at the bar after a show holding court and there would be Willem, as regular as clockwork, with that night's tax exemption forms, quill – no, sorry, pen – in hand, leading me away to the promoter's office to count up the night's takings.

Hein is now a producer of music shows and festivals for Dutch TV. That same set of Dutchmen sorted all my tours outside of the UK and America for many years after that. I became particularly close to Cable and Hein, because those two would be out on the road with me. The three of us saw a lot of mad stuff on the road over those early eighties years. At the time that I met him Cable had hardly been to England and his English was pretty poor (although better than my Dutch). In no time at all he was speaking, thanks to Dave and me, just like a cockney. He would call people 'fucking cunt' in just the same charming way that we did, with a similar cockney inflection to his voice. Cable was a tough, wiry little bloke, and like Hein immensely likeable.

We took the journalist/DJ and all-round hedonist Kriss Needs on that first Human Condition tour as our (euphemism coming up) 'assistant tour manager'. Kriss was a good chum of mine; in fact the whole group liked him. He really liked a drink. Unfortunately when he had a drink he had a tendency to get into all manner of scrapes. He returned from that tour with a fractured skull and a broken finger. Jim Walker had a detached retina. And we all had a good time.

I began to find the Human Condition sound of a three-piece (albeit occasionally augmented with saxophone) a bit limited. Our shows were a bit erratic but on our night we were a powerful and uncompromising band. Nevertheless, I fancied expanding the band to a five- or six-piece. At the same time Jim Walker seemed to be seriously questioning the idea of being a drummer. I think that he felt that PiL had been his big chance and that was it, he was doomed to never make the big time again. I respected his position and didn't try to talk him out of it. Within a few years he had completely given up drumming. I couldn't help thinking it was a shame. He was a very good drummer.

I continued playing with Animal. I encouraged him to experiment with different sorts of modes. Middle Eastern and folk ones were particularly to my liking, whereas blues and jazzy stuff (generally) felt a bit tired and clichéd. I would fit my bass lines to his modal melodies. I began my own record label and began releasing my own stuff. I called the label Lago, after the name of the town in Clint Eastwood's *High Plains Drifter*, which was one of my favourite films. Eastwood's example of self-sufficiency and artistry has been an absolute inspiration to me over the years.

I soon learned the ropes in regard to running a label. It was around that time that Mark Lusardi left Gooseberry and started his own studio in Britton Street in Clerkenwell. I became a regular client there. Mark and I enjoyed many jolly japes at that time.

The bloke that I went to for mastering and cutting my records was a bloke called 'Porky', who had a cutting room in Portland Street called 'Porky's Prime Cuts'. He was a Scouser, and always worked with a pint of beer in his hand. A very good bloke, he was very gregarious, and, more importantly, very good at his job. His back door opened on to an alleyway, which also had the entrance to a pub in it. I think it was something like fifteen paces from Porky's room to the bar of the pub. Friendly waitresses, who to a woman were Antipodeans, served the beer. Porky was very tight with Noddy Holder from Slade. Noddy would often hang around Porky's. He struck me as a very easygoing and down-to-earth bloke. I remember that the custom with Porky was to scratch a nutty message of your choice on the inner ring of the lacquer disc. This of course meant that all the vinyl discs that were pressed from that lacquer would have the same nutty message at the end of the grooves. If you hold those discs up to the light you can see those messages.

I went to a place in Portobello Road to get the records manufactured. I had to pay cash up front. I think that the actual factory was across the Channel in France, near Calais somewhere. I seem to remember that the records would be delivered on a Friday around mid-morning. I would arrange for Lightning, who were a record wholesalers, to come and buy a large part of what I had just got pressed. I would then put the rest of the stock in my van and take it to places like Caroline Exports, which was owned by Richard Branson. I would sell them a few, before moving on to various stores around London (Lynchy at the Megastore was always good for a few). I would finally finish off over at Rough Trade Distribution, which by that time had moved to King's Cross. I would save the few that I had over to sell at shows. I also used to knock a few T-shirts out. A very nice bloke called Alan up the Harrow Road would print them for me. Margaux did the design for those shirts. It was very ahead of its time in that it was quite ethnic and colourful. We also used that design for the cover of the *Bedroom Album*. It featured me as a Mogul emperor sort of a bloke. I made that album at home on a Portastudio. I really had no intention of releasing the stuff. However, one of the people who worked at Rough Trade came to visit me at Dellow House and heard the recordings. He went nuts for them, and insisted that I released them. I initially said no because I felt that it was just a rough series of sketches. However, in the end I relented and put out the record. I couldn't believe it; *The Bedroom Album* did a good few thousand. It was all down to that bloke.

That whole period was very important to me in regard to preparing me for the future. I would spend hours walking around Wapping listening to all sorts of music on my Walkman. The music of Miles Davis's electric period along with Mohamed Abdel Wahab was the stuff that I caned the most. I spent a lot of time alone and would really be off in another world. Beautiful theories and truths would come to me as I walked. It would be years before I could really actualise this stuff sent to me from the realm of ideas. My most vivid memory of that time comes in the form of a fragrance, cinnamon. London Docks and the nearby St Katharine's Dock are where all the spices and peppers were offloaded and stored. Their gorgeous aroma lingered for many years. That smell also reminds me of my childhood.

# Chapter Eight: Nil by Mouth

## NIL BY MOUTH

I also suffered intermittent bouts of illness throughout 1981. This had started when I was in PiL. I would get quite bad abdominal pains. I suffered attacks of diarrhoea and severe vomiting. I would actually vomit bile and blood. (It got a bit like the girl in *The Exorcist* except that my head didn't spin around, and to the best of my knowledge Satan didn't speak through me.) I would also develop a high temperature around the time of these attacks. The attacks would come every few weeks. At first (around the end of 1979) they had taken the form of occasional abdominal cramps, but they had grown in both severity and duration, until a couple of years later I ended up being hospitalised. I had to have a drip put in my arm because I was severely dehydrated. I also had a high white cell count. I was in a lot of pain and they put me on morphine. I remember that was the first time that I ever prayed in desperation. I prayed for the pain to stop. I had a fever and as per usual I started getting mild hallucinations. I kept talking to the nurses about a helicopter on the roof. Of course, there was no helicopter on the roof. I told the staff that the helicopter was great for emergencies, and that it was quicker than an ambulance. Strangely enough the

Royal London Hospital, ('The London') at Whitechapel did utilise an air ambulance service some fifteen years later. I also told them that in the future I would live near Manchester, and that it would be possible to fly there (Manchester) from an 'airport in the docks'. Unfortunately the Hattie Jaeques-type ward sister got wind of my ramblings and thought that I must have been on LSD or something so they kept a close and stern eye on me. The truth of the matter was I hadn't been taking anything. I hadn't even been drinking for a week or two. I just couldn't manage it.

*I don't think that I have ever foretold the future like that before or since. There have been a few times when I have gone to do sessions, and the bass line reverberating in my head before the session subsequently fits the track (which I have never heard before) like a glove. Of course, I would love it if a voice in my head said something like, 'The winners of the FA Cup in 2011 will be...' I am not a betting man but I think that I would be straight down to the bookie's if that ever happened.*

All this must have happened around April 1981 because I remember listening, once my temperature had subsided, to a radio commentary of Spurs versus Wolves in one of that season's FA Cup semifinals (Spurs won narrowly, even though they were by far the dominant team throughout and should have won by a hatful. They went on to win the cup that year). I was put on to a surgical ward. They came very near to operating on me, because it turned out that a bit of the gut just beneath my stomach had twisted around a bit. Even though the kink had righted itself the surgeon didn't see the point of me lying about taking up a bed so he wanted to cut that bit of gut out. I actually went as far as having the orderly come and shave me the night before the scheduled operation. However, there was a Persian doctor there, a gastroenterologist, who saved my bacon. He had a word with the gung-ho surgeon and asked him to postpone the operation. That was a result because no one wants a general anaesthetic, as well as the general grief of an operation, unless absolutely necessary.

Because The London is a teaching hospital, when the student doctors had their exams to do, the surgical wards were closed to all but the most urgent of admissions. All the 'regular' operations in regard to things like ulcers were put on hold at that time. They didn't want to discharge me because, although my symptoms had diminished, it was felt that they could just as quickly return, and that my condition could possibly be life-threatening. So typically for me I sort of fell between the cracks. I remember that by that time there was only one other bloke on that ward. An old Polish bloke called Michael, a smashing bloke. I must admit that the nurses spoilt me rotten. They were typical of the nurses of that time, hard-working angels. I had plenty of visitors. Margaux came in quite a bit. Holger Czukay came to visit with his Luftwaffe gear on, I recall that caused a bit of a commotion. Island Records sent over a massive bouquet of flowers and a mountain of fruit, and a hamper of food, which was very nice. Glorious spring weather ensued and I would sit out on the veranda of the ward, which fortuitously overlooked the hospital gardens, sipping tea and smoking fags.

To be perfectly honest, whenever I see Michael Caine in his convalescence scene in *Alfie* I am reminded of that time. I recall sneaking out with Lynchy and Vince on a couple of occasions during the long afternoons. I would nip across the road to the Grave Maurice with them. I couldn't handle pints of beer, so I stuck to spirits. In fact I decided that cold beer was one of the root causes of my problem. I remember telling Vince that I was going to stick to spirits and red wine from then onwards.

To be honest, after a while I got itchy feet and decided that as I felt better I would discharge myself. The Persian doctor went mental at me, but I was quite headstrong in those days and was absolutely adamant that I was leaving. The doctor told me that it was simply a matter of time before I would be back, 'if you are lucky', he added. I thought that he was being needlessly melodramatic; however, I realise now that he and the other doctors all thought it was possible that I could haemorrhage, because twisted guts can possibly, among other things, entwine the veins next to them and are therefore something to keep an eye on. But of course, when you are young you feel that you are immortal.

*In fact from about 1992 onwards and up until the age of forty I employed a rota of people whose sole job was to gently whisper to me, 'Remember you are mortal' throughout the day. I had another mob made up exclusively of beautiful girls from the Greek islands who would wave fronds about in the summer months in order to keep me cool. Obviously that was seasonal work, so I would lay them off around the third week of August. A couple of them could play the lyre so I retained them in that capacity for the rest of the year.*

Of course, within a matter of weeks I was back again as white as a sheet and doubled up in pain. The Persian doctor showed up and simply asked if I was now ready to do as I was told. I answered in the affirmative. He put me on a medical ward and did a few tests. Eventually I was diagnosed with Crohn's disease. I was quite happy that at least I had a name for my pain. The Persian put me on a course of drugs for six months or so. I was very fortunate, because I didn't suffer any side effects. To this day I have not suffered any more attacks, and touch wood have never had another stay in hospital. On a couple of occasions when chatting socially to doctors they have told me that I must be mistaken about that diagnosis, because I appear to be pretty healthy. Nevertheless, it's true.

I recall one very funny incident at that time. Before the surgical ward was cleared there were a load of youngish blokes present; most of them were having operations on bleeding ulcers. The atmosphere got quite boisterous, and in the end the ward sister had to put her foot down quite severely. Anyway, I remember that a rather posh junior doctor visited one of these geezers in the bed opposite me. I seem to recall that he (the patient) was a young docker from Tilbury. The screens went around and I heard muffled voices. Suddenly I heard the patient raise his voice in anger and indignation. All of a sudden the doctor came flying backwards through the screens, and he scurried off red faced. 'Do you know what that dirty bastard wanted to do?' the bloke asked me. 'No,' I replied (of course, I knew full well, the doctor was looking to do a rectal inspection). 'He wanted to stick a finger up my 'arris, the dirty c***,' said the bloke. 'Well,' I said, 'they need to do that to check there are no obstructions.' 'Obstructions? Obstructions?' the bloke shouted. 'Why the f*** would I have an obstruction up me arse?' The ward sister came and told him to lower his voice, then gave him a good telling-off. He was as meek as a lamb with her. He went all contrite. I considered winding the bloke up – you know, asking him, in the manner of a shrink, what the problem really was... did he actually deep down fancy the junior doctor perhaps, was that why he had reacted in such an extreme way? However, even I know when to 'leave it'. The bloke was 'wrapped very tight' and I feel sure that he would have gone for me. Most likely my drip would have been detached in the ensuing melee.

## BODY MUSIC

An A&R bloke called Ashley Newton phoned me while I was in the hospital and asked me if I wanted to team up with a guitarist called Ben Mandelson to make an 'African'-style record. I said that I would give it a go. The result was a record called 'Body Music Mokili.' Everyone else on that session, apart from Pinise Saul, the South African vocalist (a very sweet and easygoing woman), the engineer and Neville Murray (the percussionist), seemed to be English ex-public-schoolboys. Those blokes were OK but I didn't really feel at home. That was the first time that I made the link between (what is now called) 'world music' and English public-schoolboys. The world music scene is absolutely awash with them. Many of these toffs seem to fancy themselves as intrepid explorer cum Lawrence of Arabia sort of characters.

*I think that most of that lot were also in a group called*

*3 Mustaphas 3. When performing with that band they would adopt, for their stage act, Albanian names, and wear traditional Albanian garb. To be honest I couldn't take that seriously, even though they did seem to love the music of that region. I thought that it was stupid and insulting to dress up and treat the music as part of a comedy routine. Only daft ex-public-schoolboys would have done that. However, Ben Mandelson, to give him credit, is a proper player. You would call him a musician.*

Whatever, 'Body Music' didn't turn out too bad, it was a sort of potpourri of various African styles. To be honest I would have preferred to have kept it very modal and done a more stripped-down percussion-led dance record, something in the line of Manu Dibango, for instance, but with a heavy bass line. I liked the way Dibango mixed various African styles in his records, but no matter what the style, his stuff grooved. (I was also a fan of Nigeria's juju style of music, particularly that of King Sunny Ade, who was signed to Island at that time.) However, I knew full well that at that point I would never be trusted enough to be given a budget, to go off and make a 'world music' record for a major label where I would be allowed to chose my collaborators, so I made the most of it.

The best thing about the 'African' session was the friendship that I forged with Neville Murray. We got along very well with each other. In fact he was just the bloke that I was looking for. I asked him to join me in a band with Animal. It was around this time that I saw an incredible two-part BBC documentary called *The Romany Trail*. As the title suggests it highlighted the two routes that the Roma people (or Gypsies) and their music took when leaving Rajasthan. Some went through the Middle East and then over the Mediterranean and into Andalusia. Others went through Europe, yet again terminating in southern Spain. The programme makers featured music from places as seemingly diverse as Skopje in Macedonia (where the clock of the town hall had been stopped many years before in an earthquake) and Cairo, where one of the musicians they featured was also revealed as being a porn star. (Those Cairo musicians were known as Invaders of the Hearts. From that time on I used that phrase for my bands.) I particularly remember the performance of 'El Chocolate', a legendary flamenco singer, when the programme reached its conclusion in Andalusia. That documentary made me blubber like a baby. I was very moved by it. (I got that lovely 'at home' feeling to the power of ten.) I watched *The Romany Trail* over and over on video. I wonder if it is still in the BBC vaults.

*The best dub record that I have ever heard dates from that early eighties period. The mixing engineer was a bloke called 'Groucho'. He did a mix of the King Sunny Ade album* Juju Music. *It is truly outstanding. Groucho's first session was with PiL. He also engineered a lot of the* Snakecharmer *album. I could never understand why he didn't become a big name.*

## THE INVADERS OF THE HEART

I wanted to add tonal richness to things. I really fancied getting a keyboard player on board. To be quite honest I wanted a few jazz chords knocking about and acting as a tonal bedrock for that stratum of sound that lives a floor or two above the bass. By God, sir, I make no apology for that. Neville knew of a very capable musician called Ollie Marland. We hooked up with him and it went very well. He was the son of a headmaster. Although he was a nice middle-class boy he affected a bit of a mockney accent, in fact he really was a chameleon sort of a bloke, but that didn't bother me too much because he was such a good player, and he was also up for a good laugh. Ollie was in no way, shape or form what I would call a creative or innovative player, but my God, the bloke, when pointed in the required direction, could play anything. To this day he is the best 'proper musician' that I have ever come across. I learnt so much just watching him, in regard to chord shapes and chord developments. He had 'great ears', and just being around somebody like that improved my abilities in regard to listening, not only to pitching, but also to how every instrument should/could sound. There is a track on the *Snakecharmer* album called 'Hold On To Your Dreams' that gives a great example of Ollie's playing.

I was playing my bass with a much funkier edge than I had done previously. I was incorporating little 'pull-offs' and slaps into a lot of my lines. Larry Graham is, of course, the governor of those particular techniques. Owing to the fact that I was adding percussion I wanted to get away from the dominating and sometimes cumbersome sound of ye olde rock drum kit. I didn't want a heavy-handed drummer drowning out Neville. Instead I wanted a drummer who had deft qualities, yet who could still hold a groove. Believe it or not that requirement in a drummer is still a tall order. People that can do both don't grow on trees. The first bloke we got on the skins was a geezer called Cliff. He was deft, but didn't hold the groove quite as strongly as I would have liked. Eventually we got a chap called Lee Partis. Lee wasn't spectacular but he really did the job, plus he had a good sense of humour. He now plays with the Oysterband.

On the way up to Manchester's Hacienda Club to play our debut gig (booked by Mike Pickering, who went on to form M-People) we gave a lift to a trombonist called Annie Whitehead, who was going back home to Oldham. Indeed, it was within the northern brass band scene that Annie had learnt her trade. Annie sat and played her trombone in the bus, and of course I was completely won over and asked her to come and play with us that night. She effortlessly got to grips with the Eastern modes that we were playing. On top of that she understood the mellow reggae way of trombone. To be honest I had, up to that point, still been looking for a trumpet player (the higher register cuts through the heavy bass and hand percussion better than tenor sax and trombone); however, Annie was such a good player it made no difference to me.

It really was a unique sound. I can remember the journalist

Richard Cook coming round to interview me at Dellow House. I can't remember what magazine he was writing for; maybe it was *NME*. I played him some rough recordings of 'The Invaders'. I recall that he was knocked out by the unusual blend (for the time) of instruments and styles. Neville's congas vied with the heavy electric guitar of Animal, while I got Ollie and Annie playing off (as well as with) one another in ways reminiscent of Shorter and Zawinul. I was really getting close to the 'total' form of music that I was looking for. However, in the studio we couldn't quite get what I was looking for. The really explosive performances tended to be when we played concerts. The exception was the eponymous twelve-inch single 'Jah Wobble And The Invaders Of The Heart'. That had the required beautiful blend of Eastern sounds and a dub sensibility. The production had more in common with the rave

Typical Invaders of the Heart backstage scene: Hein Fokker holding a large Walkie Talkie keeps everything on schedule for 'show time', whilst Neville and Ollie skin up. I'm dozing off (the calm before the storm), as I clutch a large glass of JD. A bored Dutch girl looks on

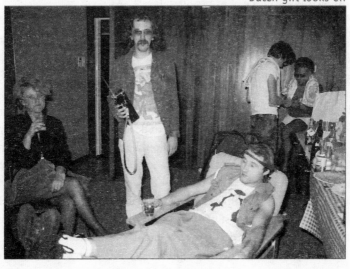

productions of the nineties than it did with other recordings of that early eighties era.

That line-up toured through Europe extensively. We also did a long tour of America and Canada in 1983. I think that was probably the craziest tour that I ever did. My drinking was really getting out of control by this point. Ollie and Annie also liked a drink, and the three of us would hammer the Jack Daniel's. At least Animal stayed on the beer and didn't hit the spirits, but even so he too would get hopelessly drunk. Neville and Lee didn't really drink a great deal; however, they did like a puff, as I recall, especially Neville. (On the few occasions that Nev did get pissed you really knew about it, because he became a lunatic.) In the course of two months we gigged our way down from Canada to New Mexico and from New York to LA and back again. When we got to LA we played a place called Madame Wong's West. I got bang on the charlie again for the first time in a couple of years, so things started to really get crazy. One mad thing after another happened on that tour.

However, one incident really stands out in my mind. We were in an industrial city on the East Coast. As soon as we walked into the club in the afternoon something felt wrong. It is now the sort of feeling that I associate with the use and sale of class A drugs, especially cocaine. The place felt a bit seedy, nothing unusual there, but this place was extra seedy. The people there were reminiscent of the baddies in David Lynch's *Blue Velvet*. The tour manager didn't like the vibe and he asked the club-owner for half our gig fee up front in the middle of the afternoon. Well, in a way that's nutty. Really you should ask for all of it up front, as I subsequently started to do as a matter of course, or trust the promoter. Well, the main bloke went mental. There was a really edgy, 'cokey' vibe with everyone. He started to threaten the life of the tour manager. He started saying that if he (the tour manager) was found dead in the local river nobody would care and there would be no 'comeback' on him (the club-owner), because he was 'the police'. He pulled out a revolver (I think it was a .38) and was pointing it at the tour manager. All his people and our driver Frank (a real tough guy who was a semi-pro wrestler) talked the club-owner into putting the gun down ('Man, put it down, man, this is crazy, this makes no sense, man'). At that point (because I had a drink in me) I piped up. 'You have to shoot him, mate, you have no choice, if you don't you will lose face, and your position as leader of the pack will be usurped.' The whole room went deadly quiet, and the club-owner stared even more intently over the top of his gun at the tour manager. He was sweating and his eyes had narrowed. Even he didn't know what he was going to do. For a few seconds everything was on a knife-edge; it could have gone either way. The hand holding the gun was shaking slightly, and his arm was fully extended. Frank, our driver, said, 'Wobble, man this is serious, man, you gotta be quiet, man, leave this, man, just back away.' Everyone started to implore the club-owner to put the gun down. To give the tour manager his due, he held his nerve quite well all the way through the ordeal. Frank moved towards me and edged me towards the door; he then suddenly grabbed me and manhandled me out through the door. Well, after that the club-owner took a shine to me. He said that everyone in my touring party, apart from me, was an arsehole, and that he wanted me to stay and have a drink with him and his pals. So the band went off and I stayed at that venue, in the back bar, drinking and coking it up with him and his crew. To be honest they weren't very good company. It was all a bit grim and humourless. It really was a *Blue Velvet* scenario. I was waiting for Dennis Hopper to turn up with his gas inhaler (at least he would have livened things up a bit). There were a few hookers and all that on the firm as well. I remember feeling awfully alone the next morning when I woke up.

The tour manager was really a good geezer about it, to be honest. He was resentful initially, but within a few days I think that relations were back to normal. Neville and Animal still talk about that tour. It was 'double mental'; there isn't the time to recall everything. It would make a book in itself. Prince, of all people, came on stage with us in Minneapolis. He licked my bass strings and said, 'Mmm, nice and greasy, just the way I like them.' I got him muddled up with the gay disco artist Sylvester. So consequently I didn't know what the big deal was.

The night before we departed for that North American tour I was still in the Island Records Fallout Shelter Studio in St Peter's Square, along with Ollie and Animal, finishing the *Snakecharmer* album. The producer was the renowned New York dance producer François Kervorkian. 'Frankie', as we called him, was an expatriate Frenchman, although you would never have known it; he had really found his spiritual home in the Big Apple and conducted himself very much in the fashion of a typical brash New Yorker. I anglicised his name as I always do with the names of French people that I work with. (I am happy for them to call me 'Jean' if they so wish.) We really took to him and had a lot of fun making that record. However, he did have his hands full with us. I remember standing up on the recording desk right in the middle of the session and urinating on to it as I danced. I had become overexcited while listening to our music. I was quite intoxicated as well. My actions caused a terrible amount of damage to the desk, a few thousand pounds' worth in fact, and delayed the session while spare parts were ordered. It was because of that delay that we ended up still recording the album right up to our departure from Heathrow for the US tour.

I learnt much while making that record. It was the first time that I had ever come across a programmable digital drum machine, in the form of a Lin Drum. Within a couple of years nearly every other record seemed to feature a Lin Drum. The 'Lin' constituted a major part of the eighties sound. Jim Walker and Jaki Liebezeit provided the other beats on *Snakecharmer*. I remember a funny episode in regard to Jaki during that session. He was playing along with the Lin drum. He kept on stopping, because he reckoned that there was a small timing discrepancy in the Lin Drum's beat.

He felt that the Lin was drifting ever so slightly out of sync, even though everything had been programmed and quantised correctly. Jaki was absolutely adamant. No one else in the studio noticed anything amiss. I think that Jaki was talking about a difference of around a couple of beats over the course of four minutes or so, i.e. the Lin was wavering ever so slightly in and out of time. To be that sensitive to subtle tempo changes is a very rare thing. I must say that I got Jaki playing to beats and machines quite a few times over the years and never knew him to complain the way he did that day. He became really irate and performed an insane angry half-time cross-rhythm over the Lin beat. The LEDs on the Lin flickered, and then the machine began to waver before eventually dying. I swear a puff of smoke actually came out of the back of the machine. It appeared that Jaki had destroyed it with the power of his beats. I was reminded of the occasion when a large oak table split at the same time that Jung and Freud were arguing while sitting at it. I remember that Frankie Kervorkian wouldn't have it that there was anything mysterious about that. As far as he was concerned that particular Lin Drum was faulty and that was that; there was nothing of a supernatural nature going on. However, I must say that I have never to this day seen a rhythm box die like that. It was all rather dramatic.

The Edge from U2 was also on that record. I remember when he first came down to the studio to meet us. As he walked in I was having a screaming match with Frankie. We both took a minute out to greet him and then continued to assail each other. The Edge played well on the record. He was a very nice, easygoing bloke. He came and hung out with us on our US tour on a couple of occasions. Frankie introduced me to the New York loft scene. At that time in Manhattan there were a number of unlicensed dance clubs as well as the famous Paradise Garage Club. I was in New York, on and off, quite a bit that year.

The famous nightclub Danceteria became a regular haunt of mine. It was crammed full of pretty girls. It was just the right side of decadent. There would be dancers in cages and standing on the bar, sort of prancing about. On one occasion I remember that there was a camp bloke dressed as Robin Hood, he even had all the proper arrows and all that, dancing on a sort of pedestal. One of our party, I can't remember who, surreptitiously took one of the arrows out of the geezer's arrow pouch and then stuck it quite forcibly into his arse. I actually think that quite a bit of blood was drawn. It caused a bit of an uproar and we had to make ourselves scarce. You can rest assured that I took the errant member of our party to task. I don't think that he had spiteful intentions, but nevertheless it was a stupid and reckless act. I bet for starters that the dancer bloke had to go for tetanus injections.

I recall going way up into the Bronx with Animal on a handful of occasions. I must say that it was a pretty rough manor. It looked like a war zone. I can't remember the name of the club that we went to, but it was certainly the first time that I had seen a metal detector on the door of a nightclub. It was a non-stop diet of rap music, which was of course still in its infancy. We met a few of the rappers on that scene. We also frequented a bar in Harlem called, I think, Harry's. It was run by an English bloke, which, considering the area it was in, seemed quite unlikely. Anyway, we pal'd him up. He kept a revolver behind the bar. One afternoon the bloke asked us to keep an eye on the bar while he went to run an errand. He was only out for a few minutes, but when he came back he got a shock. Animal had reached around and got the pistol out and he was pointing it at my head and then back to his own. When the bartender bloke saw that he went as white as a sheet. He quietly but firmly asked Animal to put the gun down. He pointed out that it had a 'hair trigger'. Drunk as I was, I realised that I had had a close shave. I also remember drinking with Animal and Ollie in a busy midtown bar, quite near to the *New York Times* building. It really was my sort of bar, very raucous and full of a real cross-section of people. There were quite a few hookers in there as well as newspaper workers.

I was wearing trousers with turn-ups on them. I flicked my cigarette towards the floor, but unfortunately it went down the turn-up, without me noticing. Unbelievably the whole trouser leg went up in flames. Everyone had to chuck their beer on it to put it out. So I was left standing there with a trouser leg missing. But I wasn't too bothered, I just carried on, until a girl in the bar kindly went and opened her shop up for me so that I could be kitted out in new strides. I really loved New York, for many years it was for me the most exciting place on earth, nothing could compare to it. However I think that in the last few years it has lost its mantle to London. Present-day London has now got that manic energy that the Big Apple had. Of course, similar to New York (especially Manhattan) during that period, it can also on occasion wear you out; sometimes it's just too big and there are too many other crazy people.

## AN ANGEL COMES

Another momentous thing had occurred while recording *Snakecharmer*: the birth of my first child, Hayley Angel Wardle. Her middle name, Angel, was my idea. My first sight of her was in an incubator. As she lay there she looked like a little angel. She was born a few weeks premature, and weighed less than five pounds. It turned out that Margaux had a condition, not terribly uncommon in pregnant women, called pre-eclampsia. I was around on the night that Margaux was taken into hospital, in fact for once I had behaved like a responsible adult; I had noticed that Margaux had swollen joints and was not feeling well. She was also acting a bit weird, although that in itself wasn't too strange (only joking). I insisted that we go to the hospital, so I took her up to Bart's. They admitted her immediately. Thank God I had shown some presence of mind because not long after I left she began to haemorrhage. She was rushed off for a Caesarean section. If she hadn't been in the hospital when she began to haemorrhage there's a good chance that both she and Hayley might have come to grief. So at least I got one thing right.

To be honest I was not prepared for fatherhood. I had quite unrealistically told Margaux when she told me that she wanted a baby with me that, OK, I would go along with it, but she had to realise that I would not always be around to help. Of course, once you set eyes on your child your instinct to be a father kicks in. Consequently my attitude changed and I wanted to care for my family. However, I was now dealing with responsibilities that I was not well equipped to deal with emotionally. Really I just wanted to go on being a musician, i.e. continue to go on tour, record and listen to music. However, 'playing and listening to music' converts in other people's minds to simply messing around. I was in a typical musician's predicament, earning money, but not on a steady weekly basis. Margaux didn't want to be a working mother so I felt that the onus was on me to bring home the bacon. Margaux had completed a graphic design course, but struggled to get work, so had returned to being a waitress. However, she wanted to devote her time to being a full-time mother. So I started doing minicabbing, while at the same time trying to keep the music going. However, it is very difficult to be a part-time musician, let alone a bandleader. You end up in a part-time groove and it is hard to do things on a proper professional level.

I think that the musicians in my band started to think that I was no longer serious about running the band as a full-time professional outfit. My general behaviour didn't help things either. Things suddenly changed very fast. 1983 had been a great year. I had become a dad. The band had toured extensively as well as making a great album and EP (*Invaders Of The Heart*). I was only twenty-four and had a cracking big band (which had a unique sound) and my own record label, as well as having a deal with Island Records. However, by the middle of 1984 everything was spiralling out of control. I was finding out how quickly things can change in life (especially in the music game). I was drinking heavily and was back on the cocaine and speed. I was becoming, on occasion, an angry drunk. To be truthful the next couple of years were very difficult for me (and Margaux for that matter). Looking back, I realise that I put myself under needless pressure. I took everything so seriously. I really started to get in a panic. Over the years I have identified the tendency to needlessly panic as one of my worst characteristics.

The scene in the latter stages of *GoodFellas* where Ray Liotta's coke-addled character Henry is trying to keep it all together in the middle of domestic life really reminds me of my life in the mid-eighties, as do a lot of the ugly scenes from Gary Oldman's *Nil by Mouth*. Although I was drinking and drugging heavily I made sure that I was straight on the occasions that I looked after Hayley. I tried my best to stay off the booze and powders, but every week or two I would crack and go on a binge that would last two to four days. However, when I was straight I would make sure that I spent time with Hayley. I would take her out and push her for miles across London in her pram. By the time she was two I was taking her to the pictures and then going to get a burger afterwards. We would often do that at the Elephant and Castle because that wasn't too far from where Margaux's flat was. On other occasions I would take her up West. From a young age she loved the movies. It is no surprise that she became an actress. I remember taking her to see *Labyrinth* (which featured David Bowie) and *Little Shop of Horrors* among others. (Her mum began to regularly take her to the Italia Conti stage school, which must have given her a great leg-up in the acting game.) I would not claim to have been the most consistent dad in the world but for all my addiction problems I wasn't the worst either. Margaux did her best but generally seemed pretty fed up with things. I will say this for her: she never drank or did drugs and she kept her flat very clean and tidy.

The mid-eighties was a horrible time for me. Thatcher's reign was at its zenith. I remember walking through Covent Garden on a summer's evening at that time. It was not long after the Falklands War. The place seemed to be full of yuppies drinking champagne. I felt totally alienated from the society that I lived in. I found it to be a very ugly time. It surprised me how many Brits bought into Thatcher. It seemed obvious to me that our culture and society were in the first stages of being unravelled. Everything was for sale. Everything had its price, but nothing was truly valued or understood.

Ghastly plastic pop was the order of the day. People's desire for heavy bass or for music that took a few chances was at its nadir. I had become sick of people ignorantly asking me why I wanted to play 'kebab house music'. The development of Docklands was under way, and the first Porsches arrived in Wapping. (One or two of those came a cropper.) Suddenly my favourite haunt by the river, the gardens adjacent to the old Port of London Authority houses at Wapping Reach, was out of bounds to all but the residents of those houses. From that time onwards the gate into the garden was locked. Local people were now denied the beautiful view from Wapping Reach up towards Tower Bridge. I recall Angus MacKinnon taking some publicity pictures of me and Animal on some wasteland near where I lived near The Highway. Suddenly a security man appeared demanding the film from the camera. (He didn't get it.) We were astounded; we couldn't understand what was going on. It all made sense when we found out that Rupert Murdoch was moving his operation from Fleet Street to that site.

Before too long the plant was up and running and the area soon turned into a war zone. I recall that when the printworkers' dispute proper had first started I tried to return back to Dellow Street to feed my cats when my van was surrounded by Old Bill. They refused to let me into Dellow Street, even after I explained to them that I lived there. In fact I nearly got nicked. Their behaviour was outrageous. The cats went hungry that night. I ended up doing a few stints on the picket line directly outside Murdoch's News

International plant. In fact I can remember managing, against all odds, to get into the plant with a bloke called Ed Shipton. Ed was the younger brother of a pal of mine called Bob Shipton. On the night in question there were the normal scuffles around the picket line. Ed and I simply cut away from the pack and calmly walked through the front gate along with some workers going into the plant. When we got in there we didn't know what to do so we simply jumped up and down like lunatics while waving and shouting at our 'comrades'. We were immediately manhandled out the front gate by a number of burly constables. Another larger disturbance started up across the road. The police ran over to deal with that, which afforded the opportunity for Ed and me to slip away. An elder cousin of mine called Billy Dennison was very active in regard to protesting against Murdoch's Wapping site, as was Terry Penton.

*Billy Dennison's heart was well and truly broken, as was his wife Valerie's, when his beloved son John was stabbed to death in the mid-eighties. Billy Dennison was the first person to publicly highlight the horrors of knife crime in this country, in conjunction with the* People *newspaper. As a kid I idolised Billy. He was a giant of a man. But he was very sensitive; he really knew how to get on a kid's wavelength. Not long after young John Dennison's death one of his best mates was hit and killed by a truck speeding away from Rupert Murdoch's Wapping site. It was all so very sad.*

I must say that I had mixed feelings about the printworkers' dispute. All those 'closed shop' union members that I was familiar with, be they dockers, market porters or printers, guarded their privileged positions jealously. Jobs were often handed down from father to son. I hardly ever encountered any sense of socialist principle or values with those blokes. In fact they were normally quite reactionary, in my experience. In regard to that dispute I felt that I was protesting more against Thatcher and her ilk than I was supporting the printers, to be honest.

## JOHN BARLEYCORN TAKES CONTROL

By that time I was behaving very unpredictably. I began to have blackouts when drinking. I could be a very angry man during those blackouts. These scared the life out of me. I would wake up and not have any knowledge of where I had been or what I had been doing. I was never sure who I might have upset or offended. I never knew for sure how people would react to me when I walked into the pub the next day. By this stage I could, at times, still drink my normal quota of booze, which was approximately one large bottle of Jack Daniel's (the Old House at Home stocked it just for me), a few Guinnesses and a couple of bottles of wine. However, there were other occasions when, after just a couple of drinks, I would be completely pissed. I couldn't work out what was going on. I didn't realise that my liver was no longer able to cope efficiently with my booze intake. (I tried hammering the speed again in an attempt to keep myself going while drinking; however, it only made things worse.) The whites of my eyes and my skin had a yellow tinge. When sleeping after drinking I would increasingly lose control of my bladder. On a few occasions I woke up in the open air with wet trousers in the cold light of day. On those occasions I would be full of shame and remorse.

A few people tried to talk sense into me but I wouldn't let them get close to me, so I laughed them off. I particularly remember Jeffrey Lee Pierce from the band the Gun Club pulling me up. The Gun Club were on the same touring circuit as us and our paths crossed on a couple of occasions. Jeffrey had observed me getting stuck into the JD first thing in the morning, and he knew from his own experience where I was heading. Sometimes it's funny how life turns out; I ended up getting sober, but Jeffrey, from what I understand, never got himself sorted out, and he died horribly prematurely in the mid-nineties.

I would sometimes look very shabby. I would do my best when in drink to stay away from Margaux's. I would stay in the East End.

People would be a lot more forgiving to my behaviour there. When I came off a bender I would have the shakes. I would normally, by that stage of proceedings, sport a long thick beard. I would pay a visit to Chris's barber shop in Cavell Street in Whitechapel. I had been going there since I was a kid. Chris was a Greek Cypriot who liked a bet. Actually he liked a bet very much indeed. Chris was a very cheerful bloke. 'Hello, my friend,' he would say, 'you have been on the beer again.' But he was never judgemental. He had a very nice way, did Chris. He would give me a haircut and a 'hot towel' shave. He would also give me, as he did everyone, a tip for the gee-gees. However, I felt that I had enough vices without taking on a new one so I took no heed of his equestrian recommendations.

*I still like to have a proper shave; nowadays I go to a Turkish place up Tottenham High Road. They use the lighted tapers there to singe off the hairs on the ears. When I come out of there I feel like I'm twenty-one again. My skin feels as soft as a baby's.*

I would at that point probably not have eaten for a day or two, or maybe three, so I would then go up to Paul's café (now Nico's café) right by Bethnal Green tube station. They do some great 'two-plate dinners' there. I would have dishes such as braised hearts and mashed potato or fried steak with onions and chips, with two fried eggs and several rounds of crusty white bread and butter. I would then feel, temporarily at least, as right as rain and would pop over the river to be with Margaux and Hayley. I would then return to the minicabbing. Working through the night would take my mind off the booze and the drugs. I would get the sweats at night, but I got used to that. Everything would be OK for a week or two, before 'the thirst' crept up on me again. Of course, it's a lot more than a thirst, it's an obsession that nags away at you, a compulsion. My mind would race and I would be a bag of nerves. I always had been a 'nervy' sort of bloke, but by now it was ridiculous. I knew full well that 'just one drink' would never be enough. Once I had succumbed to the compulsion to drink that was it; I just could not stop. I had to follow the bender through to its predictable conclusion. I once heard the process described as a man on fire running into the sea in order to extinguish the flames and (inadvertently) drowning. I think that is a pretty accurate metaphor.

The gradual decline of the alcoholic is not without pathos, but it can be amusing in a tragic sort of way. However, to be honest it does tend to have a very selfish, self-centred and self-indulgent aspect to it. I think that most psychiatrists working in the field would agree that gross emotional immaturity is one of the most noticeable aspects of alcoholics. I realise now that I had gone backwards in regard to emotional development at that time. In many respects I was more sensible at eighteen than I was at twenty-five.

## THE HITCHER

I can remember many crazy events and situations all over the world. Dave Lynch reckoned that I was just like Rutger Hauer's character in *The Hitcher*. Obviously he said that in jest, as I never actually strung anyone up between two trucks or put a human finger in a serving of French fries. However, I do admit that I could be an absolute fucking nightmare at that time. I remember an occasion when we were touring in America. We had been driving for seventy-two hours with just a few stops. Everybody had been at the charlie and was shattered. We got to our motel and everyone hit the sack immediately and that was it, they were spark out, because they had hardly had a wink of sleep for days. You see, I had this French motto, 'Deprivation Dormir'. Sleep deprivation; no one in the group was allowed to sleep for days at a time. If you nodded off someone would scream in your ear like a sergeant major, 'Wake up!' Well, on this particular occasion everyone was exhausted and went off to bed knackered. However, typically, I just couldn't sleep. So I hatched a plan. I got hold of a few cigarette lighters and used them, set to the max, continuously, two at a time, until the gas ran out, heating the round metal doorknob on the outside of my hotel room door. Eventually it glowed a dull red. I then phoned the band one at a time and told them that there was a dire emergency, 'honestly, I swear', and that they must 'come to my room immediately'. First down was Nev. He knocked on the door. 'It's open!' I said loudly. He came through the door with a look of utter astonishment and pain on his face. I actually smelt burning flesh. He went absolutely mental at me. I apologised profusely and gave him a wet towel to wrap around his burnt hand. After a minute I asked him if he wanted me to do it to the rest of the band. He enthusiastically assented. So I gave the door knob a quick 'heating'. The same process was repeated until the whole band were in my room with towels wrapped around their hands. There was nothing to do but continue partying, so out came the Charles and the Jack and we got down to it (again). They promised to exact revenge on me, but of course they weren't as pathetic as me, so when it came to it they couldn't be bothered.

*The other jape that I liked to pull was to surreptitiously get into another band member's room. I would then lie under their bed. In one hand I held a bottle of Jack, so that I could have a glug, while the other hand would be immersed in an ice bucket. In the end my hand would go numb with the cold. Eventually they would go to bed. Timing is crucial here; too early and you simply scare them, too late, i.e. when they are fast asleep, and they can act very unpredictably. So I had to gauge it so that they were a few minutes into REM. I would then reach my freezing hand up to brush over their face. If you time it right they don't scream, they just sort of gasp.*

*Sometimes I have known those people to potter about their room for a while and not go to bed. In that situation it is quite acceptable to grab their ankle with the freezing hand. I have also known some of these people to subsequently become violent. On those occasions I simply took hold of the bedsprings to prevent them turning the bed over and would implore them to 'stop being so unreasonable'. If you are faced with one of those funny beds that don't have an 'underneath' then you may have to resort to the wardrobe; personally I prefer to get behind the shower curtain. In this situation there is no fannying about with ice buckets. You simply pull back the shower curtain, at the opportune moment, and roar like a lion. To be honest I brought that one out of mothballs after a show in Sheffield a couple of years ago. Jean-Pierre Rasle, the French bagpipe player, was in his room making Mark Sanders and Chris Cookson, my guitarist, a brew. Of course, they were in on the jape. He came into the bathroom to fill the kettle. When I pulled back the shower curtain and roared he actually fell backwards into the khazi. For me that was a real result.*

*To be honest, over the course of time (through the seventies and eighties) everyone got pretty worn out, most of all me. I completely burnt myself out. Please don't think that I pull those sorts of pranks on a regular basis nowadays. It really is 'once in a blue moon'. It's the kind of thing you do when you are in your early twenties. It still makes me smile, though.*

*In my thirties I still did japes but they were a little bit more involved. I remember one night lying in bed with my wife Zi-Lan. I had stealthily tied a bit of invisible twine around my big toe, which was attached to a bit of wood jammed behind the headboard of the bed. I pulled on the twine a couple of times. She was immediately suspicious and insisted on seeing my hands. I swore innocence. I waited a while and then did it again. I then said, in convincing fashion, 'Oh God! They're back.' She closely scrutinised my face, but if I say so myself I was pretty convincing. I called out, 'Are you the spirits of the undead? If so knock twice.' 'Knock! Knock!' was the reply. Zi-Lan's grip tightened on me. I was now acting really scared. 'Have you come for me?' I asked. 'If so knock twice.' 'Knock' was the answer. 'Have you come for Zi-Lan? Is that who you've come for?' 'Knock! Knock!' I then looked at Zi-Lan in terror and screamed as loud as I could and started pulling on the twine like crazy. 'Knock! Knock! Knock! Knock!' She pulled the cover back and saw the twine.*

THINGS BEGIN TO GO AWRY

By the summer of 1985 the Invaders of the Heart had virtually ground to a halt. Animal had already left by then. He wanted to do something more rock oriented. Not long after Animal split he had an audition with Nina Hagen, who was a big star at that time. She was about to embark on a world tour. He phoned me to tell me that he had got the gig. I was well happy for him. He then astounded me. He explained that although he had got the gig he had decided not to do it. I went mental at him and asked why, because for him it was so obviously the perfect gig. 'I'd miss everyone down the pub,' he said. There was no changing his mind. I have never forgotten that. To be honest I was annoyed with him for some time. I felt that it was a typical working-class cop-out. Mind you, Dave is a happy bloke. I don't think that he has any regrets. His son Jack is turning out to be a very capable guitarist.

I told everyone that I could no longer regard being a musician as a full-time job. I told them that I now had other responsibilities. Ollie had got a plum gig as Tina Turner's MD, which really goes to prove the bloke was no slouch. He was absolutely delighted, because that was the sort of stuff that he really wanted to do. I was happy for him, but gutted as well. (I knew that realistically speaking the Invaders was over. Animal had gone, and so had Annie and Ollie.) However, before he clinched the Tina Turner gig we had made another album for Island called *Neon Moon*. There is a track on that album called 'The Beast Inside Of Me' which highlights the battle I was having with 'the bottle'. We also did some recordings for my label Lago. One of these was a twelve-inch single called 'Voodoo'. The singer was Polly Eltes, who was one of the top models in the seventies. Hers was the face that was associated with Biba, and she was on the cover of one of the Roxy Music albums.

*By this time excellent musicians such as Harry Beckett, the trumpet player, and B. J. Cole, the pedal steel player, were performing on the records as well as at my shows (Harry did all the shows from the end of 1983 through into 1985). I'm proud to say that they both still occasionally perform with me, as does Neville Murray. Annie Whitehead still came to do shows with me in the nineties. In fact she recently did a show in London with me. Ollie I never set eyes on again until last year when he walked into the dressing room in LA. He is now a resident of that city. It was funny, just as he walked in I was being well and truly schmoozed by a mother and daughter firm. (The mother was suggesting that I put her rock-singer daughter straight in my band.) I didn't recognise Ollie at first, because his hair had gone a bit grey, but his face was the same. It was great to see him. He laughed when he saw what was happening. He said that it looked exactly liked the scenes that he remembered in our dressing rooms all those years ago.*

So by the mid-eighties I was burnt out. Apart from the booze and drug problems, Island Records had been a nightmare to deal with. After *Snakecharmer* they had waited until the very last moment before picking the option for the next album up, which meant that I had gone months before getting an advance from them. Also by this stage things were getting very bad in regard to independent distribution. RT, my label's distributor, were about to go bust, so all in all things weren't too clever.

At that time Dave Robinson had joined Island from Stiff Records as the MD of the company. I didn't have anything to do with him. However, I did have to deal with the head of A&R that he had appointed. A bloke called Nick Stewart, another of the many toffs that I have met along the way in the music game. He had been a captain in the British army so was known as 'The Captain'. The Captain had a secretary called Anna. She was in her forties. She was very posh in a Joanna Lumley sort of way. She liked everyone to call her 'Auntie'. It was all very silly as well as being patronising.

I became very familiar with the long journey over to Stamford Brook on the District Line. Unless I went and pushed them nothing got done. I think that I reminded The Captain of his squaddies; consequently he wasn't going to rush to do my bidding. As far as I was concerned neither of them were the brightest lamps in the street. Then again maybe they were just pretending to be daft. It certainly felt like a joke was being played on me. I even ended up having to 'float' my own record, financially speaking, because it was taking so long for the advance monies and studio payments to come through. As far as I'm concerned that mid-eighties period was the nadir in regard to Island Records. Thankfully I would be there when it reached its zenith again in the mid-nineties. I didn't realise at the time what valuable experience I was getting in regard to the music industry, and how to handle it when the going gets rough.

I was in bad shape. My band was effectively defunct. My Lago label had run out of funds, and my drink and drug binges were getting longer and more intense. I used to hang out with Adrian Sherwood, the reggae producer, quite a bit. He was a mate, and because we shared the same dealer, we would often take gear together. If I was short of funds I knew that I could go around to Ade's for a line or two, and a beer to cheer myself up. Skip Macdonald and Doug Wimbish would often be there as well. Adrian was good company and always up for a laugh. Kishi, Ade's missus at that time, never seemed to complain. Little Annie, the singer and poet, used to stay at his house at that time.

Out of the blue I received a call from a German promoter asking if I was interested in coming over and doing a tour of the German-speaking nations along with Jaki, Holger and some other German musicians. I only gave people the telephone number at Dellow House, not at Margaux's. Business people, such as this promoter, would only tend to call in the day. I would either not be there or I would not answer the phone, preferring the call to go through to the answerphone. This promoter was a bit suspicious of me. He had heard that I was a bit of a handful and that I had a bit of a problem with the booze and drugs. I allayed his fears. I remember telling him (in a slightly slurred and over-controlled voice) that he shouldn't believe the stories about me, that a lot of people were jealous of me, and so made up stories about me that put me in a bad light. I told him that the most I did was sink a couple of pints after a show, and that I absolutely abhorred the taking of drugs. The bloke was totally convinced that I was a nice chap who was one hundred per cent reliable.

I then devised a plan to take my mate Shrew on tour with me. His job would be to 'prevent me from drinking'. I told the promoter that I needed a 'personal roadie' to come on the tour to make sure that I was OK. Happily the promoter agreed to this. On the day of our departure for the tour Shrew showed up at Dellow House. We were scheduled to take an early afternoon flight out of Heathrow. Shrew came around to get me up at around 11 a.m. For all my intentions about staying sober I suddenly changed tack, and suggested that we go over to the Old House at Home for a swift beer before setting off. Shrew tried his best to dissuade me, but there was no changing my mind. I remember that after the Old House we moved over to the Britannia in Cable Street, which was run by a very nice Irish family. They were so convivial that towards the end of my drinking I was in there as much as the Old House.

Well, three o'clock came and we were still in there. We had well and truly missed our flight. Shrew got on the blower to the promoter. I can't remember the cock-and-bull story that he came up with, but it must have been a good one. To be honest Shrew was fed up with me. He just wanted to get on the plane and get on with it. Now, however, I decided that we should travel down to Dover and then get the ferry to Ostend. From there we would get a train to Cologne. Well, that was what we did. By the time we got to Ostend and got on the train we were both mad drunk. I recall that I smashed Shrew's nose quite badly with the bass case; I did it in a bad temper as I was putting it up on the luggage rack. We then had a brawl, but by the time the authorities were summoned we had the good sense to stop fighting. We managed to stem the flow of blood from Shrew's nose and claim that it was an accident, which it was. We also tidied up the mess in our compartment. There was quite a bit of blood on the floor and all that. I distinctly remember a middle-aged German lady coming up to me on that train and taking hold of my arm; with a tremendous look of compassion in her eyes, she said, 'Such a shame, you are so young.' She could see exactly what my problem was. I felt ashamed and brusquely pulled my arm away from her.

Eventually we arrived in Cologne station well past midnight. The promoter was waiting there to meet us. I strode out on to the station concourse. He looked slightly alarmed at my wild appearance; he was probably even more alarmed at how Shrew looked. He put out his hand for me to shake. However, I ignored it and grabbed him by the throat. Shrew maintains that I then pushed the promoter up against a wall and screamed, 'RIGHT, YOU F****** C***, I WANT BOOZE, BIRDS, DRUGS AND GRUB AND I WANT IT NOW!' The poor bloke, it must have been such a shock; this was very different to the affable geezer that he had spoken to on the phone. He really was horrified.

We drove that poor promoter mad. The next day Shrew took umbrage at a framed poster on the wall of the posh apartment where we were staying. It was, if memory serves me well, an illustration of an ice cream coming out of the sea. Shrew thought that it was unrealistic and so pulled it out and screwed it up. When the promoter came to pick us up he had a fit when he saw what had happened to the poster. Apparently it was an 'original' art deco print. It was worth a lot of money.

*Funnily enough, for many years I too was disgusted by anything art deco. I had a sudden realisation years ago as to why that was. The Arsenal's old ground, Highbury, was of an art deco style. My extreme dislike of anything to do with Arsenal had led me, albeit on an unconscious level, to associate any form of art deco with that club.*

Well, that trip quickly turned into an absolute debacle. After that first mad night I calmed down and stopped drinking. We had a couple of rehearsals and they went OK. The first night of the tour was in Aachen and it went well; Jaki and me were really 'locked in' with one another. Holger was floating all his Dictaphone stuff over the top of us. There was another bloke on keyboards and a guitar player (I think). But after the show I started to drink again. I ended up getting involved in a very nasty brawl. I think everyone was getting a bit freaked out with me. Holger decided that he didn't want to do a tour with an unstable and sometimes violent drinker like me on the firm. The next night we did Cologne. Before the gig I demanded money from the promoter up front for the rest of the tour. There was a capacity crowd in the hall that night. About twenty minutes into the gig I gave Jaki a cheery wave and walked off stage bass in hand. I had the money bulging in my side pocket. It was a slag thing to do. I had never done anything like that before and I have never done anything like it since. Shrew and me went running off backstage and shot out the stage door. Hein Fokker was waiting there in his car with another Dutch bloke that I used to call Robin Hood. I called him that because he always dressed in green. We shot off across the border into Holland. Well, my behaviour wasn't too clever in Holland either. It was really getting near the end for me. I was starting to lose it. I was getting close to cracking up.

## I KNOW I'VE GOT A PROBLEM

For some time I had known that I was an alcoholic. I had gone down to Bancroft Road library and had a look at books dealing with alcoholism. I come across an author called Max Glatt, a psychiatrist specialising in the treatment of alcoholics. He was a very clever Jewish bloke, who had fled the Nazis in the Second World War and had subsequently ended up in the UK. I read a slim paperback by him, which described, indeed graphed, the spiritual and physical descent and subsequent deaths of alcoholics. I realised that I was getting pretty low down in terms of that graph. However, I did note that Max Glatt pointed out that it was possible for alcoholics to recover. So I was lucky that from an early stage I

This photo was taken when I was 'bang on it' in regard to booze and drugs. You can see from my eyes that I'm not a happy camper

©Sheila Rock

knew that it was possible to 'get well'. I knew in my heart that, for blokes like me, 'getting well' meant that I had to stop drinking completely. However, up to that time I was not ready to do that. Now, though, matters were coming to a head.

I used to go drinking with my mate Bob Shipton at that time. Bob worked at a factory over in Shoreditch. On a Friday I would go over there to meet up with him in the Spread Eagle. We would both surreptitiously put half a gram of whizz into our pints; that is how the weekend would start for us. Within half an hour we would be rubbing our chests as the palpitations kicked in, thinking that a heart attack was looming. (What we did was very dangerous. To take that much whizz in one go is flirting with death.) A half-hour later we were ready to take on the world. I started doing lots of speed again, hoping that it would stop the alcoholic blackouts. However, it just made things worse. Even close friends were getting a bit disturbed. I was getting increasingly psychotic. There was a girl called Marion – to this day we are friends – who lived on the

St Katharine's estate in Wapping. At that time she was working as a booker/tour manager for me. One night after the pub me, Bob and Marion went back to her flat. The next morning I thought that we had all had a great time the previous night. However, I could tell from their faces that there was something wrong. It turned out that I had spent hours the previous evening continuously checking the cupboards in the flat for interlopers and/or bugging devices. I was certain that members of Mossad and the CIA were concealed in the flat.

A similar thing happened at a recording studio called Southern Studios in Wood Green. I was supposed to do a recording session with Al Jourgensen and his group Ministry. I was desperately trying to stay on the dry that night. Al was very disappointed that I wouldn't share his Glenfiddich whisky. He nagged and nagged. So in the end I took a tipple. I don't think that anyone who was in the studio that night will ever forget it. My recollection is hazy to say the least. (But not so hazy as to not realise that I quickly became aggressive and paranoid.) The bloke who owned the studio was called John Loder. Eventually he calmed me down and took me away. Luckily for me all those people were very rock and roll so the police were not called. Well, I gave that bloke Loder a torrid time that night. He was desperate to drop me off… anywhere. I got him to take me to a restaurant in Whitechapel that I knew would still serve me booze. I insisted that he come in with me. When inside I caused mayhem; fortunately the geezer that ran the place really liked me and stopped the staff from attacking me mob handed. The boss of the place actually gave me another double brandy and told me to go home. Unfortunately I then ran amok across London. That double brandy was my last drink.

*To be honest I have found writing about the tail-end of my drinking and drugging quite wearisome. It got really ugly and messy. There is a lot of stuff that I won't go on about. Not out of feeling shame, although I did feel plenty of that emotion at the time, but because it's boring. It would also be a form of self-indulgence. I think most people are familiar with the descent of minor celebrities into, as the tabloids always put it, their 'drink and drug hell', and to be honest, although I might like to see myself as being different to those celebrities, in essence my behaviour was probably pretty similar.*

# Chapter Nine: New Start

SOBRIETY

I ended up at Dellow House on the morning of 23 October 1986 seriously wanting to top myself. I had one of the one-sided razors that we used for tape editing in those days in my right hand. I held it against the wrist of my left hand. However, I could not do it and I hated myself for that. I absolutely loathed and despised myself. I felt that I was pathetic and weak. I thought of all the people in the world who had problems that were not of their own making. I now had a daughter to look after, and another on the way, and I was behaving like this. I felt like a bad machine, I had a serious fault. I felt that I was beyond repair. I felt that I should have had the balls to put myself out of the game by opening my main cables up, and do everyone a favour.

I knew that if I was going put my affairs and my life in order I needed to stop drinking. I knew that I could not achieve that on my own. I knew what I needed to do. I had crept late into an AA meeting a few months before that. I knew that the people in AA knew what they were on about in regard to the drink. So I put down the razor and I phoned AA. Weeks before, when I had first phoned AA, they had offered to send someone out to see me; however, my pride would not allow that. Of course, I now demanded that somebody was dispatched forthwith to me. Well, a couple of hours later a bloke from AA called around to have a chat with me. He was practically a neighbour. He ran a scrap-metal yard in the East End. People in AA called him 'Metal Mickey', after a cartoon character of the same name.

I was in pieces. I had the shakes bad and was engulfed in self-loathing. I was severely depressed and disturbed. The bloke from AA sat with me for a long time. He got his girlfriend, a nurse, who also happened to be in AA, to come and check on me. The bloke and his girlfriend were very close to running me up to St Clement's mental hospital at Mile End. Instead he sat with me chatting away while plying me with hot sweet tea. He told me his story. I really listened, as best I could. I began the task of taking down the barriers that separated me from the rest of the world. From that time onwards I have never felt alone in the way that I had done in the previous twenty-eight years. As I write, twenty-odd years later, the emotion still wells up when I think of that conversation with a bloke who was a stranger to me. The profound sense of apartness and loneliness that I had always felt deep in my heart was lifted that evening.

*I don't think that extreme feeling of loneliness is the exclusive preserve of alcoholics; I think that it lies at the heart of the human condition. However, I think that alcoholics of my type are inclined to make a song and dance about everything, and so tend to make the mistake of thinking they are the only ones who feel that way.*

I suddenly had a glimpse at another way of life. I am full of gratitude at having received 'the message'. Having the burden of the addiction removed and everything that comes with it is akin to coming out of a form of (self-imposed) isolation.

*The first thing that I did was sell my bass and put the money that I'd received for it through the letter box of Margaux's flat. It was a Gibson short-scale, I think. The original bass that I had in PiL, the black Fender Precision, was sold by me to the Jesus and Mary*

*Chain a couple of years before that. They were delighted to have the bass that had been used on* Metal Box. *My attitude was 'Yeah, whatever, hurry up and give me the cash so that I can fuck off down the pub toot suite.'*

I started to regularly attend AA meetings. And that of course is where the hard work began in earnest. For the first time in my life I felt unconditionally accepted. I felt part of a family. I was in a group of people that had my best interests at heart. That alone was such incredibly powerful medicine for me. I underwent the familiar withdrawals from alcohol, the shakes and sweats and all that. However, something was different now. Those withdrawals were not all engulfing in the way that they had been in the past. I sailed through them. At that time there were very few people as young as me (twenty-eight) around AA.

In the East End the majority of AA members in those days were either Irish or Scottish. I felt at home immediately. AA at that time, in the East End at least, was a different kettle of fish compared to what it is now. It was very tough and down to earth. There was certainly no 'therapy speak'. The 'rehab industry' as we now know it did not exist at that time. Owing to the homeless hostels, there were a lot of 'low bottom' drunks around the East End, especially Whitechapel, so therefore there were constant reminders, all around me, of what would happen if I 'picked up' again. However, I soon realised, thanks to the good advice that I received in AA, that it wasn't simply about not drinking. After all, alcoholism comes in the man (and woman), not in the bottle; I had to begin to address the underlying factors of my alcoholism. That in turn would mean changing my outlook on life. I knew I had to do that. It was about 'change or die'. So I worked the Twelve Steps of AA. I still do today. Don't get me wrong; I'm not a bloke who lives in 'AA rooms' or goes to AA conventions. Please God I will be twenty-three years clean and sober this year (2009) on 23 October.

*You may wonder why I drank the way I did. Well, to be honest*

*I always had a pathological attitude to drink, right from the word go. Whenever I drank I lit up like a Christmas tree. In fact, talking of Christmas, my mum remembers me doing a bottle of green Chartreuse one Christmas time, when I was aged around thirteen. She remembers me sliding down the wall and saying, 'Mum, I feel terrific.' She had intended for me to simply have just one or two glasses but in no time I did the whole bottle. Whenever I drank it was as if all the tension (and fear and anxiety) left my body. I used to get panic attacks around the time of reaching puberty. At the time I didn't know that they were panic attacks. I felt that my heart would stop beating, because it would be pumping so hard and fast, and I would have trouble catching my breath. I felt that I was about to die. When I drank, those symptoms quickly disappeared. I felt joined to the cosmos; everything would turn from monochrome to colour. It was like the Holy Spirit had entered me. However, even then I knew that there was a price to pay. Once I had started I could not stop. In those early days I would not suffer blackouts, but I would get awful hangovers. It was as if the highs and lows that I received from booze were more extreme than most people's. I learnt early on when employed on straight jobs not to go to the pub at lunchtime, because a couple of pints were no good to me. I could never understand why my workmates were content to meekly go back to work at five to two. I tried not to drink if I needed to do stuff. I never saw alcohol as something that enhanced a meal or my experience of a party, or anything like that. Once I started drinking it would turn into the main event. I now completely abstain from alcohol one day at a time. Asking a bloke like me to 'count units of alcohol' would be like asking a lion to only nibble the leg of a wildebeest.*

At the time of 'getting sober' I was halfway through recording another album (which was eventually called *Psalms*). It was, allowing for the shoestring budget and my state of mind at the outset of the project, a very good record. You can clearly hear the various fusions of world styles and production techniques that were to become so popular within a few years. I did most of it with a co-producer called Mel Jefferson. To be fair he did a first-rate job.

The record featured the reggae singer Bim Sherman, who sadly is now deceased, and Julianne Regan, the vocalist from the band All About Eve. The record afforded me valuable experience in regard to writing with MIDI. I was also making good headway with my lyric writing. Angus MacKinnon did the artwork for *Psalms*. He used the *Book of Kells* as inspiration.

As soon as *Psalms* was finished (around mid-November 1986) I went looking for a job. I had really had it with the music game (and to be honest I think it had had it with me). I wanted a break. Since I had joined PiL in 1978, eight years previous, I had helped make about twelve albums (that I can remember) and done a lot of shows, mainly with bands that I had put together. I had done all that without management or any real help. I was burnt out. I wasn't tired of music but I was really tired of the music business and most of the people in it.

Another big factor was that I was broke, not only that but I had pretty large debts that needed to be dealt with, plus of course I had a family to take care of. Indeed, Margaux and I had another baby on the way, so I knew that I had to get an income pretty quickly. I applied to both the Post Office and the London Underground. In the meantime I got a temporary job, as a courier, driving a van for a company called A to Z, who were based in Clerkenwell. I couldn't do minicabbing because my car was falling apart. In the New Year I was notified that my application to join the Underground had been successful, and I was duly dispatched for training at the London Underground Training School in Wood Lane in West London, just over the road from the BBC Television Centre.

## ONE LAST KICK IN THE GUTS

*However, the music business had one last blow to administer. Out of the blue I got a call from Island Records. A bloke who held a fairly senior position at the company asked me if I wanted another deal. He suggested an album for Island's Antilles label. It was to be a record that leant towards jazz. He suggested a sum of money equivalent nowadays to around £60,000, and asked if that was sufficient. I was completely taken aback. I quickly agreed that I could make a great album for that sort of money. We literally shook hands on the deal. I thought that it was a miracle. It now seemed that I could wipe my debts clean in one go. Luckily I had the presence of mind not to give up my (new) day job, which was just as well because the bloke never called me back again. Furthermore he wouldn't take my phone calls. I was never sure if it was a wind-up or if somebody higher up had vetoed it, or even if the bloke was on coke at the time and simply bullshitting. I bumped into him at a function a few years later, at a time when I was back in the music game with a vengeance, but neither of us mentioned the 'incident'.*

## KAFKA (GOING UNDERGROUND)

What a Kafkaesque world I had entered. The Underground at that time was split into two main sections, which were Train Crew and Station Staff. You also had the 'P Way men' and the 'Fluffers'. The P Way men were the blokes who maintained 'the permanent way' (or track in other words); you would mainly see them at night. The Fluffers were the teams of ladies who would clean the tunnels at night.

The first thing I did upon joining the Underground was to undergo basic training. They rushed yours truly and the other rookies through a number of procedures, most of them related to health and safety. The instructors tried to copy the demeanour of British Army sergeant majors, so they would suddenly turn to a new recruit and shout stuff along the lines of 'Smith, you are working at Theydon Bois station, during an off-peak period, it's a lovely sunny day, at a quiet suburban station, you are sitting in the station office picking your nose and drinking your tea, when there is a knock at the door. It is a most lovely and gorgeous blonde bird that stands before you sticking her chest out. She informs you that she has dropped her purse on to the tracks. What are you going to do? Ring and inform the line controller, bother him with a small detail like that, or are you going to be a man, Mr Smith, and jump down on to the line, while taking care of course to avoid the live rail? I mean, there is no train due for ten minutes, what's the problem? ARE YOU GOING TO BE A MAN? ARE YOU GOING TO HELP THIS POOR UNFORTUNATE WOMAN? WILL YOU JUMP DOWN AND IN THE BLINK OF AN EYE RETRIEVE HER PURSE?' Smith meekly replies, 'Yes, Mr White [fictitious name], I would jump down and retrieve her purse.' Mr White becomes incandescent with rage. 'NOOOOOOOO! YOU JUMP DOWN AND I'LL HAVE YOUR GUTS FOR GARTERS, LAD! YOU MUST INFORM THE LINE CONTROLLER ABOUT THE INCIDENT, DO YOU UNDERSTAND ME?!'

*Of course, when you are out on the job a few weeks later you soon find out what happens if you bother the line controller with something trivial like that. The real point of the exercise is that they have a bit of paper signed by you acknowledging that you were shown the 'correct procedure' in the event that you inadvertently kill yourself or someone else.*

They would follow a question like that with something along the lines of 'Brown! You're making your station inspection when you notice a light bulb has gone out in the store cupboard, you can easily reach it, so what do you do? Do you call Maintenance like some helpless old tart, or do you behave like a man and do it yourself? WELL?' Brown ponders his answer and quite logically decides that it is a trick question, similar to the one posed to Smith, and answers accordingly, 'I'd call Maintenance, Mr White.' Mr White, hamming it up for all he's worth, explodes, 'CALL MAINTENANCE! YOU LAZY OLD TART, MR BROWN! YOU DO IT YOURSELF!'

There would follow more questions about light bulbs: what

about if there was another bulb slightly higher yet still within reach, what do you do? No problem; change it yourself, right? 'NO! ALWAYS CALL MAINTENANCE WHEN THE BULB TO BE CHANGED IS OVER SIX FOOT FROM THE FLOOR!' It really was Franz Kafka territory.

While working as station staff my main duty was being a ticket collector, predominantly at very busy tube stations in central London like Covent Garden, Piccadilly and Embankment. I got recognised by people a lot when I was collecting tickets. I didn't mind at all, I would often have a joke and a laugh with them. On a couple of occasions people went to the nearest record shop and bought one of my records and then brought it back for me to sign.

*Sometimes when I was working an 'early turn' at Embankment I would leave our flat off Blackfriars Road at around six in the morning and walk down through the South Bank and over Hungerford Bridge. I would see loads of teenagers and punters in their early twenties queuing up to get into a club in Villiers Street. I was quite intrigued. It was of course the very beginning of the Acid House scene. Within the year I would be working with some of the people on that scene.*

Sometimes while working on the tube a sense of devilment would overtake me. I remember performing platform duties at Tower Hill station on a day when there were some bad delays. So I was faced during the evening rush hour with the massed ranks of glum-faced commuters. Suddenly it all seemed so absurd, and I could not resist getting on the public address system and announcing in classic PA style, 'I used to be somebody, I repeat, I used to be somebody.' A slight ripple went through the sullen hordes, but overall there was no reaction.

After a few weeks I got called in to see the inspector who was in charge of the group of District Line stations that I often worked at. He asked me if I fancied 'going on the trains'. I was duly dispatched back to Wood Lane for training as a guard. From Wood Lane I was sent out for 'on the job' training to Leytonstone

Depot, which is on the Central Line. The duties of a guard were pretty simple. The main task was opening and closing the sliding doors at every station. You looked down the train to make sure that nobody was stuck in the doors. When all the doors were closed a couple of pilot lights would come on and you would press a button that rang a bell in the driver's cab. Admittedly there were a few other things that needed attending to, like preparing trains for service, for instance, but basically it was down to opening and closing doors.

Guards also needed to learn to drive the trains. This was in case anything happened to the driver, such as being taken ill, or having a heart attack. So this led me to taking the controls of a westbound Central Line tube train at Stratford station. As the train sped down into the tunnel I turned to the instructor and yelled something along the lines of 'Fucking hell! I love this!' He laughed and said something like 'OK, watch your speed, son'.

Sometimes people would either fall or deliberately jump under the trains. In the job this was known as 'one under'. I remember that upon finishing my training I was transferred to the Northern Line. Golders Green was my depot. My first memory of that place is sitting in the canteen having a cup of tea. A bloke ran in and shouted, 'One under!' The whole place went demented, geezers were banging their mugs on the table and shouting and whistling. It meant that they didn't need to go out on their turns because the service was 'up the wall'.

Privately of course the drivers weren't so full of bravado when it came to facing incidents of 'one under'. I remember an Indian bloke who was driving the train ahead of mine on the southbound somewhere around Clapham Common. There is a bit of a curve in the line there, so you have to slow down. Well, he reckoned that as he came around the curve there was a bloke with his head on the line looking up at him. As he went over him there was a spurt of blood up the side of the driver's cab. It turned out that the bloke had walked fifty yards or so down the tunnel from the station.

(I must admit he was a lot more committed than me with that one-sided razor at Dellow House.) I had a cup of tea with that driver at Morden, the last stop on the line. He was badly shaken up.

## HELLO, NATALIE

It was while I was working at Golders Green Depot that my second daughter, Natalie, was born. I was there for the birth, which took place at Guy's Hospital. The delivery ward was right up near the top of the big tower that lies at the heart of the Guy's complex. It was a very long labour and Margaux had to endure quite a bit of pain. But what a beautiful day it was, in high summer. As soon as Natalie was born the midwives placed her in my arms. I swear that she looked at me in a way that was totally cognisant. At that time Margaux and I were getting along as well as we had ever done. Everything was pretty sweet.

## A FEARLESS AND SEARCHING MORAL INVENTORY AT NEASDEN DEPOT

Not long after that I was transferred again, this time to the Jubilee and Bakerloo. I was quite happy to get off the Northern, which is still dubbed 'the misery line' by passengers.

The stretch between Morden and East Finchley (via Bank) is the longest continuous tunnel on the tube system at 17 miles 528 yards. On some 'turns' you would be down in the tunnel for the whole day. (Camden to Kennington to Morden to Camden to Morden, etc.) In summer especially it would do your head in. Plus I would find myself coughing up black mucus. My new depot was to be Neasden over in north-west London. I ended up doing a lot of 'sleet nights' there. Sleet nights occur in winter when freezing conditions threaten to ice up the points. Train crews are dispatched at regular intervals to spray the line with a form of antifreeze. I also did a lot of regular night turns, where you do the last and first trains. You spend nearly all the turn sitting at the depot. I was happy to do that because I am, as you now know, a night bird, plus the wages were good (time and a half).

While doing these nights I was working on the fourth step of Alcoholics Anonymous which is 'We Make a Searching and Fearless Moral Inventory of Ourselves'. I was dreading somebody asking me, 'What are you writing, John?' Can you imagine that? What would my answer have been? 'Well, mate, since you ask,' I would have replied, 'I'm just knocking out a fearless and searching moral inventory of myself.'

So there I was at Neasden Depot in the middle of the night peeking into all the nooks and crannies of my soul, while the blokes around me were following their various pursuits. A few of them would be drinking, in half-arsed fashion, a few tins of Harp and all that (I bet that doesn't happen nowadays), others would be playing cards and gambling, while a few others would be playing table tennis.

*Actually in the yearly tournament I finished runner-up. There were much better players than me but I was a very dogged and single-minded player. I would just hang on in there and my opponents would eventually make mistakes.*

Similar to when I was collecting tickets, I got recognised a few times, but I didn't mind and I was happy to have a chat with people. One day a bloke from the *Guardian* newspaper came up to me while I waiting at the end of the platform to start my turn. I had a natter with him and he wrote about it in the paper. Whenever I signed autographs, the other members of staff who saw me would go bananas. They would be intrigued and consequently would start pumping me for information on my past.

*Around that time I was listening to a lot of music. Salif Keita's Soro album was a big favourite as was Anita Baker's Rapture album. I also listened extensively to the new wave of Miles Davis albums that were released in the eighties. There were some very good tracks on those albums. I think 'Tutu' was probably my favourite. At that time funky slap bass was very much in vogue and Marcus Millar, who was Miles's bass player at the time, was the prime exponent of that style (which had been originated by Larry Graham all those years before). I loved the fact that Davis refused to get stale and predictable. Yet again he had found another up-to-date setting in which to display his talents.*

## NEVILLE CALLS ROUND

In no time I had my appetite back in regard to playing music. Neville came over to our flat in Southwark and asked me if I was going to get another band together. He told me that he felt that I should start up the Invaders of the Heart again. I said that I was bit out of touch and that we would need to find completely new musicians. If we were to do it I wanted to make a fresh start. This time around I wanted to avoid the thick, rich tonality that comes from 'jazz chords'. In fact I didn't really want too many chords at all. I wanted drones and simple melodies with few notes. He asked what sort of players I wanted. I told him that we needed to find either a guitarist or a keyboard player who was familiar with Eastern styles, especially stuff from the Middle East. Within a couple of weeks he came up with the name of a guitarist, Justin Adams.

*Neville had some serious reservations about Justin because he was another ex-public-schoolboy. Remember, that's how Neville and I first met, among a gaggle of ex-public-schoolboys. I must admit that for a number of reasons I wasn't, generally speaking, crazy about them. However, in regard to Justin, I was willing to keep an open mind. I also encouraged Neville to keep an open mind. I decided that I would meet with Justin and see what he was like. I had, after all, made friends previously with Angus MacKinnon, and he certainly wasn't a terrible person. Anyway, my temperament is such that I am always willing to give people a chance, no matter what side of the tracks they come from. Additionally, I would like to think that the arts generally and music particularly are a place where you can meet people 'halfway', no matter what their background. Additionally, even then I knew that if you were automatically prejudiced against toffs, you were in danger of being 'hoist by your own petard'. You can fall into the trap of unthinkingly treating other people with an air of moral superiority and distain. After all, inverted snobbery is just as boorish as, er, snobbery is.*

## THE OLD ETONIAN

Eventually I hooked up with Justin and found out that he was actually an ubertoff. He was Eton educated and his father had been the British ambassador to Jordan and his grandad had been a judge at the Nuremberg trials. When we met the subject of jobs came up. I told him about life on the Underground. He told me that he hated the thought of work. He had done half a day of a temporary job at Westminster Housing but had left the post for good at lunchtime because he couldn't handle it! Half a day of work in his whole life! Of course, the fact that he didn't have to worry about work of any kind meant that he could, if given notice, make himself available for rehearsals, which was admittedly quite handy.

Because of his father's job he had spent time in Jordan and subsequently developed a fondness for various types of Middle Eastern music. Although he was enthusiastic about my project, I did sense the vague underlying lack of urgency that is so typical of the 'resting toff'. For them the wolf will never truly be at the door, they can afford to wait calmly for the right opening to come in life.

*I met very few working-class boys and girls in musician circles (other than in the rock and reggae scenes) at that time. However, I did meet lots of musicians, most of them mediocre, from well-to-do backgrounds. I was always amazed at how laid back they were, even though they were, for the most part, late twenties/early thirties,*

*with not a lot, it seemed to me, going on. I could not understand*
*why they were not unhappy with their lot. I was also amazed at the*
*unsanitary conditions that they chose to live in. (Then again they*
*are like actors, who can quit the role that they are playing at any*
*time, and stroll off the stage.)*

Whatever, Justin's genuine love for, and basic knowledge of,
Middle Eastern stuff won the day for him, as did his honesty; he
didn't try to pretend to be something that he wasn't. At that stage
he did all that was asked of him, which was basically speaking,
at the beginning at least, to play Middle Eastern-tinged guitar
melodies over heavy bass lines and beats. As a musician he was
very raw at that time; however, he understood perfectly well what
was required of him. I quickly put any doubts I had out of my
mind and he was accepted into the fold.


## THE BAND GROWS

The two other blokes recruited for the band at that time were
keyboard player David Harrow and percussionist Ned Morant. Ned
was a typical 'London boy'. He was very likeable and easygoing.
We rehearsed on my evenings and afternoons off at either The
Point studios, where David Harrow worked, or at Alaska Studios
in Waterloo. Out of the blue I got a phone call from my agent,
Willem Venema, in Holland. Somehow he had heard that I was
clean and sober and he offered me a tour. As chance would have it
the Underground informed me that I had to take my one-month
annual leave all in one go because I had been there for over a year
without taking any time off. So as well as taking a family holiday
I went off touring the Continent with my new band for a couple of
weeks.

Our first date was in Neuchatel in Switzerland, just across the
border from France. On the way there we stopped for the night in
Dijon. I had a great night's kip, and I vividly recall waking up on
that first morning and stepping out on to the small balcony, which

The Invaders
Mk II

overlooked the town centre. It was a glorious spring day, bright and breezy. The smell of fresh bread and croissants was wafting up to me from the patisserie below. I stood there soaking it all up. My first clean and sober tour. I felt great.

It felt good to be playing and hanging out with a band again. However, the tour finished and that was it. It was back to the Underground. There was absolutely no hope of a major record contract at that time.

*To be honest, at that point I was not certain that I even wanted to get back into the music business full time. My first priority was to support my family, and there did not seem like a snowball's chance in hell of doing that via my music. At that time the only income I had from music was via PRS payments.*

On my return from the tour I got moved to Hainault Depot on the Central Line, whereas I wanted to go to Leytonstone Depot. There was something about the vibe at Hainault Depot that I didn't like. I couldn't quite put my finger on it. I remember that a few blokes felt like that. So I wanted a transfer immediately.

However, I received a call from a friend of mine called Maxine, telling me that there was a driving job going at a haulage company that she was working for. The company in question was situated in Bermondsey in South London. She said that the governor was a very good bloke, and that as long as you kept your nose clean, he was a diamond. So, on the spur of the moment, I ended up putting my resignation in to the Underground. I am proud that I left that job with a good record of employment. I had managed to keep my head down and do what needed to be done. My duties for the haulage company mainly entailed taking pallets of paper about in a big old 'Box Luton' van. I used to be backwards and forwards through the Rotherhithe Tunnel all day long.

I was still doing one or two shows with the band and we were getting a little bit of a reputation, plus I could still pull a crowd, so the situation was far from hopeless. I remember that we did a show at the Astoria with the Irish band Stump who were good lads. There were about a thousand people there, not a bad turnout.

Our show was scheduled to finish around 11 p.m., at which time a rave was going to begin (I still called events like that 'discos' at that time). We did a good show and as soon as we were finished the crew at the Astoria were asking us to clear our gear off the stage because the rave was going to start. I went to get the van so that we could load up. When I got outside the Astoria I couldn't believe my eyes. There must have been about five thousand people out there vying to get in. I hadn't realised how big the rave scene had got. At that time a lot of promoters, agents and artists were worried that the 'live scene' would completely disappear under the onslaught.

Among the crowd of ravers were a few prize hooligans that I knew. They came over and started talking to me. They were really friendly and hugged me. I was a bit taken aback because they weren't the sort of geezers that you would expect to do that. It was as if all violent tendencies had been removed from them. Their eyes looked a bit glazed and dilated. They were very chatty and quite clearly were in a euphoric state. I quickly realised that they were on drugs but I could not work out which one it was. I thought that maybe it was a combination of drugs, cocaine and

LSD possibly. But then I suddenly realised that they must be on the new drug, 'E', that I had heard so much about. I knew that a couple of my band regularly used 'E', but I had never actually seen them on it.

Over the next few months we did a few more shows, but absolutely nothing was happening in regard to interest from major record labels (although I did make a couple of tracks for the indie label Nation Records, which was run by Aki Nawaz and Kath Cannonville). We really needed to do an album, but of course we had no money. At that point I wanted to bring in a real drummer but yet again we could not find anybody who seemed to fit the bill. Around that time I paid a visit to Holland. I think that we had a show at the famous Melk Weg club in Amsterdam.

While there, by way of the Dutch contingent, I met a drummer called Michel Schoots. He was a good mate of a sound man called Hugo, who was a pal of mine. (The distinctive Ovation bass, which I play to this day, was lent to me at that time by Hugo.) So anyway, Hugo introduces me to his good mate Michel, who is the drummer in a group called Urban Dance Squad. 'The Squad' had quite a bit of success in both Europe and the States in the early nineties. Upon hearing Michel play, I realised almost immediately that he was the bloke that we were looking for, in regard to doing some recording. Jaki Liebezeit had obviously been a big influence on him. I wanted to continue to utilise the Middle Eastern themes that we had developed. But I also wanted something else. I wanted what I would term a spooky, European sort of sensibility. I certainly didn't want Anglo-American rock music. That meant that we had to be able to play spontaneously, and a real drummer is crucial in that situation.

I had at that point a few ideas for recording an album, in a way that would not cost an arm and a leg. I thought that if we did a tour of Holland we could utilise the talents of both Hugo and Michel. We could record all the shows, via Hugo's stereo mix, straight on to DAT. But more importantly we could, in between gigs, set up at a venue or some other space, and record in a very live and relaxed fashion, yet again, straight down to DAT. Hugo and Michel immediately knew the place that we could use, The Freefloor, in their hometown of Utrecht. We did not use headphones, we used proper gig monitors, as well as a PA. Instead of Hugo making the best sound that he could in the hall, he tailored the sound to suit the DAT recording. My idea was that we could take the stereo mixes back to a cheap studio in London and bounce the DAT tracks down in stereo to another DAT machine as we did one or two overdubs. I planned on having big and powerful live tracks from Holland, and so only anticipated the minimum of 'overdubs' (really it was a crude form of 'cut and paste', i.e. collage) in London. This was in the early days of digital recording, and I really wanted to take advantage of the clean digital sound. If you had tried to make an album that way using analogue tapes you would have had to endure lots of accumulated tape hiss in the 'collage' process. The tracks that we left Holland with were absolutely outstanding. Better than I had dreamed of. Both Hugo and Michel were exceptional.

As well as the Freefloor recordings we had also done some some fabulous ad hoc recording of some sessions at the Bungalow Park that we stayed at near 's-Hertogenbosch. I say we, but for that trip I only brought two other musicians with me, Justin Adams and Dave Harrow. That was simply due to lack of funds.

Justin and Dave were so much more animated than they had previously been. They had never done anything like this before. It was a buzz for me seeing them so happy and inspired. As musicians they were both novices, but that was a good thing. You could never make an album like that with session players. Justin started to let go of himself. Dave Harrow started to discover a world that lies beyond the four-square regularity of Acid House and other sorts of 'sequenced' music (that's not to say that sequenced regularity is a bad thing). I was a few years older than both of them and it was nice to be able to give them the sort of musical experiences that I had enjoyed over the years. Harrow had a nice melodic and atmospheric sensibility. It was ideal preparation that he had worked with the poet Anne Clark because I started doing more spoken-word stuff on that album; something that I had flirted with in the past. One of the tracks was called 'A13 (The Ancestral Trek Eastwards)'. It is about the main road that goes from the East End out into Essex. I tour-managed as well as doing the driving on that tour. The vehicle I hired for the tour was a brown Montego estate. The resulting album was called *Without Judgement*. There is a bit of dialogue in the movie *Apocalypse Now* when Marlon Brando's character Colonel Kurtz talks about 'reason defeating us'; he also talks about the need to act 'without judgement'. That bit of his monologue is what inspired the album title.

As soon as the record was done I set about getting a deal for it. I utilised a few of my contacts and got in to see two or three record company A&R men. I recall one of those meetings very well. I had known the A&R bloke in question for a good few years. He was vaguely like Simon Cowell off the telly (only a bit camper). A lot of music business people had that look and vibe back then. In the past the bloke had always been quite respectful to me. But now something had changed; he assumed that I was down on my luck and started to go through a cruel little routine. He looked me up and down and said, 'Cor, haven't you put on weight?' and 'Oh dear, you're losing your hair.' (I mean, look, I could accept that now, but at the time I was about 12½ stone, 'in shape' and my hair was only showing the first signs of thinning.) He played the tape of *Without Judgement* but would keep doing 'stage yawns' and fast-forwarding the tape. He then said, 'Na, you won't get anywhere with that,' and slung it back to me. 'For starters you're too old,' he says. 'What about production, why don't you go into production? Let's see if I can help you.' Without saying who he was calling he picked up the phone. 'Jah Wobble,' he says down the mouthpiece to whoever it was on the other end.

'Yeah,' he said in reply to the other A&R man that he was calling, 'that's what I said,' and he looks at me and mouths the words 'too old'. He said the best that I could do was to try and get jobs producing up-and-coming bands' demos. I can't explain how or why, but I didn't get a rush of blood to the head, or feel tempted to scare, intimidate or assault him. I felt calm and unruffled (I wish that had always been the case then!). I simply told him that I wasn't interested in doing demos. I couldn't wait to get out of his office to tell people how funny the encounter had been. I was about thirty and I was too old as well as being fat and bald! (Perhaps I smelt as well.)

*Not too long after that my star was just beginning to go into the ascendancy again. I was doing a gig for Gary Clail in Brighton, it was a sold-out show. Skip Macdonald, Doug Wimbish and Keith LeBlanc were in the band as well. My own thing was starting to go well, and as soon as the gig was over I was looking to get back to London. I was supposed to stay in Brighton that night but some important business had come up in London and I needed to get back. Bobby Marshall (a bloke who has really done me a good turn or two over the years), who was Gary's manager at the time, yelled for silence in the packed and buzzing dressing room. 'Who is going back to London tonight? Wobble needs a lift.' Well, who steps out of the throng but that same bloke from the record company. 'Sir,' he says to me, 'it will be an honour,' and gives me a bow, like I was royalty or something. He then stepped forward, grabbed my cheeks (the facial ones), and then looked me right in the eye and said, with a voice full of conviction, 'I knew you'd be back.' I swear on my mother's life that is a true story. The music business: you couldn't make it up. On the way back to London I simply listened to him drone on about what I should and shouldn't do to enhance my career. Neither of us mentioned his performance a few months earlier.*

# Chapter Ten: Solo Success

## THE BLOKE FROM MODERN ROMANCE

A couple of years before that time, I had started knocking about with a geezer that I had met in the 'reformed drinker' circles that I now mixed in. His name was David Wilkerson. He had been in a group called Modern Romance. His stage name was David Jaymes. Everybody that I knew hated Modern Romance. It was Morrissey who famously said, 'I'm sure there are worse bands than Modern Romance, but seriously, can anybody think of one?' So I had to put up with a fair bit of ribbing from one or two people, especially Margaux, who had sat there on a few occasions watching me lambasting them when they made their *Top of the Pops* appearances.

However, I wasn't too bothered by a bit of mickey-taking and all that, because as far as I was concerned Dave was just another bloke who had (supposedly) got into difficulties with drink and drugs, and deserved a fair crack of the whip. Although Dave was three or four years older than me, he was still younger than just about everyone else that I knew in 'those circles'. (Nowadays there are far more youngsters knocking about.) He was yet another ex-public-schoolboy, albeit minor, from Woodford Bridge, a well-to-do suburb that straddles the East London/Essex borderlands. He was, with me at least, a hail fellow well met, suburban sort of a bloke, who seemed happy to come over from Essex and pick me up in his car so that we could go to meet other ex-problem-drinkers.

To be honest, Dave only ever seemed to pay lip-service to the 'getting clean and sober' process that most of us were going through (you could call that process the beginning of taking responsibility for yourself and growing up). I did sometimes wonder why he bothered knocking around 'those circles' at all because he didn't seem to be too enthused by it (it isn't everyone's cup of tea). I suspected that his real problem was simply his fall from grace from being a pop star. Modern Romance's time in the spotlight had come and gone. Consequently he'd gone off the rails for a bit. But whatever, he wasn't drinking or using. He occasionally had a vibe similar to a spoilt child, but I basically liked him, and considered him to be a friend.

Dave's overriding ambition was to get into artist management. If he couldn't be an artist he'd be the next best thing. He did have a couple of fledgling acts under his wing but, as I'm sure he would still admit today, he had a hell of a lot to learn. He was very keen to be helpful. He had a few quid and offered to lend me money to go over to New York, to visit that city's New Music Seminar, in order to secure a deal for *Without Judgement*.

I hesitated to accept his kind offer because I do not like owing money. However, after some persuading from Dave, I agreed. I have never borrowed money like that before and I haven't since. Up to this time we had simply been mates, and I was happy with that, and to be honest when money comes into it you do worry about a friendship. I was aware that the offer probably wasn't entirely altruistic. Dave was desperate for credibility, and credibility, surprisingly, was something that I still seemed to have at that time (shame that it doesn't pay the rent, of course). I think that Dave hoped that he could get some credibility by association. He had said that he was thinking of going to the seminar anyway, but I'm pretty sure that if I hadn't accompanied him to New York, he wouldn't have gone alone. But whatever, he was an OK bloke most of the time, and he was doing his best to be as helpful to me as he could.

A couple of London-based indie labels had shown interest in *Without Judgement* but had not offered enough money, so I gambled and went off to New York. The New Music Seminar was a hellhole, your worst nightmare: several thousand music business tossers all in the same place. On the last day of the seminar I succeeded in doing a deal for *Without Judgement*. I licensed the European rights to a company in Belgium. I recall that once the deal was signed, some three or four weeks later, I took a day trip with my daughter Hayley to Ostende on the fast catamaran service from Dover that used to run in those days, in order to deliver 'the parts' (the lacquer and the artwork). Hayley loved the chips in Belgium.

A few weeks before going to New York I had sent a tape of *Without Judgement* to Celluloid Records. I was familiar with some of the records that Bill Laswell had done for that label. I thought that it would make a good home for *Without Judgement*. I had heard nothing so assumed it was a non-starter. However, on the eve of the trip I received a phone call from Bill's then right-hand man, the guitarist Nicky Skopelitis. It turned out that Nicky had belatedly got his hands on the tape, checked it out and liked it. He had then played it to Bill, who also 'got it'. I was due into New York a couple of days later. How's that for good timing! I had been aware of Bill from the first thing that his band, Material, had released in 1979, a short-cassette release (that's how it came out in the UK) called 'Temporary Music'. It was funky, as I recall, but with a certain idiosyncratic sensibility, especially in regard to the bass, that I now associate with Bill.

Anyway, I went over to meet Bill, and felt on the same wavelength immediately. It turned out that his favourite album was the same as mine, *Dark Magus* by Miles Davis; at that point hardly anyone knew that album, so to meet someone who also rated it highly was a pleasant surprise for me. Within a few weeks he flew me back to play bass on the Ginger Baker album *Middle Passage*. I didn't actually meet Ginger at that time because his drum parts were already 'down'. Bill paid me better than he needed to and put me in a very nice Fifth Avenue hotel. Nicky Skopelitis met me at JFK with a limo and took me there.

*The staff at that hotel were Hindus, and to this day I don't think that I have ever met such happy hotel staff. I remember I was having a shave in the nice bathroom there one morning, before going off to the studio. I suddenly felt a tickly sort of sensation on my (bare) right foot. I looked down and saw a little mouse standing on my foot looking up at me, with its bright and inquisitive eyes. I do think that you get a better class of mouse at posh hotels.*

I'd already jacked in my job working at the haulage company. I didn't want to muck the governor Ray about, because he was such a good bloke, and I knew that I would be working on that album for a few weeks. He told me I could come back any time that I liked. So when I finished putting the album together I was going to call him. However, I saw that a warehouse near to where we were living in Southwark was advertising for a delivery driver, and the wages were well above the normal rate. So I applied for the job. The geezer who interviewed me thought I was a bright spark and asked me if I would be interested in another vacancy that they had, which was for a warehouse manager. So I ended up managing a warehouse! It turned out that the manager and drivers who had been working there previously had robbed them blind, and consequently they were looking for a trustworthy person. The wages were pretty good, but what a horrible job. Most of the deliveries would be taken off the vans by forklift trucks, but once every couple of weeks a delivery would arrive from France on an artic (with an extra trailer). There would be crates of glass piled (actually crammed is a better word) floor to ceiling and wall to wall. It would not be on pallets, therefore we couldn't use a forklift and had to 'handball' the stuff off the lorry and into the warehouse. Half a dozen of us would be at it from eight in the morning to six or seven at night on those days, without a break.

I really had a problem with two people at that place. There was an old boy, semi-retired, who was a virulent racist, and the other was the owner's son, who used to swan in and talk very rudely, without good cause, to the employees. He particularly liked to steam into (verbally speaking) the Chinese driver. I think that his father had been a successful market trader, and sent the son to, yes, you've got it, public school. He was one of those war-games blokes. He was your worst nightmare, arrogant and disrespectful. One morning I had our truck routed to go all over North London, when the owner's son comes in and demands that one small box of glass goes off to his pal's restaurant, which was somewhere in deepest Surrey, well to the south of London. I told him that was mental, and that it would be better to send it by courier, because otherwise it was going to screw up the whole schedule. He shouts, 'Just put it in the van, wanker!' Two seconds later he was out for the count. Everyone was patting me on the back, even the racist. Somebody lifted my arm in the air the way you would a boxing champ. That was the last straight job that I did.

*I recall that there were a few occasions when we were so busy on that job, trying to get orders out, that I loaded up the van and did some deliveries myself. (I knew London like the back of my hand and could get the job done much quicker than anyone else.) I delivered to the kitchens of some of the top restaurants in London. They were absolutely filthy. I remember that one of those places had stacks of cold fancy desserts left near the bins. They were covered in flies. I assumed that they were 'out of date' and being binned. But then a waiter came and took a couple and plated them up. I was appalled. Actually waiters and waitresses always say that the posher the restaurant, the dirtier the kitchen. On another occasion I delivered a box of beer mugs to a West End club in the middle of the afternoon. I walked down the stairs into the gloomy club, to be*

*confronted by a solitary drinker sitting at the unattended bar. The
bloke was George Best. I needed a signature for the delivery. What
a nice bloke; he took me to the offices upstairs to get the manageress
to sign for me. I recall that the manageress was a bit of a looker. I
assumed that George was waiting for her.*

Margaux wasn't too impressed that I'd lost the job at the
warehouse. We were really starting to fall out with each other
again. It wasn't just losing the job; that was no more than the latest
(major) excuse to have an argument. For years we had carried on
in a way that was reminiscent of Richard Burton and Elizabeth
Taylor in *Who's Afraid of Virginia Woolf?* I suppose that modern
phrase 'co-dependent relationship' comes into play. There you
are in what is supposed to be the closest relationship in your life,
treating each other, for much of the time, abominably, far worse
than you would a dog, or even an enemy. At times we really
brought the worst out in each other. It was a shame, because since I
had quit drinking a few years before we had, for a while, got along
as well as we ever had. However, over the years things had grown
rather tempestuous between us, and of course 'tempestuous' isn't
really great for your kids. Within a few weeks I left and went back
to Dellow House. There was, as they say, no one else involved. As I
recall Margaux started acting classes around that time.

*Eventually we divorced. Although I probably sound rather glib
about the marriage break-up, it wasn't something that I took lightly.
It left me with a crushing sense of failure. I don't think that she felt
too clever either. I was granted joint custody of Hayley and Natalie.
It is very awkward to talk about Margaux, because since the divorce
we have never spoken, or even set eyes on each other, for that matter.
As I look back at my life and write this book, the failed marriage is
without doubt the saddest single thing. It is like a big chunk of my
life that in regard to this book is ring-fenced, with 'Do Not Enter'
signs up all the way around it. I have no wish to embarrass her in
any way, but I have to say something. What am I supposed to do?
Write her out of my history?*

The band was still getting gigs but there still wasn't a sniff of a record deal. I wasn't sure what to do, persevere with the music full time or get another job. I even started to think that maybe I should go and train to do something else. I had a chat with an older and wiser mate of mine (who had spent much of his life as a submariner). I asked him what his view was on my predicament. He didn't actually answer my question. Instead he asked me some questions. Firstly he asked me if I felt as if I had a special talent for music. I quickly replied, 'Yes.' I didn't have any doubt about that. He then asked me if I believed that the talent was of my own making. Again, without hesitation I replied, this time, 'No.' 'Do you believe God gave you this talent?' he asked. 'Yes,' I said. 'Well,' he said, 'don't you think that he would like you to use the talent that he has given you?' That bloke would always say, 'You already have the answer to any question that you may ever ask yourself.'

I decided that I would devote myself single-mindedly and wholeheartedly to the making of music. There would be no more half-measures. Around that time there were some changes of personnel in the band. David Harrow went and was replaced by a bloke called Mark Ferda, who was a mate of Ned Morant's.

*Dave Harrow was such a fool; it was as if he went out of his way to get sacked. He tried being slick and clever on one occasion too many, so I sent him up the road. Being a nice bloke I set him up with a regular gig with Adrian Sherwood. I warned him to keep his nose clean with Adrian. However, from what I heard he blotted his copybook early doors with Adrian. Well, believe me, there are no flies on Adrian. He is an astute bloke from the suburbs. Adrian absolutely adores a pound note, and knows all about being slick, so he won't put up with a bloke like Harrow queering his pitch. Consequently he tormented Harrow until he began to tow the line. There is another side to Adrian, which I am reminded of every time I see Ricky Gervais's David Brent character on TV. Similar to Brent, Adrian could on occasion be incredibly gauche, to a toe-curling degree, without coming close to ever realising it. For me that was his most likeable aspect.*

Ferda was Welsh and came as part of a pair. The 'other half' was another Taff, a drummer called Nick Burton. Nick only lasted a year or so with me. More importantly I drafted a girl into the band called Natasha Atlas. For months I had been looking for a singer who could handle Eastern modes and quarter-tones. We had tried a couple of singers, and even gone as far as doing a few shows with those singers, but I had not found anyone who felt right. Eventually I got a call from Kath Cannonville, of Nation Records . She had heard about a singer who split her time between Brussels and Northampton. That singer was Natasha Atlas. It turned out that Nat worked in Latin forms of music as well as Arabic. I heard a tape of her singing some Latin-flavoured stuff. Immediately I knew that she had something special. I got her to come down to London for an audition. It worked very well. We already had a whole host of Eastern-flavoured dub tracks. I got her to do basic question-and-answer stuff with the guitar while the keyboard droned and the rhythm section kept things grooving. I also drafted in a player called Dawson Millar. I knew him through Annie Whitehead. Dawson is a knowledgeable percussionist, and is particularly adept on darbuka. We were starting to get a nice balance in the band. I can still remember the first gig that Nat did. It was a London show. She lost her purse and all her money straight after the gig. She got into a right old state. I soon learnt that was pretty typical of Nat; anyway, I paid her again for the night and she was over the moon.

The crowd absolutely loved her. Not only because she sang well but because she belly-danced as well. I thought that we were on to a winner; Nat augmented the band perfectly. The new line-up was starting to gel. It was still far from perfect, but I did feel that it was a band that was both hip and futuristic. I felt that we were by that stage good enough to play large festivals. I was convinced that audiences would really like what we were doing. However, to my dismay, neither agents nor promoters were in the least bit interested. I made contact with a bloke called Basil Anderson at Peter Gabriel's Womad organisation. It was obvious that our style would really suit their festivals. In fact I had played at the first-ever event at London in 1982 at the ICA.

*What a mental gig that was. It was like a musical nuclear reactor going into meltdown. I had the infamous John Stevens on the skins. John had done his National Service in Germany, where he struck up a friendship with Jaki Liebezeit. I recall sitting at a bar once while John Stevens lectured me on 'the need to be calm in life, and not to react angrily'. The lecture went on and on. Eventually it was 'last orders!' followed by the dreaded 'time, gentlemen, please!' John broke off from lecturing me on 'good karma' and asked the governor for another drink. The governor rudely declined. In an instant John was over the bar and at his throat. So much for calm! John was a very lively character as well as being a great player.*

Womad seemed to be getting pretty active again in regard to putting on festivals. They were also forging ahead with their record label, Real World. I was hoping that we might get some festival gigs as well as scoring a record deal. Basil was a very friendly bloke, out of Bristol, if memory serves me well. He came up to London to see the band and immediately saw that it 'fitted the bill' at Womad perfectly. He arranged for me to go down to meet the powers that be at Womad. I went down to Womad's base at Box in Wiltshire by coach from Victoria Coach Station. It was the day after a massive storm and the journey took ages, there were fallen trees everywhere. I ended up having to change coach three times. To be honest, when I arrived my heart sank. It was so horribly upper middle class. There was no buzz. Basil took me around to meet everyone. The impression I got was that the senior people that I met simply assumed that Womad's only black employee had got some cockney bloke in for a chat, and so fucking what. Nobody was that interested. However, Basil was a very good bloke and he persevered and got us on the bill for the following year at a couple of Womad festivals.

*Of course, within a couple of years, when we were flying high, the more senior Real World and Womad employees were all over me like a rash. Suddenly I was an 'old friend of Womad'. They would look to chisel me down on the money, as they came on like they were Oxfam or something. However, for all their bleating about lack of funds, I knew that the main management and administrative people would probably be on OK wages, and so why, I asked myself, shouldn't my band and I be on good wages? I suspected that for Womad it was ultimately more about building the 'Womad brand' long term than it was about anything else. Consequently, I always made them pay top dollar. There were quite a few women working there. Some of them seemed a bit cranky. Justin Adams wittily dubbed them 'the mad women of Box'. I found the vibe at Box to be pretty similar to that of Richard Branson's Manor Studios. Richard Branson and Peter Gabriel are definitely two lords of the manor, Branson literally, of course. They are both capable of being very charming and attentive when you are in their presence. Vince even remembers Branson making us a cup of tea at the Virgin offices one afternoon. I must admit that Branson always seemed very easygoing and affable.*

*Peter Gabriel came on stage once and put his stage 'cloak' around me once at the end of an Invaders set. Which to be honest he didn't need to do; he was being nice. I can also remember a bizarre occasion when the two of us ended up besieged in a Jacuzzi in America. It was not that long after his massive 'Sledgehammer' hit. We were both part of a Womad package tour. He was still extremely popular in America at that time. We were staying at the same hotel. I was in the deserted pool area, chilling out, when Peter walked in. We sat together in the Jacuzzi having a slightly tentative and awkward conversation about music, when suddenly he was spotted through the windows. Suddenly there were literally dozens of his fans stood gazing in at him. So we sat there chatting away in our swimming trunks while being stared at by loads of vacant-looking Yanks. It would have been a bad idea for him to go outside. The fans had that* Night of the Living Dead *vibe about them. I think that they would have eaten him alive. Eventually Security came and fucked them off. Sometimes you have to feel sorry for those big stars. At times they look so forlorn and lost.*

*I had met Peter a couple of times before that at the Womad recording weeks. I would sit in his studio playing the bass with some great players from all over the world. Some of the stuff was pretty mediocre, but the odd track was dynamite. I recall doing some stuff with a percussionist from Cameroon. That geezer was dynamite. He was outrageous. A couple of years later I bumped into Peter at a reception for Brian Eno. We started chatting, making small talk and all that. I asked him what had happened in regard to the stuff with the Cameroonian player. Were there any plans to release it? Suddenly the old 'toff shell' came up. It was as if I was the gardener and had asked a damned impertinent question, and he got all cold and frosty. In an instant I saw another side to him. I already knew that he was as much a businessman as an artist. But suddenly he appeared to me as if he were an art collector, like Charles Saatchi. Only instead of acquiring paintings, he acquired music.*

*Whatever, my relationship with Womad did have an upside. That has to be admitted. I did OK out of them. I earned some dough, and played at some lovely locations around the world. I always preferred the overseas Womad festivals, because generally speaking they were better organised than the UK ones, which, in those days at least, had on the organisational side of things a vibe similar to what you would probably encounter at a Middle England church garden fete. It really was an unappealing mix of rank amateurism and upper-middle-class insincerity. The regular hired workers were generally OK. I particularly remember a Canadian girl called Karen. She seemed to do the work of ten people.*

## BOMBA

Bobby Marshall did me another good turn at that time. He approached Andy Weatherall about doing a remix of one of our

The early
nineties
arrive and
I become
ever more
comfortable
within my
own skin

tracks. At the time Andy was involved with the Boy's Own record label. Andy was a big PiL fan, and was very familiar with my stuff, so it was an easy deal to put together. The track in question was 'Bomba'. We recorded the track at my mate's cheap little rehearsal and recording studio in Waterloo. Andy Weatherall did a great job of deconstructing the track, without turning it completely into something else, which is something a lot of remixers tended to do in the nineties.

Andy Weatherall's involvement, and the resulting Boy's Own release, did us the power of good. Boy's Own went through London Records, so the distribution and marketing were very good. The record made a bit of a splash, particularly around the clubs. I did a fair bit of promo for the record in the UK and so my presence started to reassert itself. At the same time *Without Judgement* came out on the Continent and made a bit of a stir. Yet again there was a fair bit of promo to do. I recall that the record label over there was a bit taken aback at the enthusiastic press response, so all in all things were pretty positive.

However, there were still no offers from any of the majors in regard to the band. Unfortunately Island Records were still a bit 'asleep at the wheel' at that time, so there was nothing doing there. I knew that I could quite easily secure a deal with an indie label. However, if I had done that, I would not have got the recording advance that I required. It wasn't just the recording costs that needed to be considered; it was a sizeable band and the running costs would be considerable. I knew that I would need to put at least some of the band on retainers. I can't say that I was terribly worried. I had a faith that everything would be OK and that we would get a deal. I was seeing a very nice girl the other side of London at that time. I used to stay over at her flat. She was a blinding cook, and good at massages, so I was well fed and pampered and all that. I was perfectly happy. I managed to see plenty of my daughters; it wasn't always easy getting access but generally it was OK. In those days I wouldn't let them meet my girlfriends; I knew that wouldn't go down well.

## OVAL RECORDS

Dave Jaymes was really trying his best to help. He had got himself a cushy number at a music publishers called Eaton Music, which was run by one of his old mates. His main function seemed to be taking people out for lunch. He used the job to make contacts and to network. On one of those lunches he was out with a bloke called Charlie Gillett and he slipped him a cassette. Charlie had a small independent label called Oval Records. I was familiar with the label and its releases. Gillett had a partner called Gordon Nelki. Charlie also had a show on Radio London. I had listened to that show on a few occasions and thought that he sounded like a nice bloke. Nice Charlie. They contacted me and we sorted out a meeting. They both really liked the tape. They hit me with a thousand questions about the personnel in my band and about how I thought the band should be recorded and marketed. I started to realise that 'nice Charlie', although definitely a music fan, was a bit of an energy vampire. He would 'crowd in on you', asking lots of questions, some of them bordering on the personal and intrusive, without ever really giving anything of himself away. (In my experience people like that have often got quite an anaemic sort of look about them.) Gordon always seemed to be a fairly morose figure at Charlie's side, never saying much. He seemed to be pretty world weary. He vaguely reminded me of Clement Freud, whereas Charlie, by way of his general demeanour, reminded me of Ron Noades, the old Crystal Palace chairman. Gordon, a Jew, had been a dentist in a former life. Charlie had been a schoolteacher. They were a funny old pair. I realised early on that I had better keep an eye on them. Charlie was as much a crafty small businessman as he was a nice-sounding DJ. But fair's fair, to give him his due he saw the potential of the thing right from the off.

A couple of days later they faxed me an offer. I thought it was, after everything we had discussed, derisory. I think that they offered around two and a half grand as an advance. I ignored it. To be honest, when people utilise that 'coming in very low' tactic, I think that they are just testing the water to see if you're naive. With me there is no point in doing business like that; you may as well be up front. If you're up front with me I don't see it as a sign of naivety or weakness, I see it as honourable, and you will quickly win my respect. At that point we can start meeting each other halfway. Whatever, I knew full well that they were hooked and would be back with another offer. They got back in contact with me and I told them that they had to get serious. And they did.

Although Oval was an independent company they had a deal whereby they could, depending on the project, get funding, manufacturing and distribution via East West Records, who were major players in those days. The head of East West was another Jewish bloke called Max Hole. (Of course, we immediately knew him as 'Arse'.) I found him a tad vulgar and crass, but then again I felt like that about many people that I had encountered in the music industry. I would chat with him but what he had to say went in one ear and out the other. One thing he seemed good at was recruiting capable staff, which to be fair is half the battle. Women seemed to run most of the major departments there. They were not all particularly likeable but my goodness they were efficient. We were very lucky to be at East West at that time. We had a hit album, *Rising Above Bedlam*, and a hit single, 'Visions Of You', and all the consequent palaver that comes with even a modest amount of commercial success. 'Visions Of You' featured the vocals of Sinéad O'Connor. I met Sinéad by way of a bloke called Kevin Mooney. I knew him from the time that he was 'going out' with Jordan (the girl that worked at the shop Sex). Kevin was one of the original members of Adam and the Ants, one of those people (similar to Jordan) that you couldn't help but take a shine to. He was a London (Irish) boy (out of Woolwich, if memory serves me well). In 1991 Kevin was in a rock band called Max with a bloke called John Reynolds, who was the drummer. John was married to Sinéad at the time. Via Kevin, I became friendly with John and Sinéad. Shortly after meeting Sinéad I played on one of her album tracks. John did a lot of the 'fixing' and sorting out for Sinéad at that time. He sorted it out for her to come and sing a track for me.

*I think that you had to be seen as a 'happening person' to appear on John's radar. Nevertheless, I got on well with him. My time in the music business has been peppered with those sorts of symbiotic relationships, with hail fellow well met sorts of blokes.*

'Visions of You' was the last track that we recorded for *Rising Above Bedlam*. I always enjoy the build-up to the last track of a songs-based album. You know that you are nearly there, but realise that maybe you can make your good album a great album by pushing yourself just a little harder, as you enter the home straight. I started the process of writing 'Visions'. I have written and co-written many compositions, I can't remember the exact circumstances of many of them; however, 'Visions' is one that I can recall well. As usual it started with the bass. To start with I recorded the bass line, with a click track, on my Portastudio. I also recorded the drone. I did that simply so that I would remember the line. If you know the song you will recall that it has a simple yet hypnotic four-note B-line (albeit with a few 'fills'). It is in the key of D. (D and C are the best keys for me to sing in.) I then recorded a rough demo of the bare rhythm track, at John Reynolds' flat (at that time he had an eight-track demo studio set up in one of his bedrooms). John supplied two loops, one of drums and one of percussion. I never asked him where he got them from, but the percussion one especially did the trick, it was a real peach. At that stage Justin put down a simple, sparse rhythm guitar part. I took the track home to Dellow House with me, and got cracking on the lyrics. I lay back on my bed and wrote them. I can vividly remember that. I swear I could hear the song clearly, with Sinéad singing, in my head, even before we recorded it.

*At that time I was five years clean and sober. I was really feeling the benefits of that process, spiritually, mentally and physically. I tended towards a feeling of well-being for much of the time. I felt incredibly vital and alive. Consequently my lyrics refer to no longer being 'numbed out'. It felt at that time as though my feelings were thawing. I also talked of no longer being 'drenched in shame'. (Sometimes alcoholism is described as a shame-based illness.) Basically I was beginning to feel good about myself. Elsewhere the song talks about the heart and mind 'meeting'. In essence I was saying that I was becoming a less 'fragmented' person. I also sung about circles (meaning cycles), and how 'Hell can be a circle too'. I was simply referring to the 'vicious circles' that keep us locked in unenlightened states of mind, to the extent that you end up 'living in hell'. The chorus part ('I love visions of You') refers to God. God as I felt I'd glimpsed him/her/it working through (quite ordinary) people in the process of life. (Of course, the word 'God' is totally insufficient.) That God felt like an inherently and infinitely warm, loving and humorous force that was somehow immanent. It certainly didn't feel like a force that you turned to for mere consolation, and was far removed from the Old Testament God of my youth. It felt like an irresistible wave that you gently swum with. The chorus lyrics and melody are a mantra pure and simple to the manifestation of God in our world.*

Sinéad loved 'Visions'; she lost herself in it. She never got paid a penny for the track. She didn't want anything. That to me was typical Irish generosity. However, I didn't feel good about that, it didn't feel right. I decided to give John Reynolds a slice of the publishing. If it hadn't been for John I would never have made the connection with Sinéad.

'Visions' was the the first single to be released from the album. *Rising Above Bedlam (On An Elevated Section Of Motorway)* went on to do well in terms of sales; thanks largely to the success of the 'Visions' single it 'crossed over' into the mainstream. 'Erzulie', 'Everyman's An Island' and 'Soledad' are my other favourite tracks on that album. The title, by the way, was inspired by two elevated sections of motorway: the M6 that runs through Birmingham, and London's Westway, the A40(M). Whenever I drove along those roads, normally during the wee small hours, I would envisage myself rising up over the insane terrain of modern man.

So everything was rosy. We were really in business. It was time to go on the road again. The only shows that I can remember in 1991 were in the Far East (Japan and Hong Kong respectively). It was my first time in the Far East and I fell in love with it. Now, at the beginning of 1992, we were off to Italy followed by a drive down through Monaco (where, most unusually, it was snowing) to Cannes in France, where we were to play the annual Midem music seminar, which I found to be very similar to its New York counterpart. There had been some personnel changes in the band by this point.

I had drafted in a French girl called Margot Vynia for the previous year's trip to Japan and Hong Kong. She was a blues/soul-type singer. She did some spoken word and backing vocals on 'Everyman's An Island'. She was a nice girl, but very easy to wind

The naive 'fresh off the boat' look

up. She had a typically hippy libertarian ethic. She would loudly complain about 'fascist' immigration officers and the like when we were travelling. I would pretend to get very hot under the collar at her attitude, and tell her that 'you can't have every Tom, Dick and Harry strolling in a wholly unregulated fashion across international borders'. She would get very upset with me. Of course, I didn't mean a word of it. She was so earnest it was like shooting proverbial fish in a barrel. She thought that I was a very horrible and reactionary 'Roast Boeuf'. The funny thing is, now that I'm middle aged, I do have some sympathy for the views that I stated at that time.

That year was the first year of the Mercury Music Award. We were nominated for *Bedlam*. That was the night that I found I was sitting next to Jeannete Lee from my PiL days. As I said earlier, she was good company. We didn't win it; Primal Scream did, with their album *Screamadelica*. Funnily enough I played on that album too. The track was called 'Higher than the Sun'. It was another Andy Weatherall remix.

*I first met the Primals in Glasgow in the early eighties. They were still young lads and had been refused admission to one of my shows. So I snuck them in and gave them a beer each. Funnily enough, that Glasgow show sticks in my mind. I slashed all the tyres of our own tour bus so that I could stay drinking in Glasgow the day after the gig. I recall making a show in front of the driver, going on about 'mad fucking Jocks' and 'senseless vandalism'. However, I think that he knew full well that I was behind it. I always liked the way they drank in Glasgow, a beer with a chaser, ad infinitum. That was my way of drinking. I felt very much at home there.*

In between touring we went back into the studio. We were playing quite a few shows, all over Europe and America. By that stage we were using a coach that was owned and driven by Tom Hain, the brother of the government minister Peter Hain. Tom and his brother both used to run with me as part of Tottenham's infamous 'Yiddos crew'. Tee-hee, only joking; Tom was of course another posh friend of Justin's. To be fair, one or two of Justin's upper-crust pals came in handy at times.

It was during the Oval/East West period that I appointed David Jaymes as manager. To be honest I brought him in simply to act as a buffer between me and Charlie Gillett. I swear that Gillett would use up an entire roll of my fax paper every two days with his endless questions ('in regard to the drum roll on the beginning of verse 2 of the song...' etc.). It really did my head in. It was a smooth transition getting Dave in, because he had been helping out, increasingly, with stuff such as booking travel and hotels, for a few months. I had been reluctant to give him the role of manager. I had been hoping that he would have a runaway success with one of the other acts that he was managing, or get offered a job as an A&R man or something. I had hoped that if he had success elsewhere it would let me off the hook in regard to employing him. That might sound a bit strange; however, I had strongly suspected that our friendship would end if we did too much business together. Friendship is far more important to me than business.

Not long after starting a new album for Oval, there was a dispute between Gillett and me. I felt that Gillett had begun to cross a line, in very specific ways, in regard to interfering with the process of making the new record. I was a bit surprised because I felt that he was interfering in a way that he hadn't done in regard to the commercially successful 'Rising Above Bedlam'. He had drastically upped the ante in regard to clipping my wings over 'artistic control'. He must have known that his actions would provoke an argument with me. I told Gillett, face to face, that he was 'needlessly rocking the boat', and 'to be careful not to sink it'. I felt that it could turn out to be a bad business for all concerned. He sort of laughed me off; in what I felt was quite an arrogant and cavalier sort of a fashion. His voice and demeanour were very different to that of 'nice Charlie' on the radio. Not long after that, Gillett sent a long fax to David Jaymes, justifying his actions. The communication was presented in very reasonable terms, and attempted to gloss over what I felt were his unjustifiable actions. I felt that under the surface the argument wasn't really about 'the music', rather it was a classic case of a (needless) control issue situation. Things could have been handled very differently. For me the whole affair had a strange undertow to it.

A couple of weeks after that I got a call from an engineer at a London music studio. It was immediately clear that 'the problem' was still very much alive. Well, all bets were off. I really would have thought that Gillett and Nelki would have read me and the situation far better. After the trials and tribulations that I had gone through in the past, did they really think that I would suffer this? I really wasn't looking for a 'music business scrap' (I'd already had more than my fill of them), but OK if they wanted one they would get one. Max Hole, to give him credit, did try and rectify the situation, but to no avail. I was determined to get out of the situation, and within a month or so I was completely free from that deal. It's very unusual to be released from a deal like that, 'cleanly' and quickly. The parting of the ways was by mutual agreement. The truth be told, I think that in some respects they were quite relieved to see the back of me.

*Of course, Gillett has never, since that time, played one of my records on air. But never mind, I'm still here and earning a living. In the late nineties I met Ian Dury. He too had once been on the books of Charlie Gillett and Gordon Nelki at Oval. Similar to me he had fallen out with them. We had a good laugh about 'the odd couple' as we compared notes (Ian wasn't bitter in the slightest). He was one of the most special people that I ever met via the music game. I had briefly met him once before, with Sid, outside the Roxy circa '77. Sid had jokingly squared up to him. Ian held his walking stick in the air above his head and said something like 'off with you... you scoundrel!' His whole demeanour was totally Dickensian and theatrical. He then burst out laughing, as we did too.*

*John Lydon and John Gray were big fans of Kilburn and the High Roads, and they introduced me to his music. I loved his album* New Boots and Panties. *Just about everybody I knew did. When I met Ian again he was suffering from cancer. We were both doing a bit of promo at the BBC. He was a geezer. When I met him I could sense that he didn't have too long. I sensed an incredible well of compassion in him. It was like a fucking force field. I do not mean compassion as in 'pity', I mean something way beyond that. You can hear the essence of that compassion in his lyrics and vocals. 'My Old Man', for instance, hums with it. I saw him one more time after that at a charity night that he organised at Walthamstow dog track. He made a point of getting his people to track me down to get me there. I was absolutely honoured. It was a great night. All the best, mate.*

My then lawyer George Babbington talked to me about the Oval situation. He informed me that it was very hard to get recording deals at that time (there was a recession on) and that I could well find myself unable to get another deal. However, I did not have a shadow of a doubt that we would get an even better deal elsewhere. And we did, with Island Records.

It was very nice deal. On the strength of it I also got a very good publishing deal with Warner/Chappell. I had a mate in that company called John Brice who had been aching to sign my publishing. He is still a good pal of mine to this day.

TAKE ME TO GOD

We embarked on recording an album that I would title *Take Me To God*. By the way, the title is a request, even a plea, to the music. It's as if the music is some sort of vehicle. I knew that it was going to be an important record. I was determined to finally fuse all the disparate strands of my music into one coherent whole. It really was a large and ambitious undertaking; it was to be (what we used to call) a double album. I fancied a return to the richer tonal sounds and different musical genres that were evident in the earliest manifestations of the Invaders of the Heart. I wanted to 'paint a huge mosaic'. I reasoned that I might not get the chance again. Consequently there was a whole army of guest players and vocalists. I ended up doing a lot of lyric writing for that album, not all of it in English. Like many English people I am lazy in regard to learning foreign languages; however, I learnt that if I used an English/Spanish or English/French phrase book (and dictionary), I could eventually come up with something that was OK; certainly it would be enough to approximate the basic sentiments that were required. I had used that approach on *Bedlam* in a limited way and on *Take Me To God* I took it farther and it came up trumps. I would have been happy for the vocalist to write lyrics, but quite often when you ask vocalists to do that they stand there frozen, like rabbits caught in the glare of headlights, no matter what nationality they are.

I wanted *Take Me To God* to have a large emotional and spiritual range, yet I didn't want it to take itself too seriously or be in any way portentous (or pretentious for that matter). So even darker tracks such as 'No Change Is Sexy', a track that among other things discusses murdering shop assistants and eating their livers with olive oil and a sprig of parsley, still raise a smile (well, they do with me), with their delivery and juxtaposition of images. The title is a reaction against nineties psychobabble and the (at the time) fledgling 'rehab' industry. It also mischievously argues against the notion of change and 'maturing' being good and desirable things; which of course they are. Really I just wanted an opportunity to poke fun at 'Californians with strange haircuts and symmetrical teeth'.

*'No Change' is essentially a paean to sick co-dependent relationships, and their unholy union with pornographic videos, kinky sex, takeaway food and violence. For me the regular ingestion of takeaway food equates to a lack of connection with any nurturing or (internal) mothering instinct. Violence in that context is also to do with lack of connection. Sex in those circumstances, especially sex that is either overtly or covertly sadomasochistic, is, I think, a form of 'papering over the cracks', or to put it another way its primary function is as a displacement activity. The more these compulsions are indulged the more old patterns are perpetuated. Emotional development is prevented. The real soundtrack to this 'chronic lack of connection' is the sound of traffic moving down an urban stretch of motorway as heard from a motel room.*

*In regard to this 'mothering sensibility' I recall that over the years I came to quite like aspects of hospitals (when they weren't doing unpleasant tests) and other institutions. To me they were places where you could be 'looked after'; places of certainty (the London Underground when I worked there was a bit like that). They were places of 'being mothered by proxy'. I am not at all surprised by those blokes who freak out when they have to leave prison and so immediately reoffend so they can get behind bars again.*

*The counterpart to 'No Change Is Sexy' was another spoken-word track called 'I Love Everybody'. For the first time in my life I felt a strong and consistent feeling of empathy in regard to the world. At that time I would have 'turns' that were quite pleasant. For instance, I would on my regular sojourns up Roman Road market see deities (in the form of regular people), all around me. I would try not to stare at people because obviously that can appear rude; it can of course also be disquieting for the person being stared at. I began to take very long walks across London. Sometimes*

*I would walk up the River Lea all the way to Waltham Abbey. I recall that on one occasion, while walking on East London's sewer link late in the afternoon, I looked towards the western sky. To the east lay a wilderness of junkyards with the empty carcasses of cars piled forlornly on top of each other; a pall of acrid smoke hung in the air above them, while the junkyard dogs barked incessantly. The colours of that western sky were to my mind totally outrageous and unrealistic; they consisted of an incredible fluorescent bluish backdrop, which was overlaced with a lurid powder pink. It was an awesome sight. It was how you would imagine the sky would look on a foreign planet. I was quite overcome; it struck me violently, like a bolt out of the blue, that everything was temporary and fleeting, a mere temporary 'coming together' of various factors (and that even those factors themselves were insubstantial). Of course, looked at that way 'everything' is 'nothing'. At that time I was quite scared by that notion, because ultimately it spelt death to my ego and to all the things that I considered permanent and 'fixed', such as identity and personality. Most scary was the thought that I might well not have a soul – well, certainly not in the way that I had believed up to that point. I realised that the comprehension of emptiness was the essence of liberation. That 'emptiness' is certainly not a cold lonely void; it's a vast region of consciousness where anything's possible.*

*On other occasions (at that time) I would feel that I was in some way 'being absorbed into the world'. It was as if 'my' subatomic particles were striving to be absorbed into the universe. I would feel literally as light as a feather. This sort of feeling would come and go. When it wasn't there I wouldn't particularly miss it. I still did 'normal (blokish) things', played/watched football, had girlfriends and took my daughters to the pictures and all that.*

## STEAM

*Take Me To God* was quite a complex beast to put together. It wasn't unusual at that time to work a sixteen-hour day. I absolutely loved it. My days would often begin with a trip to Ironmonger Road baths, where I would take a swim followed by a nice bit of 'steam'. There were two old boys who worked there in those days as masseurs; well, I say masseurs, but they had the demeanour of boxing trainers. They would really pummel you. The combination of the pummelling and the heat would really relax you. They had proper beds there where you could have a lie-down and a little kip. There was a bloke there called Michael who had a limp; he would make you a cup of tea as well as pop over to the café for you. They had a telly room there as well where you could have a ciggy. Unfortunately it's not like that any more. Some bright spark on the council decided to market it as a 'health suite'. They got rid of the old boys and the whole vibe changed. A different set of people started to use the place. Up to that time 'steam baths' had been an important part of London culture for many ordinary men and women. (It was men on Tuesdays, Thursdays and Saturdays. The Sundays alternated between men and women.) Apparently the women would all sit about doing each other's hair. There was a great democracy to the steam baths, you had all creeds and nationalities in there, and all sorts of professions were represented: cabbies, gangsters, market traders, Old Bill, boxers and jockeys. Those last two examples would often be there just before a 'weigh-in'. I have not been in for years; the last time I went in there was hardly anyone there. The vibe had gone. (However, I am told that it is getting back on track again, and I plan to drop in there at some point in the near future.)

After Ironmonger Row I would take the short stroll over City Road past the famous Eagle, as in 'In and out of The Eagle… pop goes the weasel' (that lyric refers to the pawning of an implement used in the tailoring industry), and on to the junction of Provost and Vestry Streets where Greenhouse Studios lay. Most days I was as happy as a pig in shit. I felt like I was finally being the geezer that I was supposed to be, living the life I was supposed to live. Something happened to me in that early-nineties period. I made a quantum leap as a human being, let alone as an artist. That process was encapsulated in the making of *Take Me To God*. I felt so energised. The music began to pour out of me. To this day it has not stopped. It was around that period that I considered myself to really be both a musician and an artist. I had never really felt entirely comfortable with those labels up to that point.

That was my last spell at Island, and I must say that I had, yet again, been very lucky with my timing. In that mid-nineties period it was a very well-run company. All the departments were very efficient, especially their marketing department. The record enjoyed the benefit of an extensive poster campaign. My face was plastered all over the UK for a couple of weeks. We went for a fresh-off-the-boat, naive 'Russian émigré' look, which suited me down to a tee. The idea was to create a look similar to that of the émigrés that entered the East End at the turn of the last century. The finished photos were given a sort of a sepia finish, which accentuated the early-twentieth-century look. A photographer called John Sleeman took them.

He also did the *Take Me To God* cover, under the direction of a bloke called 'Calli', who ran the Island art department. (He was one of those blokes who permanently wore leather trousers. That normally indicates that the person in question is a graphic designer.) Sleeman utilised a technique where my band and I stood, absolutely still, in a room that was completely 'blacked out'. Sleeman would then open the shutter on his camera, which was on a tripod, and sort of 'paint' everyone with the light from a torch. It gave quite a ghostly effect. It was quite reminiscent of an old painting, which was of course the point. Everybody who appeared on that album is on that cover somewhere.

I turned us all into caricatures of ourselves. I decided what characters the band should be. I got Justin to dress as a district commissioner of the British Empire, I turned Neville Murray into a scary-looking Haitian-style policeman à la Graham Greene's

*The Comedians*, I got John Reynolds to be a blacksmith, because I liked the idea of him looking like he did something physical and rhythmical. It was also slightly 'in-jokey', because John liked to act as if he was gauche and not very clever sometimes, as he played up to 'being the drummer'. I made Mark Ferda into a creepy Victorian undertaker; somehow I always felt that he had that sort of vibe about him. Jaki Liebezeit I turned into his hero Buster Keaton. I became a vaguely Christ-like figure, revealing my sacred heart. As the artist, I was well aware that everybody loved me, but would be quite happy to nail me to a cross when the time came (please, no comments about a Jesus Christ complex).

# Chapter Eleven: Changing Times

We were doing gigs throughout the making of *Take Me To God*. Once we finished the album we hit the road with a vengeance. By this stage we were mainly doing festivals; I particularly recall the second of our two Glastonbury performances in 1994. We had already played a show earlier in the day on the main stage. In the evening we played the jazz stage. I really wanted to 'push it out there'. I felt that we had done our basic thing earlier in the (breezy summer) day. Now it was the night-time, my time. Just as we went on a geezer got shot (not fatally) to the side of the stage. I took the band 'off script' pretty early on and kept it there. It really grooved. I was calling the band in and out, and at times taking the music off the edge of a cliff and bringing it back again. The band was really focused; all their eyes were fixed on me as I cued them in and out. They weren't the best players in the world but they were playing as a unit at that time. The music would compel me to do lots of slow-motion movements around the stage. I would intersperse these with insane 'Spotty Dog the puppet' dances, while side-on to the crowd; I would enjoy turning my head and smiling inanely at the crowd for 'a minute or so too long'. Occasionally, I would feign, in time to the music, heading and volleying spectacular goals.

Yet again there were one or two changes to the line-up of the Invaders. Natasha had left in early 1993 to be replaced by Ali Slimani. The impossibly beautiful Christina Amran replaced Nat in regard to belly dancing. I also got Christina to do some backing vocals. She was a big hit with the audiences. There was no animosity with Nat about the split, in fact we started 'seeing each other' for a while. Nat was absolutely crackers, but I was very fond of her. Most people saw her as an exotic diva, but in fact she reminded me far more of Julie Walters (who I considered to be very attractive) than Oum Kalsoum. Nat's mum was from Northampton, and Nat did have a bit of what I would call a 'Midlands way' about her, which is no bad thing, not as far as I'm concerned anyway. I recall the occasion when Nat introduced me to her mum. I put my hand out in readiness to shake her hand. Nat's mum bent forward, as you do, and sank her teeth into my arm. I looked at Nat and said, 'If she doesn't stop in five seconds I'll punch her in the head.' Thankfully she stopped before it came to that. Fortunately the skin wasn't actually broken. I didn't really mind the incident. In a way her mum was 'speaking my language'. To be honest I have bitten a few people in the past. I find it a strangely comforting pursuit, especially when accompanied by deep throaty growling. If anything it's a sign of affection.

I met Ali Slimani while doing a soundtrack for a Channel 4 feature on dance. Ali and a few of his chums were being filmed in front of a blue screen doing 'rai dancing'. By coincidence there was a French Algerian girl there, also working as a dancer, who I had met years before in Paris. She introduced me to Ali, and we immediately struck up a friendship. He was working as a waiter at various London hotels. Like most Algerians he sang, played darbuka and danced as a matter of course. I thought that it would be prudent to get him down to the rehearsal room for a bash. Ali really brought energy to the proceedings; he was a really

Me and
Natasha

©Echoes/Redferns/Getty Images

good geezer to have around generally, let alone as a performer. His best mate was another bloke called Ali (Mabrouk was his second name). I called Ali Slimani 'Ali number one' and his mate 'Ali number two'. (It was a similar concept to the 'four Johns set' that I had been a part of in the seventies.) The two Alis were chalk and cheese. They both came from the same area of Algiers. If you wanted a straightforward answer to a question you went to Ali number two. If you wanted to go 'around the houses' you went to Ali number one.

I visited Algeria with Ali in 1993. It was actually a bit of a war zone there at that time. Another Algerian by the name of Jaffa came along for the trip. He was a good geezer, who had settled in the UK right next door to West Ham's Upton Park stadium. Among other places we went to Tizi Ouzou in the Berber part of Algeria. We made our way to a Berber cabaret, narrowly avoiding a firefight between government forces and the Islamic militia, who went at that time by the acronym FIS. I was never really sure who was fighting who, and on that occasion it may have been a rebel Berber militia engaging the government forces. To be honest it got a bit hairy there on a couple of occasions.

Eventually we arrived at the cabaret. Well, I have to say that the female dancers were both beautiful and captivating, North African and yet fair skinned with blonde hair, I couldn't believe that. The music was absolutely first class; the sound was similar to Arabic music but with its own funky character. It was performed by a band called (in Berber) Love the Night. I thought that was the best name ever for a band.

I remember that another musician who was hanging around the place took a bit of a shine to me in more ways than one, if you get my drift. I explained to him, kindly and patiently, that although I was devilishly good looking, with fine chiselled features, I was not into geezers (the poor bloke was crestfallen); 'however,' I said, 'my friend, he very much likes to "be with man", and he would very much like to be your friend.' A short while after that I heard a bit of hollering and screaming coming from Ali, as he went about disabusing the bloke about his chances of a 'close friendship'. I made myself scarce. 'Al,' I said to him later, 'I think you do protest too much.' He went mad at me.

*A postscript to that trip to Algeria: for a time I stayed with Ali's family in Algiers. I was treated like a king, they were fantastic hosts. The atmosphere of the flats where they lived was not unlike some blocks of council flats that I knew in London in the sixties and seventies; basically it was very convivial, everyone mucked in. A short time before I arrived two blokes wearing Ray-bans and designer jeans and tops had walked into the courtyard of their apartment block and shot a couple of people, seemingly at random. That was getting to be a fairly common scenario at that time in Algiers. What absolutely shocked the Algerian people was the western appearance of those assassins. They had become accustomed to what they perceived as typical mujaheddin veterans coming back from Afghanistan committing terrorist acts, i.e. blokes with thick beards and Islamic robes killing people in the name of God. Their world was absolutely rocked because these latest killers wore clothes that made them indistinguishable from all the other young men wearing Armani and Gucci. That was such a new thing. Everyone was really twitchy, because just about everybody else was now a potential terrorist.*

I was really reminded of that trip during the aftermath of the London tube bombings in 2005. Yet again, as in Algiers twelve years earlier, the main concern of the public debate was how can you possibly distinguish and identify these young men before they commit their dastardly acts? I have to say that the scariest geezers I met there were a notorious anti-terrorist squad nicknamed the 'Ninjas' because of the balaclavas that they wore over their faces. We went through a few pretty heavy roadblocks while we were over there, but nothing like the one the Ninjas were manning. They were very tasty. Now I have had guns pulled on me on a couple of occasions, and that was very scary (on both occasions the ends of the barrels looked as big as the entrances to the Blackwall Tunnel), but these blokes had a tank with them. They flagged us down and then the tank slowly swivelled its turret until it was pointing straight at us. We had been driving down the dusty road between Camus' home town of Oran and Algiers, windows down, blasting out the rai. As usual me and Jaffa did this game of chanting loudly as soon as we spotted a roadblock (normally something puerile like 'the workers united will never be defeated'), just larking about; we would steadily decrease the volume as we approached the roadblock, and then sort of say, 'Hello, Officer, nice day, isn't it?' just as we pulled up. This used to really freak Ali out, which is precisely why we kept on doing it. Ali would go mental, worried that the soldiers might hear us chanting our nonsense and misunderstand, and confuse us with terrorists, with potentially fatal consequences. As usual we started doing it on this occasion. As we got near to the roadblock we saw the masks and realised that this was a bit different, so we piped down quicker than usual. We had to get out the car and all that and eventually they reluctantly let us go, literally slinging the passports back in our faces. They really didn't like the look of us. I thanked God that I had a government visa stamped in my passport. I think that saved the day.

## BIG BAND GETS BIGGER

The size of my band seemed to swell by the day at that time. At some gigs we had as many as thirteen musicians and singers. The 'regular vocalists' were a pretty diverse bunch; apart from Ali there was Ximena Tascon from Colombia and Trevor Rennie (Spikey T) was the reggae singer/toaster of the band. Trevor was from Tottenham, and fittingly was a follower of the Spurs, as of course is Neville. Trevor would, apart from singing and chatting, do an old-school type of toasting, which was quite reminiscent of I-Roy. He knew that I was very partial to that. We would occasionally have ad hoc five-a-side football games versus teams that would generally be made up of African musicians on our travels around various festivals. Ali and Trevor were both OK players. I don't think that we ever got beaten. The regular vocalists would sometimes be augmented by singers such as Sinéad O'Connor and Annalise Drecker for some shows. Annalise really had character, she was very pretty, but a bit of a tomboy. Her dad was one of Norway's top football coaches. She did the 'Becoming More Like God' video with me. I have done a handful of videos over the years, but that one is my favourite; it was directed by Peter Christoffersen. Throughout that nineties period I had a great roadie called Dickie Daws who was a fervent atheist. I used to initiate as many arguments as I could between Dickie and Ali, who was a Muslim, as well as Christina, who was a born-again Christian. I would get them 'at it' and then stand back and fan the flames as best I could. Dickie hailed from Cornwall. I used to very much enjoy telling Dickie that he was damned and was going to Hell, owing to his 'immoral behaviour'. Dickie absolutely relished our 'believer' versus 'unbeliever' battles, just as much as I did. Dickie was my favourite person in that group. He was a very genuine bloke.

## THIS TIME I REALLY DO TOP MYSELF

For a couple of years at the beginning of the nineties I went to see a therapist. Since I had stopped drinking and drugging in 1986 many things had changed. I felt like I was really on a roll in regard to (finally) growing up and developing and fulfilling my potential. I had long since come to realise that drink and drugs in themselves were not 'the problem'. That's not to say that I didn't totally accept the fact that I had to continue to completely abstain from the use of alcohol and drugs (that had ceased to be an issue back in 1986). The maelstrom of active alcoholism had long since diminished and I had, via the AA programme, had a good look at myself. I had got the ball rolling; however, I felt that I would benefit from talking to a qualified and experienced person. The shrink I ended up seeing was a Polish woman; that was ideal for me because I tend to get on quite well with Slavs.

Obviously it wouldn't be appropriate to go into all the ins and outs of that process. (But I can tell you that I didn't break down in floods of tears, or pummel a teddy bear while screaming abuse at it.) For me (and I expect everyone is a bit different), the help came in diverse ways. Firstly she gave me great practical advice about how to deal with life, and how to avoid the sort of negative cycles that had dogged me so much in the past. Secondly she was invaluable in regard to dream analysis. *Don't get me wrong, I don't think that dream analysis, or analysis of the unconscious, can provide all the answers to life's problems, but they can certainly come in handy.* I generally tended towards having nightmares rather than dreams up to that time. What nice dreams I had before that time (leading up to analysis) were confined to sexual/musical areas (sometimes they would combine and I would get literally 'turned on' by the music. The music would become personified in the female form). Suddenly that had changed; the sexual/musical aspects were still there but they were now in a bigger and somehow more meaningful context. At that time I found myself getting incredibly vivid and significant dreams. Some of these were quite beautiful and moving. Others were disconcerting and intense. On other occasions all those effects were mixed in together.

I remember one of these dreams well. It was situated right in the middle of the Clichy estate. I was standing by one of the massive rubbish bins (which used to get set alight on a regular basis by the local tearaways, so that they were always blackened and charred). There were the legs of a dead body sticking up and over the edge of the bin. I knew with certainty that the legs of the dead body were 'mine' and that I was also 'the murderer'. The police were in attendance; they had parked up and were approaching me, in that cautious and stern way that they do when they know that they will probably be nicking you, i.e. they had already somehow identified me as the suspect. All the tenants of the estate were lined up on the landings silently bearing witness to my situation.

It was a really hot, muggy day. The air was totally dead. It was a WPC that questioned me; she was a petite brunette, and not unattractive. She asked me if I was the killer of the corpse that was lying in the bin. I answered in a hesitant and non-committal way, 'Well, yes and no, you see you're going to find this a bit hard to believe, but actually it's me in that bin, my "old body", I don't need it any more, but it is my body so it isn't actually murder.' All the time the police were looking at me with hard, stern faces. I had the urge to laugh manically, as much as anything to relieve the unbearable tension that I felt hanging in the air, but I knew that would only make things worse. The policewoman stepped forward and put the handcuffs on me as she cautioned me. I was led away. I thought it strange that the arresting officer was a young WPC. I remember thinking (in the dream) that I might need to call my shrink to get her to explain (to the court) the ramifications and consequences of 'spiritual growth'. One of those consequences, in my dream at least, was the development of a new physical body. When I awoke it took me several minutes to realise that it was a dream and hadn't really happened. When I told my psychiatrist about the dream she was delighted. She saw it as a sign of progress. And so did I.

## SESSION MAN

Throughout the nineties I was very much in vogue as a session bassist. I did sessions for quite a few artists/producers. One that I remember well was for Rachid Taha, the French-Algerian singer. Steve Hillage produced it. I was very impressed by both Rachid and Steve. They both really knew what they were doing and what they were aiming for. Steve also produced The Orb's session that I played on. I knew both Alex and 'Thrash' from that band. I think that Steve really got the best out of them. It was thanks to Steve that I got my publishing on Blue Room.

A lot of other things happened in that period. I had started doing goju-ryu karate pretty seriously. I had begun instruction in 1992. For a few years I would train hard for fifteen hours a week or more. I trained with a sensei called Chris Rowan, firstly at his dojo in Old Street, before he relocated to Shoreditch (before it became an area burdened by a huge number of total and utter tossers). I have a lot of respect for Chris; he upped sticks as a young man and bravely went off to study under the Japanese master Yamaguchi (who was known as 'The Cat'). Eventually Chris gave me a set of keys to the dojo and I would go down there on most afternoons to train on my own.

## TELEVISION

Apart from flying all over the world doing concerts, I also had to do promo tours to support the record. Sometimes that process is quite gruelling; you can for instance find yourself in New York, still jet-lagged, getting up for a breakfast meeting with journalists at 7 a.m. before whizzing of to La Guardia airport. You then spend large parts of the day on little propeller planes flying up and down the Eastern Seaboard, visiting radio stations situated in towns and cities in the states of Massachusetts, New Jersey, New York and Rhode Island. (Of course, that's just a small segment of America. The sheer vastness of the States can take your breath away.) You get back into New York at 6 p.m., where you do more interviews up until 11 p.m. You would after a few days do the same on the West Coast, before moving on to Atlanta, Austin and other Southern states and cities, and then to Chicago, the Midwest and Canada. You would then fly back to Europe, where you would repeat the whole process, flying from cities such as Paris to places like Berlin and Copenhagen, etc. Sometimes the procedure feels like an attempt to 'break you' psychologically. You are asked the same daft questions, over and over and over. It truly is 'Groundhog Day'. You start to doubt that 'you' really exist, or that there is a thing called 'truth'.

However, some interviewers are interesting and it ceases being an interview and becomes more of a stimulating conversation. Sometimes those journalists are pleasantly surprised that you are more than willing to have quite a deep conversation. They don't realise that you are as lonely (and as thirsty for conversation) as a desert island castaway. (Metaphorically speaking there is 'water, water, everywhere, but not a drop to drink'). Sometimes the accompanying press officer will have to nag you both to stop because you are falling behind the allotted schedule, and there is a growing queue of journalists waiting to talk to you.

One bit of promo does stick in my mind. It was in the UK and was for the telly. The show was Jools Holland's *Later*. At the time we did *Later* it was a relatively new programme. It was totally unfamiliar to me because I had never seen it. I was astounded when I was told that we had to jam along with Jools Holland at the top of the programme and smile. I thought that was a bit strong, to say the least. To be honest I regarded Jools Holland as a glorified pub pianist. I had seen him on *The Tube* a few times in the past and found something vaguely contemptuous in his demeanour. I didn't have an axe to grind about it, but I certainly wasn't going to play along with him (or his producer Mark Cooper for that matter). I instinctively knew that the programme was all about 'the *Later* brand' (and Cooper and Holland), rather than about the guests or the music. I refused to do an interview, and rather than smile I turned my back to the camera. I also went well over the agreed time limit; when we had finished the song that we were performing I called in a dub version. They were furious, not that it stopped them using the inspired 'overtime' dub performance on a 'best of' compilation of the programme. It surprised me that *Later* was not actually filmed live from start to finish, as it appears to be, but rather it was filmed in segments. To me it was like an ersatz version of *Ready Steady Go*, but without the naivety. (Not that I'm that fussed about music programmes on the telly.)

Island Records were really worried about me upsetting Mark Cooper. Indeed, he was all red faced and indignant. He reminded me of Captain Mainwaring from *Dad's Army*. (I was praying for him to come and confront me; alas he didn't.) Cooper was considered an important person in TV and Island Records were terrified at the thought of incurring his wrath. (Indeed, Cooper is still a 'big fish'. His name comes up as 'executive producer' at the end of most BBC documentaries that are related to music and performers.) I told Island that they were the company that had Bob Marley. I suggested that they roar like the Lion of Judah, have some pride, and tell Cooper that he was a jumped-up two-bob chancer and he could fuck off. I suggested that they make their own TV show. They should have taken my advice. To me Cooper was one of the new breed of cynical media manipulators, rather than being what I would call a 'proper TV person'.

A couple of years ago I read an interview with Cooper about the fifteenth anniversary of *Later*. He said that he and Holland were worried that artists would not be happy to go along with the opening format of the show, where everyone plays along (in more ways than one) with Holland. They were apparently surprised that performers on the show didn't complain about the format. I think that they knew full well that they were chancing their arm. However, by then 'the tail wagged the dog' and artists were happy just to be on telly and consequently meekly played the game. Cooper said in the interview that I was the only artist to ever give them a hard time. I'm very proud of that.

*Around that mid-nineties time I also met a number of people who I would describe as the spawn of Thatcher. In regard to those people, there is marvellous director's commentary that accompanies the classic British film* Get Carter. *That film was made in the early seventies by Mike Hodges. In his director's commentary on the DVD, Hodges refers to the ruthless, greedy and ambitious Cliff Brumby character (that's the bloke who gets chucked off the top of the car park in Newcastle) as the dawning of a new type of greedy (Thatcherite) Englishman. By the nineties I was observing lots of Cliff Brumbys. In fact they were now running the show. The Brumbys that I encountered were probably the thin end of the wedge as compared to the likes of Jeffrey Archer, Jonathan Aitken and Conrad Black.*

We did a lot of TV around that time. To be honest, television is not my favourite medium. I suspect that most musicians probably feel that way; however, I would by and large, at that time, be content to get on with it and keep the record company happy; plus I knew full well that those TV appearances would not be that numerous, so I wasn't too fazed by it. I was often up for a laugh, so anywhere I went, TV studio or otherwise, I tended to have fun. I found that the appearances that I fully expected to be extra painful often turned out to be easy and straightforward. I dreaded the Saturday morning kids' show performances, for instance. At that time it was *de rigueur* for anyone with pretensions to pop chart success to go on those shows. Surprisingly I found that the presenters were generally very down to earth and straightforward to deal with. They were not pretending that their shows were something more than what they were. They didn't take it all too seriously; after all, it's only the telly.

## NEVER MIND THE BUZZCOCKS

Another bad experience of TV came a few years later, when I appeared on the programme *Never Mind the Buzzcocks*. Initially, I wasn't too sure about going on there. I had seen it and thought that it was a bit of a student, 'after the pub' sort of a programme. The small promotions company that set up my appearance were gutted when I turned it down. I had employed them to get press reviews and a bit of radio on whatever album I had out at that time. I hadn't asked them to get telly stuff for me so I was a bit surprised. Initially I had turned it down because I knew that there was a good chance (owing to the rather snide and sarcastic nature of the show, and the nature of me) that I would end up clashing with somebody. However, in the end I decided not to be too precious about it. When I called the promotions people back they were delighted. They like to curry favour with the people that run those sorts of high-profile programmes. It looks bad on them if they say that they will deliver and then fail to do so. They fret that their phone calls will no longer be returned.

Predictably enough I did have a problem. However, the problem wasn't on camera with Mark Lamarr, the presenter, or the other guests; rather it was off camera with my 'team captain' Sean Hughes. Naively I thought that the whole programme was an off-the-cuff ad hoc sort of affair. However, it was nearly all scripted, to the point where the contestants even knew some of the questions that they were going to be getting. It was certainly like that on the show that I appeared on. It was during the script meetings (which last all day) that I clashed with Hughes. We were backstage in the dressing room going through the scripts for the show. During the process of trying to come up with gags, he had made unsavoury remarks about Jim Kerr and Liam Gallagher from Oasis in regard to Patsy Kensit. (Incidentally, I don't know and have never met any of those people; I just didn't like what he said about them.) He was rocking back in his chair, carefully scrutinising me. He was like a malevolent little toad. It was his little patch and he was King of the Castle. He could see that I didn't like the 'avenues' that he was going down. I knew full well that he wouldn't use that material on air; rather he wanted to make me, and the young blokes working on the scripts, uncomfortable. I could tell that he knew that he wasn't really a funny guy. That was obviously a problem for him. It was easy to see that he wasn't comfortable with himself.

Suddenly it was dinner time and somebody brought sandwiches in. I said, 'Oh, fuck it, I want something hot, I'm going to go to the canteen.' 'Do you swear every time you get sandwiches?' asked Hughes, still fixing his eyes on me. Now when you fix your eyes on somebody else's eyes like that it has, as far as I'm concerned, only two connotations; sex and/or violence. The idea is to dominate the person that you are staring at. I think that Hughes thought that his position was unassailable, and that he could get away with bullying even a big lump like me. I told him to be careful or he would get a slap. He sneered at me, 'Yes, but you can't do that, you're spiritual.' 'Yes,' I replied, 'but in an Old Testament sort of way,' and I slapped him. *The crack he received across his cheek was like the sudden crack of a twig breaking underfoot in a silent pine forest. I think that for Hughes it produced an astonishing moment of Zen-like realisation.*

A few of the BBC workers surreptitiously came up to me afterwards and shook my hand. One of the girls there gave me a kiss. I got the impression that Hughes wasn't terribly popular with the ordinary workers there. Even so, hand on heart, I knew that

I shouldn't have done it. I knew full well by then that there are other ways to handle things. That incident was a very rare blip. By the mid-nineties I hardly saw, or was involved in, violence of any kind. Not even low-level stuff like the Hughes incident. Jo Brand, the comedienne, was there at the time that I did it. I apologised to her, I mean, it wasn't a nice thing to see, but as I pointed out to her, he was behaving like a cunt and couldn't have too many complaints. She looked at me in a horrified fashion. She struck me as a dyed-in-the-wool middle-class Englishwoman. She is nothing like her stage persona. She was actually very prim and proper (not a criticism, just an observation). She was there to do a job and that was that. I was upsetting the whole apple cart. Sean Hughes himself came up and shook hands with me half an hour or so after the event. He apologised for his earlier attitude. I apologised for my part in things. I also apologised to the other people on the show. None of them seemed that bothered. As far as I was concerned that was it; matter closed.

Anyway, I basically ignored the script and went out to record the show. Like *Later* it's not actually live but done in segments. Once the production team is happy they move on. For years I was familiar with being a 'funny cunt' at the bar, so situations like *The Buzzcocks* didn't faze me in the slightest. Actually, most of my mates are also adept at being 'funny cunts'. We are natural performers. It is the culture that we are from, we are very good at 'larging it'. I went out there in front of the cameras and had a laugh. I recall that Mani from the Primals was there that day on Phil Jupitus's 'team'. Every time we caught each other's eye we pissed ourselves. Anyway, the show worked well; I did some funny miming routines and stuff like that.

To my surprise Hughes wrote a piece in the *Guardian* about the incident a couple of days after the event. Of course, he said that he had done nothing wrong and that I had attacked him 'out of the blue'. He compared me with the Christian Brothers, who are an order of Catholic lay teachers. (That was a fucking insult. I am more of a Jesuit sort of a bloke. Everyone knows that.) I then got a plethora of phone calls from people in the business congratulating me on my actions. One of them was a producer who had worked with Hughes in the past. He introduced himself, and then asked, 'Did you punch Sean Hughes?' I thought that he was shaping up for a row. I said, 'No, he's too little so I gave him a slap.' 'Ah well,' he said regretfully, 'that's better than nothing.' Fucking geezer was disappointed!

*There is a funny postscript to this: about four years ago I was walking down Old Compton Street in Soho. I was late for a meeting so I was steaming down the road at a rate of knots. I absent-mindedly saw a bloke and a woman walking towards me; they were about twenty yards away. As I got nearer to them I saw the bloke suddenly fling himself off the pavement and into a group of drinkers standing outside a pub. They looked at him like he was crazy. The bloke's actions had caused them to spill their beer. The girl that was with the bloke was also looking at him like he was crazy. Obviously the situation had caught my attention. As I got alongside the melee I looked out the corner of my eye. I couldn't believe it, the bloke in question was Sean Hughes! He must have seen me, steaming down the road, staring ahead of myself, and assumed that I was about to attack him. As I passed I said 'Cunt' out the side of my mouth.*

## CORFIELD STREET

In March 1994 I moved from Dellow House to a little house in Corfield Street in Bethnal Green. My Dellow House flat had consisted of one big room with a bathroom and kitchen. In retrospect Corfield Street was also small, but at the time it seemed more than adequate for my requirements. I even had a garden! (I put a big old punchbag out there.) A brand-new car nestled in my parking bay outside. One of the first things that I did was to purchase a massive television set. I was the first person I knew to have a huge telly like that. My popularity seemed to increase every time there was a big football game on telly. So everything was very sweet.

Best of all I was now on the firm with Zi-Lan Liao, the Chinese harpist. We had met in Finland at a concert a couple of years before that, and had finally started seeing each other romantically in October 1993. I really was a happy bunny. She also does Chinese dance; in those days her style was pretty acrobatic. She needed to keep in shape so consequently she would stretch for an hour or two every day at that time. She would be doing that, and I would be exercising in the garden, doing karate katas as well as punching and kicking my kick-bag. We made a 'good fit' together.

Zi-Lan was born in Guandong; she came here to the UK in the mid-eighties when she was fourteen, and she and her family settled in Liverpool. Can you imagine the shock to the system of taking your place at a tough Liverpool comprehensive school? She had been used to doing exercises in the morning and singing

Zi-Lan doing acrobatics. This picture was taken around the time that I met her

the Chinese national anthem before starting her lessons. She was astounded at how rude and disrespectful some of the Scouse kids were to their teachers. She couldn't believe that; if you had done that in China your feet wouldn't have touched the ground. Liverpool was a pretty tough environment to be thrust into. However, she was quite capable of dealing with it. In China she had been sent away aged only three to learn the Chinese harp at a boarding nursery that specialised in looking after the children of travelling performers, which both her mum and dad were.

Within a couple of weeks of arriving in Liverpool she was sent off for English lessons. Eventually she came under the tutelage of a Trinidadian woman called Loretta, who was out of Toxteth. Zi-Lan said that Loretta was extremely tough with her, and forced her to learn to speak English and to adapt and integrate into British society. Of course, Zi-Lan is now very grateful to Loretta. They still correspond by letter occasionally. (Loretta went back to Trinidad upon retiring.)

## CHINA

We took a holiday to China in 1994. It was quite a big deal for Zi-Lan to take me back to meet her relatives before we were married. It was a very interesting and enjoyable trip. We didn't only visit Canton, we went all over the place. (Zi-Lan speaks Mandarin as well as Cantonese, which made life much easier.) Even back then it was clear to see that the wind of change was blowing in China in regard to major economic and social reforms. I was surprised at the high standard of living that some of Zi-Lan's relatives had. I was also surprised at the religious freedom that people seemed to enjoy. They quite freely visited Buddhist and Taoist temples. I had expected that the authorities would still have frowned upon such activities. One of Zi-Lan's aunts was especially religious. She had some years previously been one of only two survivors of a plane crash. She had walked unscathed from the wreckage, picking her way through the burning debris and dead bodies. From that day on she had followed the path of the Buddha. She introduced Zi-Lan and me to a Buddhist holy man called Sat Bam Guam. For a while he had been the abbot at the local monastery but by all accounts he hated the inevitable politics that such a job involves. For long periods he took to sitting up in a tree meditating. If approached he would chuck fruit at whoever had come to disturb his peace.

Sometimes he would relent and hold audiences with people seeking help and advice. He was considered to be a soothsayer and saint. We were fortunate that we happened to pass by the monastery at the very time that he was giving one of his audiences. To be honest, at that time I didn't really know what was going on. I just thought that we were going to meet a well-regarded monk. Suddenly I found myself being ushered into his presence. He was an impressive-looking character. It was quite hard to tell his age, I would guess that he was in his seventies. He was quite a sturdy bloke. He had keen, intelligent eyes that weren't lacking in humour. He certainly had a presence about him. Suddenly I was jabbed in my side by Zi-Lan's aunt and told to ask him something. I could have asked something like 'How do I achieve enlightenment?' but even at that time I knew the answer to that: in shorthand it's simply 'stop being a self-deluding arsehole'. Instead I asked him, via a translator, a sincere question: 'What did you do in the Cultural Revolution?' The people around me gasped once my question had been translated into Cantonese. I had committed a real faux pas. It was not considered good manners to casually bring up the subject of the Cultural Revolution, especially in that sort of public or semi-public setting. However, Sat Bam Guam wasn't fazed in the slightest (after all, he knew he was dealing with a foreign devil who didn't know any better), and waved one hand as a sign to his people that he was not offended and would answer the question. He went on to give a beautiful explanation of the interdependence and connectivity between individuals and the state, and the past and present, etc. and how that had specifically applied to him at that time. His answer boiled down to: yes, he had stayed in China and suffered, but no, it wasn't really a big deal. I found what he had to say, even via an interpreter, inspiring. Eventually the time came to leave; as we turned to go he gestured towards Zi-Lan and me and said something, almost as an aside, in Cantonese to Zi-Lan's aunt. Apparently he said 'their marriage will be a good one'. Zi-Lan and I both laughed at that because we had no plans for marriage at that stage. But he turned out to be right, of course, so far anyway (I say, touching wood).

I really enjoyed the food in China. The Chinese are even more of a gourmet nation than the French in my estimation. However, although I had some outstanding stylishly refined dishes while there it was the simple stuff that I enjoyed the most; fried bread for breakfast in northern China, for instance, was a lovely way to start the day, as was a nice warm cup of seasoned congealed pig's blood in rural Canton. The most memorable dinner I had was also in rural Canton. It was way out in the backwoods – well, not so much woods but hills, in a place that they called a snake shack. As the title suggests it's a place that specialises in snakes. The walls of the place were covered in cages that contained writhing snakes. The name of the game was to pick your snake out; it was then killed right in front of you and quickly fried in a wok at your table and served to you. Zi-Lan, it has to be said, has got a bit squeamish since moving to the West, and she freaked out a bit. It tasted a bit like a cross between chicken and frog.

We sat there with the 'mayor' of the district, plus some members of Zi-Lan's family. The mayor had a Kalashnikov rifle propped up by the table and a walkie-talkie radio on the go. The radio was very busy; it kept crackling into life. The mayor had a few of his men out on patrol. Apparently there had been problems with bandits in the area over the last few nights. Every now and then he barked orders into the radio. He certainly was a larger-than-life character, reminiscent in some respects of the sorts of characters that the actor Joe Pesci plays. Unfortunately the mayor died in a motorcycle crash a few years ago.

As well as cages full of snakes there were huge (and I mean huge) bottles of 'snake wine' dotted around the room. These bottles contained the bodies of dead snakes. In my drinking days I would have gone crazy in a place like that. I would without doubt have made a pig of myself and quaffed gallons of wine. As it stood I was turning down offers of snake wine all night long. They were so disappointed that I didn't get pissed with them, but what could I do? Anyway, if I had started drinking I would have wanted to liberate the live snakes and had a go with the mayor's Kalashnikov; it would have ended badly for sure.

I was offered the gall bladder of 'my snake' to eat. Normally you would put it in a glass of warm snake wine to ingest it. I washed mine down with tea. It was as bitter as bitter could be. The Chinese consider the gall bladder to be a real delicacy that has health-giving properties, as it is full of 'chi'.

One of the places we visited was Guilin, which lies adjacent to the border with Vietnam. It is well known for its strangely shaped hills and mountains, some of which resemble animals. These shapes are the result of a geological anomaly. The fishermen in that area use trained cormorants to work for them. It is amazing to watch those birds dive down and then, upon returning to the boat, cough the fish up for their 'master'. The fisherman throws a fish back to the birds every once in a while. I whispered to a couple of the cormorants, 'Listen, fuck the middleman, you don't need an agent; you could keep all the fish,' but they didn't appear to understand English.

It was one of the few places in China where we had a guide. To be honest, the bloke was a bit 'on the make'. He suggested to me quite openly that I dump Zi-Lan in Guilin and cross the border into Vietnam, where there were loads of girls who we could sleep with for a greatly reduced price that he could negotiate. In fact, in some cases, he informed me, we could just sort them out with a packet of fags. All I needed to do was 'take care of him'. At first Zi-Lan and I were laughing at the cheek of the geezer. But like all bad hustlers he didn't know when to shut the fuck up, and he started to wear me out. When I declined his kind (and persistent) offers he got the hump with me. He became a bit truculent. I pushed him to find out if there was anything vaguely cultural going on in Guilin that we could visit. To be honest I wasn't too bothered, I have never been keen on doing tourist things. I find that the best stuff happens by chance when you don't try too hard. Just like making music.

Anyway, he told us about a qigong exhibition that was going on at a local 'research hospital'. I told him thanks, got the address off him, gave him a few dollars and told him that we wouldn't need him any more. We jumped in a taxi and went off to see the qigong exhibition. Now that term qigong can, in my experience, mean just about anything. Strictly speaking the term applies to practices that combine breath and mind control in regard to feats of strength and endurance, as well as spiritual, mental and physical development. This is obviously a broad area and practitioners of qigong can therefore include a wide range of people: meditation masters, healers, martial artists and t'ai chi masters, for instance (of course, these areas are not mutually exclusive). It can also refer to blokes pulling trucks along by their penises, fire-eaters and what we might term, if we encountered them in the Middle East, fakirs, i.e. it can go into circus territory, which is not by any means always a bad and unworthy thing; I mean, to pull a truck along by your penis is no small matter. Anyway, we pulled up at the hospital and were ushered into a lecture room. There were a handful of other tourists already in attendance. As soon as we were seated the show began. Three doctors and three nurses appeared. The doctors were middle aged and appeared to be consultants. They had that grave air of authority that senior doctors used to have. The nurses also looked gravely serious and purposeful. I was totally intrigued. 'What the fuck are they going to do?' I whispered to Zi-Lan.

The answer soon came. One of the doctors suddenly made a face like a goldfish at the assembled collection of tourists. He stood there like Benny from *Crossroads* with his mouth open. One of the nurses then popped a light bulb in the geezer's mouth. He looked sort of 'mock astounded'. She then plugged some bare wires into an electric socket. They all held hands in a circle. The nurse clutched the bare wires; *voila*, suddenly the bulb in the senior consultant's mouth lit up. I could not believe what I was seeing, I was truly gobsmacked. Imagine popping into the Royal London or St Mary's in Manchester and seeing the head of gastroenterology with an illuminated 40-watt bulb in his north and south.

With grave faces they continued doing various tricks, many of them electrical in their nature, for half an hour or so. At the end I expected them to pass a hat around, but no, they came out and started giving everyone a 'medical examination', insofar as they would study your irises and feel your pulse. They would then tell you that you urgently needed some Chinese herbal remedies that they could flog to you then and there for thirty dollars a box. They told Zi-Lan that she would, when the time came, probably have trouble conceiving without the right herbal remedy. She really annoyed them by saying, in Chinese, 'That's great news because I don't want kids!' It would be the last thing that they would expect a Chinese girl to say (of course, she didn't really mean it; she was just mugging them off). I didn't understand what the exchange was about at first, I just saw her laugh and say something to them, and then their demeanour changed. They really got the hump because it wasn't only us not stumping up funds; the other tourists, a selection of Yanks and Aussies, were also unforthcoming in regard to spending dough. The vibe was a bit uncomfortable and it was time to go. I felt sorry for them. Something about them made me think they were proper doctors. They were obviously desperate for funds. As we turned to leave a thought popped into my mind and

I turned around and said to them, 'Never mind all the nonsense, can you fix a bad back?' They looked at me suspiciously as Zi-Lan interpreted my question for them.

They realised that I was serious; suddenly the vibe changed. They were galvanised into action. Within seconds they got me to whip my top off, and the main doctor began to examine me. The problem was this: about six months previously, while touring in the States, I had got some shooting pains up the back of my leg. I had been training pretty hard and I assumed that it was no more than a pulled hamstring. It got worse and worse, it was very uncomfortable getting in and out of cars and things like that. The pain was of the searing, burning variety. I thought it would simply get better; I was wrong. When I got back to London things got drastically worse. The pain started to travel up my back. Yet again, like a fool I did nothing. I went to bed hoping that I would wake up and feel that it was getting better.

Eventually I was referred to a physiotherapist; however, the back was never more than eighty per cent right, so consequently in Guilin I found myself sitting back to front on a hardback chair while the head honcho examined me. He located what he felt was the exact area that needed treatment. He then proceeded to repeatedly strike the area with focused blows, utilising the backs of his fingers. This 'whiplash' technique is similar to that found in some schools of martial arts. Within a few minutes he had drawn a long protuberance out of the affected area (it was the shape and size of Alex's grotesque fake nose in *A Clockwork Orange*). Zi-Lan was chatting away with the nurses and the doctor all the time this was going on. Zi-Lan explained to me that they were 'drawing the wind out' of the affected area. It was a phrase that I had heard Zi-Lan and her family use before in regard to the treatment of sprains and other injuries.

Once the doctor was satisfied that he had 'drawn out' all the wind that he could, he attached an acupuncture needle to the protuberance. He then attached that by wire to an electrical socket in the wall. I felt the electricity flowing into the affected area (don't try this at home, kids!). God knows why I didn't feel any pain.

After about twenty minutes of that he detached the wires and put a chunk of lighted incense on the needle. He then attached a suction cup over the lump. After half an hour or so, he removed the cup. The lump had disappeared. He told me to stand up and touch my toes. I had full mobility. I couldn't believe it. He said not to be surprised if the problem came back a bit. He said that it was a shame that we weren't going to be in town for longer because if he had another few sessions with me he felt confident that he could completely sort the problem out. Well, fourteen years later, and, touch wood, I have not had the problem again.

I was very grateful and asked how much the bill was. 'No,' he said, in Chinese, 'I can't accept any money.' I started to get annoyed with him, because there was no way I was leaving there without paying. I couldn't believe this. An hour or so earlier they were rushing us for money. Now, when they had performed what seemed to me to be a minor miracle, they refused to take money from me. I asked to buy some herbs as a way of giving them money, but they laughed and said that the herb shop was shut. Eventually, after a lot of haggling, I was allowed to meet the hospital administrator and make a donation to the 'hospital trust fund'. I am eternally grateful to those doctors and nurses.

# Chapter Twelve: New Departures

## MISSION ACCOMPLISHED

By the autumn of 1994 Island Records were looking to me to begin recording a follow-up to *Take Me To God*. I was more than happy to start making another album, but I didn't fancy doing a follow-up to the last one. *Take Me To God* had a very broad scope, it covered a wide musical territory. The combination of it and its predecessor *Bedlam* had left me feeling very satisfied, insofar as I felt that I had finally captured the sound and style of what you could term the original Invaders of the Heart concept (I suppose that sound would now be referred to by most as 'world fusion'). I was exceedingly happy to have finally nailed the thing. It had been many years coming; the original line-up had been formed in 1982. Don't get me wrong, I know full well that the creative process isn't set in stone; it certainly doesn't stand still because the essence of the music is as fresh and ongoing as a mountain stream, but in a way albums can be said to document and represent certain times, places and ideas. And I certainly felt that the basic idea had been captured and documented (across a pretty wide canvas, no less).

I fancied changing tack and doing a highly stylised album that had only a few tracks. I wanted every track to be very different to all the other tracks on the album. I intended to focus on no more than half a dozen musical themes. In some respects I wanted it to be the antithesis of *Take Me To God*. I also wanted to raise the bar in regard to production. I felt that the sound of the new album should be a bit heavier and dynamic than both *Bedlam* and *God*, especially in regard to the drums and the bass. I wanted it to, metaphorically speaking, purr like a Rolls-Royce engine. I wanted it deep, heavy, assured and expensive sounding. On *Bedlam* and *Take Me To God*, I had been happy to play the numbers game with the record company, i.e. try to cross the records over and all that. I didn't mind doing all that for a short period; in fact to not do that in regard to running an expensive group like the Invaders would have been foolish.

However, I now fancied a change. I wanted to take a trip to New York to work with Bill Laswell again. Angus MacKinnon had been advising me, for years, to go and play with the players in New York. He was of the opinion that I would be on the same wavelength as them, plus I was just as focused as them. He would get slightly frustrated with me when I hummed and hawed about that. To be honest I was increasingly finding the limitations of some of my regular musicians a bit of a drag. I had used them less than I had expected to when recording *Take Me To God*. The great strength of that line-up had been its enthusiastic amateurism. Unfortunately it had by then become its weakness. I seldom felt a sense of assurance in their playing, especially in the studio; I never, save for Neville, felt that they ever really 'nailed' their parts with total verve and confidence. I would often end up spending an inordinate amount of time tidying up their parts. They were beginning to get a bit out of their depth.

## EIGHT YEARS WITH AN OLD ETONIAN

Justin Adams was the one who seemed to struggle the most at that particular time. Right from the word go he didn't seem at home, during the process of recording *Take Me To God*. His best spell with me had been around the time of recording *Bedlam*. At that time it seemed to me that he was beginning to approach finding his own 'voice', which is a pretty tall order on the electric guitar, owing to the legacy that has been handed down by the likes of Hendrix, Bo Diddley, Muddy Waters et al. (I think that only the tenor saxophone presents more of a challenge in that respect.) To be fair, he did have a bit of grief going on in his personal life at that time, and that certainly didn't help his state of mind. Then again in my view he had never really put in the hours of practice. Not to the extent that you need to. Up to then he had got by with the most basic of techniques, coupled with a passing knowledge of North African music. That had been OK for the first few years of his time with me, but it was now no longer enough, and he was beginning to come across as a dilettante.

*The strange thing is that as his playing went down the pan he showed an increasing penchant for idiotic onstage dances. I had to nip that in the bud pronto. At a show in Belgium I told him to 'stand still and be cool'. He was obviously upset, but what could I do? I cannot abide the upper classes hopping about like care-in-the-community cases at the best of times, let alone during a band performance. It's just not professional.*

I did try and talk to him about his playing on more than one occasion, but he retreated into a rather haughty 'above it all' upper-class shell (cum escape pod). I wasn't terribly surprised as I had always thought that it was entirely possible that he would revert to what I now call the 'pre-David Cameron' type of toff – indeed, he vaguely reminded me of Lord Lucan, minus the tash, at that time. (I hasten to add, the 'Lucan' comparison is purely referring to the physical similarity of the two old Etonians.) Indeed Dickie and I began referring to him as 'Lucan'. I think that as his tenure in the band drew to a close, his world had really been rocked and he was 'all at sea'. What was happening to him went against all his 'Eton conditioning'; he had no control in the situation. Underneath it all he was a scared little boy. Over the years I increasingly came to realise that a lot of those ex-public-schoolboy boarders had quite a bit in common with some of the blokes that I knew who were career criminals and had been in and out of institutions, such as children's homes, borstals and prisons, since they were very young. Both social groups had been psychologically hardened to the detriment of their emotional development. I suppose that it is one of the main points of sending young men to public school: to toughen them up and turn them into winners, no matter what the cost; captains of industry and all that.

*Thanks to my involvement with the music business, I came to realise that for the boys and girls of the elite ruling class the world truly is their oyster. They know all the strategies. They are adept at finding a cushy number, whether it's in the Foreign Office or the music business. They are very well educated, and very well connected. I have now known quite a few, both before and since Justin. They are expert in hiding their motivations and intentions. They seem to love being Machiavellian.*

*When the circumstances are right the former elite public school brigade are entirely capable of being one hundred per cent ruthless. They really know how to play the game. Having said all that I find most of them curiously 'unformed' as people; I nearly always sense that 'something' is missing. And yet these are the people that lead us. For the foreseeable future we will be governed, regulated and represented by the likes of Justin. Old Etonians, in particular, seem to abound at the moment; at the time of writing Boris Johnson has become mayor of London, while David Cameron works his way, in confident and oily fashion, towards Number Ten Downing Street.*

Anyhow, all that stands in stark contrast to his first few years with me. It's not fair to 'coat Justin off' the way I've done without mentioning the good aspects of the bloke's character. It was fascinating to watch Justin deal with people. He could be very smooth (but in a way that wasn't cloying or sickly). In fact, I don't think that I have ever known anyone with better social skills than Justin. (At his best he reminded me of Tom Conti's character in the movie *Merry Christmas Mr Lawrence*.) Out of everybody in that line-up of the Invaders, he was the quickest to understand what I wanted us all to achieve in any given situation. Sometimes, my methods can appear to be a bit off the wall, and even a bit extreme on occasion. However, he was never far behind in understanding, at least on an intellectual level, what it was all about. He understood what the 'artistic point' was. Moreover, in those first few years he was, for much of the time, buzzing with the whole Invaders thing. The good vibe brought out the best in him. When I look at the group photos from that time his happy demeanour belies the rather absurd caricature I felt he became over that last year or so of his time with me.

NEW YORK

While in New York I wanted to do a couple of tracks that were quite jazzy and that had a distinctly 'New York' flavour. I felt that we needed a virtuoso trumpet or soprano sax player. I had a chat with Bill and he suggested that we procure the services of Pharoah Sanders, somebody he had worked with in the past. I was thrilled to bits at the thought of playing with Pharoah. I had a few of his albums. I had first checked out Pharoah when I found out that he had Lonnie Liston-Smith in his band for a while. As a teenager I was a fan of Liston-Smith's. Cecil Macbee, who was Liston-Smith's bassist, was also a big influence on me. In fact the B-line to Liston-Smiths 'Hypertension' is probably my favourite B-line of all time. It drives me insane. The soul and jazz funk scenes turned me on to quite few jazz artists, people such as Roy Ayers, Johnny Handy and Johnny 'Guitar' Watson.

I went over to New York and cut two tracks with Pharoah. One of them was a groovy jazzy track called 'Hit Me'. The other track was a mighty piece of work called 'Gone To Croatan'. Bill encouraged me to play a modulating line à la 'Poptones'. The line I came up with is a funny old B-line. On a first hearing it sounds for all the world like it is in a regular four but it's actually an eighteen-beat cycle consisting of six beats per phrase. The drums for the 'Gone To Croatan' session were looped; mind you, it was a bloody long loop, eight bars or something. That loop was played by Jerome 'Big Foot' Brailey of Funkadelic fame.

That really was a fun session; I got on very well with everyone. They were all such strong players. Along with Pharoah there was Nicky Skopelitis on guitar, Ayib Dieng on percussion and Bernie Worrell on keyboards. The latter three I already knew from my previous visits to Greenpoint. At Bill's suggestion we brought in DJ Rob Swift and DXT to man the decks. That was a masterstroke; it really gave the session a hip edge. On 'Gone To Croatan' Nicky did a beautiful sad-sounding guitar arpeggio; it was simple, but had a great presence. Ayib's percussion parts fitted like the proverbial glove; in fact they set the atmosphere of the track. Bernie, who is quite a character, played with a subtle sophistication. He helped to marry, in regard to tonality, all the various parts of the track. Bernie is far more than just a funk player.

## BILL LASWELL

*Bill Laswell is a disciplined and organised producer, so therefore when you work with him all the energy is maximised and focused. We would work a six-hour day and then cut out and head back into Manhattan, and nosh fine Thai cuisine and the like, while engaging in good banter. In those days Bill's studio was at Greenpoint in Brooklyn; indeed, his studio was named after that part of Brooklyn. I recall that Omar from the Last Poets lived in a room above the studio. There were a lot of Poles in that neighbourhood,*

Me and Bill
Laswell share
a joke shortly
before going
onstage at the
Roskilde Festival

consequently the food was great. Well, I thought so anyway. I really like sauerkraut and Polish sausage. I used to stuff my face. Over the years, whenever I was due to work at Greenpoint, I looked forward to the food as much as I did to the music. Bill is a serious geezer in regard to making music. However, he's not in the least self-important or sanctimonious and has a great sense of humour. Bill's knowledge of all the pertinent forms of music and musicians is encyclopedic. Music truly is his passion.

I've done quite a few bits and bobs with Bill over the years. Our 2002 Palm Pictures release 'Radio Axiom A Dub Transmission' is one of the best records that I have ever played on. It features Gigi (Bill's missus), Nils Petter Molvar, Graham Haynes (later he would be in Solaris with Bill and me), Karsh Kale, Amina Claudia Myers and Nicky Skopelitis. Actually, playing on Nicky's 1994 release 'Exstasis' was another terrific experience. To play along with Ziggy Modeliste and Sly was a total buzz. It's a shame when those sessions are over, because you want to keep on playing. You don't want the buzz to stop.

Bill Laswell is also well informed in regard to all the arts, and in particular painting. In fact he's a dab hand with a paintbrush himself. He is an aficionado of Jackson Pollock and his work. He told me once that he broke into what had been Pollock's studio and

287

*stayed the night there. There were still thick layers of paint on the studio floor. Bill cut away slivers of that paint to take away with him. That tells you everything that you need to know about the man. He is a truly remarkable bloke; I'm very fond of him.*

On 'Gone To Croatan' Pharoah played soprano sax and flute. What he did was gut-wrenchingly moving. On 'Hit Me' he played tenor. His playing on that track was silky and joyous. It wasn't long before both the tracks were recorded and mixed. I took a cassette of them, popped them on my Walkman and walked around Manhattan for hours as darkness fell. Man, I was buzzing, floating on the glorious melancholic vibe of 'Croatan' and the 'up' jazzy joyousness of 'Hit Me'. I was exactly where I was supposed to be in life.

Back in London I got Zi-Lan to play ku-cheng on the title track of *Heaven And Earth*. She played a part that has great poise and delicacy. It flits over the bass line like a dragonfly over a lake. I also got her dad to play on that track. He is a multi-instrumentalist, so as well as playing bamboo flute, which he would see as his main instrument, he played some er-hu, which is a bowed instrument. It is similar in range to a cello. He was considered, while still living in China, as one of the very best bamboo flute players in the country. 'Heaven And Earth' has some tricky bridge parts that speed up quite severely. I was impressed that he nailed them without any fuss. After leaving China he spent some time as a studio session musician in Hong Kong, playing in the ensembles that provided the music for the (mainly kung fu) movie industry there in the seventies. Obviously in that sort of session environment you need to work quickly and without any bother.

Apart from the two tracks with Pharoah and the track with Zi-Lan and her dad, I did a couple of instrumentals, 'Divine Mother' and 'Dying Over Europe'. The former is a bit like a meeting on the celestial plane between Augustus Pablo and Arvo Part. I played the drum kit on that track, which was a first for me. The second one is inspired by the British saxophonst John Surman, a musician that I have never met, but his record 'Road To St Ives' was a favourite of mine for a good while. The other two tracks featured female singers, Natasha Atlas and Najma Akthar, on 'Love Story' and 'Om Namah Shiva' respectively. The latter of those last two tracks is a readaptation of a well-known Hindu mantra. The *Heaven And Earth* album is a personal favourite of mine.

## ALL CHANGE ON THE LIVE SIDE OF THINGS

Around that time, as well as getting tired of sloppy performances in the studio I started to get a bit weary of the Invaders' live shows. It was definitely time to look at changing things. It was just starting to feel a bit tired and stale. There were still exceptional performances, such as our 'Womadelaide' show in Australia that year, when new vigour and life were, temporarily at least, blown back into the music. But overall I felt that we were just starting to drift towards becoming a (world music) caricature of ourselves. I think that is bound to happen if you stop growing (i.e. getting better) as a band collectively and as musicians individually. We were still miles ahead of other bands in that field. However, I felt that we were beginning to stand still and I wanted to nip it in the bud before it started to roll backwards.

There were other factors at play; we had become a little bit too dependent on loops. It all becomes a bit of an easy option. A number of outfits had followed our lead. However, unlike us, most of them did not have any degree of subtlety to their playing. Their default setting was thunderous ethnic percussion loops, married to house beats, with ethnic vocals and instrumental loops floated over the top. That was the all-pervasive sound at roots/world music festivals by the late nineties. It was the sonic equivalent of IKEA furniture. An easy option, and therefore it quickly became ubiquitous. Some of those acts are still going strong. It will be interesting to see if they outlast the Swedish furniture manufacturer.

I wanted to inject the 'real playing' element back into our set. However, to be honest, with that line-up of the Invaders there was on occasion a noticeable tendency towards timing discrepancies even with the loops in, let alone with them out. Occasionally, I cringed at the clumsiness of it. Audiences probably wouldn't have noticed those discrepancies because the heavy bass was high up in the mix, and heavy low-end bass can cover a multitude of sins in regard to timing discrepancies in a band. Neville is always 'bang on' in his timing so I always instructed the sound men to make sure that he was also pushed up in the mix. (I tend to like percussion mixed high up in the mix anyway; listening to a lot of Weather Report over the years had turned me on to that.)

Apart from the aesthetic stuff, there were other problems. There were a few petty jealousies and rivalries cropping up between some members of the entourage. I could sense people vying for position, plotting and scheming, pretending to be one thing while really being another. Yet again it was the typical stuff that you get in bands that have been together touring for a few years. All in all it was pretty obvious that it was the perfect time to change things. I realised that another cycle was undoubtedly over. A few people were surprised at my decision. They thought that I had discovered a winning formula. I think they saw me as being in some way 'home and dry'. But of course you never are home and dry in life. Moreover, that formulaic aspect never really interested me, because I want the music to always be allowed to reinvent itself. That way it keeps you on your toes; plus it's more fun that way. It's like a continuous adventure.

*Some of the entourage had got desperately concerned about networking, and tactically positioning themselves, rather than about their actual playing or doing their job with one hundred per cent focus. Of course, furiously networking to position oneself in an endless world of possibilities is even more the* zeitgeist *now than it was then. It's all a bit silly really, but admittedly it did have its funny side. I recall one tragically comic little scene in Spain, at Granada, at the final show that I did with that line-up. We were playing a Womad concert near the Alhambra. The Moroccan Master Musicians of Jajouka were playing the day after we played. I stayed on to see them. Along with Dickie, I worked my way to the front of the audience, very excited about finally seeing them perform. (I wasn't disappointed; they were first class.) As the show started, I saw Justin Adams, John Reynolds and David Jaymes (the manager) at the side of the stage, schmoozing with the then boss of Womad, Thomas Brueman. They were 'grooving', awkwardly, to the music, and trying their best to look cool, while grinning inanely at each other. I thought that it looked really bad. It was embarrassing; a grotesque sideshow. I hate it when 'VIPs' stand side of stage doing that sort of thing. I think it shows no class. In fact I find it quite vulgar. However, Dickie Daws and I did take a wicked delight in it. If they had scrutinised the front row of the crowd they would have seen both of us looking up at them grinning away like Cheshire cats.*

*I bet that the three of them would accuse me of being more than a tad sanctimonious and of taking cheap shots. (I just couldn't resist mentioning that scene. It was such a vivid picture.) There were other people around that band who were far more negative than those three, and in fairness they had to think about their futures and do what they felt they had to do in order to crack on and earn money. They were terrified at the thought of returning to anonymity. I think that is an understandable fear; after all, just about everybody wants to be somebody in life.*

*And anyway, to censure people for that sort of behaviour, especially in the age that we live in, let alone in the music business, is (to steal the words of Colonel Kurtz) 'like handing out speeding tickets at the Indy 500'. However, I can't help but stick to my guns in regard to that sort of behaviour. For me it's undignified. As Blake said, 'The Fox feeds himself. God provides for the Lion.' In my book it's better to be a lion.*

## WHAT A NICE MAN JAH WOBBLE IS. I WANT TO HUG HIM

I also thought it best that Ali went up the road as well. I had nothing against him. He was a nice little geezer from a tough part of the world doing what he needed to do in order to survive in a foreign culture. I genuinely thought it would be good for him to go and do his own thing and stand on his own two feet. I arranged a meet and gave them notice that for them the band was over. It was all very amicable and we had hugs all around. I wanted to do the right thing. After all, they had been on the firm with me for a while. So to make the transition as smooth as possible and to avoid leaving them in the lurch, I proposed that we make a solo album for Ali, which they gladly agreed to. We subsequently sold the album to Real World. Ali was delighted because it kick-started a solo career for him. They all got a wedge of dough (Ali especially) and time to prepare for their 'Jah Wobbleless' future. I also gave Justin and Ali a couple of sessions each on other recordings that I was making at that time. To give myself a pat on the back, I thought that I handled the whole tricky affair very well. I just wish that the people that I have encountered in the music business had been as good to me. I had kept my side of the street clean; that's all you can do in life.

My ultimate aim was to move into a future unfettered by the various demands of a large full-time band and crew. I continued doing shows with the Invaders for another couple of years. I drafted in a number of guest players and singers after that, familiar faces like Harry Beckett, Jaki Liebezeit, B. J. Cole and Sussan Deiheim returned to the fold, as well as players like Clive Bell, Baluji Shrivastav, Jean-Pierre Rasle and Joji Hirota. I even worked with the Liverpool Philharmonic Orchestra around that time, when I wrote a concerto for Zi-Lan to play on the ku-cheng. By 1999 I had started up a new touring band called Deep Space. As well as Clive Bell and Jean-Pierre Rasle, it featured Mark Sanders on drums. As the name suggests, the music consisted of really quite 'out there' trance music. There wasn't a sampler in sight.

*So much for dispensing with large bands; a decade on and I have just finished my 'Chinese dub' tour. I had twenty performers on the road with me. That's the biggest ever. Predictably, I'm currently swearing that 'I will never again do a tour with a big band. It's all too much work etc.'. As well as Neville, Clive Bell and Mark Sanders are still on the firm with me. Both of them are excellent players. They never give less than a hundred per cent. I would still employ Dickie the roadie today if he was available. Unfortunately in 1997 he had a serious motorcycle accident. One of his legs got badly mangled. Since then he hasn't worked. He left East London and went back to live in Cornwall. We still have a chat from time to time and whenever I play the West Country Dickie turns up.*

In regard to David Jaymes the initial plan was for him to continue doing stuff for me in terms of management. But to be honest I felt that things were not progressing or developing at any level. He had never surprised me by coming up with clever ideas in regard to marketing, getting productions or making collaborations, etc. He certainly never showed a predilection for lateral thinking. He seemed to avoid confrontations with promoters and record companies, even when the occasion demanded it. So I would tend to have to go and get the tough situations sorted. I wasn't particularly surprised about the situation. To be honest I had never entirely lost my initial reservations about working with Dave. At the beginning of our friendship we had a 'cards on the table' sort of relationship, typical of pals in 'reformed drinker' circles. But I was now beginning to get a very creepy vibe off Dave. He started to remind me of Hal, the (insincere) computer in Kubrick's 2001. Kubrick used the blank lens of Hal's 'eye' to chilling effect in that film. Dave would come around, quite late at night sometimes. He would sit there scrutinising me through his big bins, buttering me up or pretending to be having all sorts of little spiritual crises that he would then seek my advice on. However, I strongly suspected that it was all just a silly sham, a sort of smokescreen. On top of that it seemed to me that he would subtly spread disharmony wherever and whenever he could. However, unfortunately for Dave there's 'no kidding a kidder', so I brought our relationship to a close. To tell the truth, by that stage it all seemed a bit silly, bordering on the absurd. It was well past its sell-by date.

Nevertheless, it had to be admitted that he had put a lot of energy into my thing over the years previous to that time. There was absolutely no way that I could deny that. To be fair, I don't think that his intentions and motives were by any means exclusively machiavellian and self-serving through those early years. I think that a large part of him enjoyed the day-to-day involvement in things, as well as seeing me crack on as an artist. When the end came I made sure that financially he wasn't hard done by, and he got a final and fair slice of the cake. Also, thanks to his involvement with me he had the credibility that he had yearned for. So he wasn't in a bad position. We had been pals for nearly ten years and that has to mean something, even if the last couple of years had been increasingly difficult. I've bumped into Dave a few times over the years subsequent to that time and we always have a friendly chat. He's back drinking again; however, although he looks a bit rough around the edges, he seems to be keeping it all together, even though he still moans and protests about his lot in life. In my estimation blokes like Dave could do with an interest outside the music industry. No matter how much success they have, they will never be happy. They are unquiet spirits marooned in the transit lounge of the music business.

## THE WANDERER

I was, effectively, being repelled by the bullshit world that surrounds the music business, by a spiritual force that felt almost physically tangible; it was as if that force was part of the electromagnetic waveband. I certainly didn't feel that I would be missing anything, because generally speaking that scene is a dead zone in regard to human development. Many of the people around it are perennial teenagers. They are deeply uninteresting. Like many teenagers they are dreary conformists. They wear the same absurd mutton-dressed-as-lamb clothes, and use the same trendy expressions non-stop.

It had been in effect my third time around the merry-go-round of the music business (PiL, then my solo thing, and then my renaissance in the early nineties). I was very bored with it all again. I wasn't bothered about playing the 'numbers game' in regard to sales. I wasn't interested in expanding, exploiting or consolidating markets. I certainly wasn't interested in developing Jah Wobble as a brand, something that more than one person advised me to do at that time. I simply wanted to make music and make a living. But in so doing I wanted to cut down my contact with the music industry to a bare minimum.

Everything was getting increasingly corporate. A lot of people around the game were afraid to voice anything like a strong opinion, just in case it got back to the wrong person. They had to appear to be everyone's mate. When people get like that they no longer have anything interesting to say. They live under a constant shadow of fear. It wasn't just the music game either; I noticed the rise in corporatism in all its forms in all areas at that time. I remember talking to a person around then who had worked in a council housing department since they left school. They told me that they were still in the same job, but that they now worked for a division of General Motors, who had taken over the franchise of running the huge computer systems that their department employed. General Motors? London councils? Housing? I thought that he was pulling my leg. Of course, we would now accept that sort of thing as normal.

Before long my record company, Island/Phonogram, would be taken over by Universal, who in turn would be merged into a French utilities company. I knew things were beginning to get really crazy, and that they would only get worse. Never mind pop eating itself; late-stage capitalism was beginning to gorge on itself. If that wasn't bad enough, Blair and 'New Labour' were banging on about the 'New Pragmatism', which I thought was simply relativism in a different guise. All the dot-com baloney was kicking off then as well, of course. Increasingly people started to talk in a way that made little sense. I yearned for space and the silence that comes with it.

There was now a terrific sense of forward momentum as well as meaning in my life both musically and spiritually (in fact there was now no difference between those two aspects). The world might have been getting crazier but I was getting better. In fact 'recovery' was no longer anything to do with booze or drugs. Of course, I still abstained from their use, indeed I still do, but in reality I was grateful for every drink and drug that I had ever taken, because it was thanks to them that I now had this beautiful life that was both dynamic and stable, which in turn led to great productivity. By default drink and drugs had been my portals of entry on to the spiritual path. Funnily enough drink and drugs themselves never really delivered, but ironically their negative effects (ultimately) did.

Don't get me wrong; I had no interest in aiming for a bland 'let's pretend everything is nice' sort of a life where there were no emotional peaks or troughs. That would have been what I term 'Mogadon spirituality', i.e. you may as well be on tranquillisers. I simply felt fully alive and sensitised. I certainly wasn't approaching sainthood. I had simply begun to grasp what it is to be human. Of course, a lot of people can come to terms with themselves and their humanity without having to go through all the silly dramas that I did.

# Chapter Thirteen: Renaissance Man

I could now tell the wood from the trees in life. I felt free to do just about whatever I wanted. One ambition I had was to get a BA in Humanities. I thought that it would be an interesting and inspiring thing to do, as well as serving to broaden my horizons and join a few more dots up. I had originally applied to go to Birkbeck College as a part-time mature student back in 1989. Initially, I was attracted by their extensive campaign of tube train poster advertising. However, at that time I had been turned down, without even getting an interview, probably because my academic CV wasn't too convincing (three O levels). It was probably just as well that I was rejected at that time, because I would not have been fully committed; certainly not over the length of four years (the duration of the course). However, things were different now as I was the master of how I organised my time. Nevertheless, I still had the problem of not possessing a convincing academic record, so I enrolled on a pre-access course at the City and East London College in Pitfield Street. The pre-access course went very well, better than I thought it might, so I decided to chance my arm and apply for Birkbeck a year earlier than expected.

I'll never forget my first evening of attendance at Birkbeck (as most of the courses are part time most lectures are held in the evenings). It was a beautiful autumn evening, as I walked through the Mallet Street entrance of the college and over the huge mat with 'London University' emblazoned across it. It was like my experience of driving a tube train for the first time, totally fresh and new. It was a total buzz: me at university! In 2000 I passed my finals with flying colours and got a BA in Humanities.

## WILLIAM BLAKE

I was grateful to Nick Angel and Mark Marot at Island Records for having allowed me to indulge myself, by going to New York to make tracks for *Heaven And Earth*. Having said that, they didn't lose on the deal; it paid its way in regard to sales. In those pre-twenty-first-century days, if you made a good classy record with good players, at a reasonable budget, and kept it 'on catalogue' (and well distributed internationally) it would go on selling a steady amount month in and month out. Over the long haul the record label would nearly always make a profit. Of course, they didn't like to admit to that, but it was true nevertheless. Indeed, there was a saying in the music business similar to the estate agent's maxim of 'location, location, location'; it was 'catalogue, catalogue, catalogue'. Indeed, it had been the constant availability of a quality back catalogue that had traditionally been one of the main strengths of Island Records over the years.

However, Marc and Nick made it clear to me that although they had played ball with me in regard to *Heaven And Earth*, they now wanted a follow-up to *Take Me To God*, i.e. they wanted a hit album. They were very keen to place me with what we would now term an urban producer. But unfortunately I was simply in no mood to do that. I had started (belatedly) getting into the works of William Blake.

By that time, over a span of nearly twenty years, a good half

A publicity shot taken around the time of my William Blake album. I saw this image as representing Blake's Urizen character

a dozen people who knew me pretty well had recommended that I read his poetry. I only knew two of his poems: 'The Tiger' and 'Jerusalem'. I identified the latter with toffs and the Proms, and the former with Victorian tiger hunts. So when people told me that I should check him out I simply patronised them and said 'yeah, yeah, yeah; I'll check it out', knowing full well that I had no intention to. I could remember Marg years before that period, telling me about him (Blake) sitting around naked in his garden. That just made it worse; I ended up lumping him in with Wordsworth et al., and decided that he must be some sort of hippy. To be honest, over the years I used to think, Why the fuck does everyone think that I'll like this bloke?

It was a geezer called Jimmy Whiter who finally changed my mind. Jim was the first person that I knew to do a degree as a mature student. Among many other things Jimmy had studied the works of Blake. He forced a Penguin paperback containing Blake's *Songs of Innocence* and *Songs of Experience* on to me. He said, 'Look, Johnny boy, I know you won't fucking look at this now, but when the time is right you'll open it.' Well, it took about six months, but eventually open it I did.

As soon as I opened the book I was mesmerised. I immediately recognised that he was 'a knower'. Of course, my awakening to Blake's genius came at just the right time. I had been instinctively drawn to making some deep and psychedelic music over the weeks leading up my 'Blake revelation'. However, I wasn't sure what to do with it; I knew that it wouldn't be suitable for 'songs'; I also knew that it would not make great instrumental music. I speculated about marrying it to the spoken word. However, I couldn't think of anything that would fit. Blake's words fitted the music like a glove. Apart from the *Innocence* and *Experience* collections I utilised 'Auguries of Innocence'. I did the voice-over. I made 'The Tiger' into a mellow reggae number, complete with synthetic horns. It really suited it.

## EMPTYING OUT

Everything in my life was sort of 'emptying out' and becoming simpler. I realise now that I was in the first stages of developing something approaching a meditative mind. I would walk for hours up the canals, sometimes all the way up the Lea Valley. I felt a great sense of freedom coupled with a strong sense of purpose, and yet at times I was melancholic. There was one area of my life that was still problematic and 'stuck'. Since Zi-Lan had come into my life things had got a bit awkward with my daughters. For some time I felt that I was being eased out of their lives. I was seeing them less and less. When I did see them they wouldn't want to be with me and Zi-Lan at Corfield Street, so I would take them up West to see a show, or go to the pictures. Sometimes I would take them to the studio with me, before going out somewhere, which they loved. Hayley would love getting on the drum kit, while Natalie would love the games room. We would have a great time, and yet when I went to pick them up the next time they would have long faces and wouldn't look me in the eye. I was fading out of their lives. I was gutted but felt powerless to change the situation. I started to see even less of them. That was not my choice. Eventually I was completely blown out by them. My calls, faxes and letters weren't acknowledged; so that was that: game over. It wasn't really a surprise, I had felt it coming for a couple of years. I knew that there was nothing I could do about it.

I won't go on about it too much because the last thing in the world I want is to cause them to feel embarrassment. I must admit that I did feel 'put out of a job'. There was so much more that I would have liked to show and teach them. I don't have any hard feelings about it, simply because I don't have the right to. They were not responsible for the problems that existed between their mum and me. At the time we lost contact Hayley was just coming up to thirteen and Natalie was eight. They are both now in their twenties. Hayley is a successful actress and has been in a number of TV dramas and movies. Natalie is a fashion student. They both work together as DJs as well, when they run their own club nights. I wish them both the very best. I wish so much that I could have been a proper dad to them.

## REQUIEM

Around that time I was cracking away with my sequencers, notepad and keyboard at my kitchen table. I started to write some really sad orchestral compositions. I wondered what it was that I was coming up with. It suddenly hit me that it was a requiem mass. I started to write choral parts in Latin. I got the Latin checked over by a Roman Catholic priest to ensure that it was accurate. (My cousin Kevin O'Donovan is also very conversant with Latin.) I also wrote some of it in English. At the mass's conclusion I utilised the words of Blake's 'Jerusalem'. I brought in proper classical singers as well as a string section when it came to recording it. I think the 'loss' of my daughters strongly influenced that record, plus the general feeling that so much of what had been so intrinsic in my life was now in the past. In a way 'Requiem' signified a rite of passage of sorts.

301

## WHAT'S UP, RON?

It was around that time that I bumped in to Ronnie Britton for the first time in years. He was not long out of prison. He was hanging out with the 'street people' at Bethnal Green tube station. He wasn't in a great way. He spoke in a fractured way that didn't make complete sense. He was telling me that he regularly talked to the Queen and John Major, and was helping them process the new criminal justice bill. I realised that this was more than just crazy drug talk; Ron had some other issues going on. Suddenly he stopped talking nutty. His eyes changed and he said something along the lines of, 'Do you remember when we used to walk for ages at night? Those were my happiest times, John, just me and you.' I had a lump in my throat. After a little while he started talking nutty again, so I cut out. As I walked up the Bethnal Green road I had tears in my eyes. Sadly Ronnie passed away just before Christmas 2008. His liver and kidneys packed up. Ronnie's Dad told me that it was a crying shame because Ronnie was getting it together. He had his own flat again, and would pop around to visit his mum and dad every day. RIP Ron.

## I WANT TO BE INDEPENDENT

So I found myself going into Island Records armed with an album based on the works of William Blake as well as a requiem mass. I felt sorry for Nick Angel and Marc Marot. Their faces dropped. I think that they felt embarrassed. They didn't know what to say. It must be hard in their position to be honest with the artist sitting directly opposite you. They really didn't want to hear about requiem masses and William Blake. I think they were worried that they would hurt my feelings. To be fair to them, they were prepared to do all they could to facilitate me making another album that had commercial potential. But I simply didn't fancy it. My head (and heart) was full of other ideas. I felt like a creative dam had burst inside of me. I knew that album after album was waiting to come out. The thought of going on to do a follow-up to *Take Me To God* was pretty uninspiring.

*It took me nearly ten years to do a follow-up. It came in the form of an album called* Mu, *which was released on Trojan Records in 2005.*

I had, after a fair bit of thought, decided that I wanted to start my own label, primarily as a vehicle for my own music. (It would of course be the second time around for me; I had run Lago Records in the early to mid eighties). I told Nick and Marc of my plans and asked them if they were interested in distributing it. Without a moment's hesitation they said that they weren't. They were in a position where they had to either re-sign me, and give me another advance, or drop me. They chose the latter. To be honest they were very helpful. They gave me the Island Records database of my punters. They knew that I was very keen to get cracking on the label as soon as I could. That was very nice of them and meant that I could get off to a flying start.

Quite a few people in the music business warned me against starting a label. They thought that it was a foolhardy venture. They felt that I would probably suffer distribution problems and that my sales would subsequently fall to a point that would be unsustainable. They also advised me that I would suffer from underfunding. They told me that I was making a big mistake and that I would, effectively, be putting myself 'out of the game'. However, I never had a moment's serious doubt about starting the label. The one positive voice among all the doubting Thomases was that of my good mate Pete Holdsworth, who is the boss of Pressure Sounds, the reggae label.

*Pete gave me some very sound advice at that time, in regard to costing and cash flow, etc. Pete was a co-founder of the On-U Sound label along with Adrian Sherwood. He is one of the very few genuine and honest people that I have encountered in relation*

A boys' night out: Pete Holdsworth, Adrian Sherwood and yours truly at Walthamstow Dog Track

*to the music business. He's as straight as a die. Over the years we have become good mates. We had similar upbringings. Pete grew up on Teesside (which is one of the toughest places that I have ever encountered). When Pete's mum died, rather than stay living with his dad, he went, aged fourteen, to live with his sister in the East End of London.*

I was confident that I could make enough money to keep the whole thing going. Although I knew that I would sell less via the indie route, I also realised that production costs, largely thanks to the new technology, were tumbling. Basically it ended up similar to being signed to a label that automatically renewed your contract every year, and gave you carte blanche to do whatever music you wanted. There wasn't a huge amount of money but there was certainly enough. In regard to selling to the masses, well, I didn't think that was something to aspire to. Who gives a fuck about them? I make music for freaks. Because I too am a freak, so I know what they like. They like that bass way up in the mix, that's what they like. Imagine how a painter would feel if he was able to sell 7,000 prints of his latest painting within a couple of months, with a minimum of fuss and without the aid of an agent or the involvement of galleries. I knew that in the long term I had it made, both artistically and commercially. It was time to take control of things. As Blake said, if you don't live by your own system you will be enslaved by another man's.

## SPINNER

I had intended to make *William Blake* the first release on my new label. However, ironically enough, I got an offer that I couldn't refuse from All Saints Records for that album. By agreeing to it I got a nice injection of cash, which came in handy in regard to funding the start-up costs of my new label. The All Saints label is run by a bloke called Dominique Norman-Taylor. He is the brother-in-law of Brian Eno. As well as releasing the *William Blake* album, he was about to release an album that I had produced for Brian Eno. That album was called *Spinner*. I had met Eno after a show in London a few months before that. He had come backstage and introduced himself. I went and did a session for him at Abbey Road Studios not long after that.

*Spinner* was a funny old project. Its roots lay in a 'soundtrack' that Eno had made for the film director Derek Jarman some years previously. That soundtrack consisted of scraps and fragments of sound, most of which were only seconds in duration. Eno simply gave me a recording of those scraps of sound and asked me to make an album. There certainly wasn't much of an album budget – I think it was around £8,000 – so I elected to do it in my home studio. Rather than simply make an 'art record', I chose to make something useful out of it. I wanted something that matched the atmosphere of my walks along the River Lea and around the Bow backwaters (where the Olympic village now stands). As I finished the tracks, I would record them on to cassette to play on my Walkman as I strode along. It was my method of testing those tracks, to ensure that they were 'fit for purpose', i.e. it was meant to be a 'walking record'.

When it was complete I sent it over to All Saints. I then went travelling, working on other stuff. Upon my return I received a fax from Eno that was quite long. In the opening paragraph he said something about wanting to be treated like 'a Moorish maiden'. A wave of tiredness swept over me; I had just got back from my travels, I was knackered and in no mood to deal with camp bullshit, consequently I got no farther than that first paragraph or so before binning it.

The next day I sent a message to All Saints that Brian and I should have a face-to-face meeting to quickly sort any problems out. A couple of days later we met mid-afternoon in a deserted brasserie in West London. I immediately asked him what his problem was. He asked me if I was happy with the record; I replied that indeed I was. He said if that was the case then the record should be released in its present form.

I had been waiting since the onset of the recording process of *Spinner* for there to be a twist (or indeed a sting) in the tail, in regard to the project with Eno. I was ready to deal with any problem quickly and firmly. I could immediately see the game. I had been given a very limited brief (as well as a very limited budget). Brian is seen to have given a raw and young(ish) talent a chance. However, when I deliver the finished record, criticism is implied in a vague and rather fey way, that I have been a tad heavy-handed and macho in the approach to the production. I subsequently have a crisis of confidence and, hey presto, Brian rides to the rescue and saves the day with some sophisticated advice of an aesthetic nature. I don't think that he is a terrible bloke; rather that way of carrying on is his modus operandi. Quite a few record producers carry on like that. It's also a common trait of film directors and interior decorators. They like to get people 'at it' in various ways, and then be seen to sail in and 'save the day'. The thing is, I'm not a Barcelona-based museum curator, or an impressionable lead singer of a rock band. I'm Jah Wobble, a geezer. I come from Stepney in East London; I'm one of the chaps. I'm a totally different kettle of fish and I haven't got time for all that nonsense.

To give Eno his due, he is a bright bloke who is quick at adapting to situations, and he quickly realised that I wasn't going to play that game with him, i.e. pretend to be 'artistic friends' and let him push me 'around the board', or be made to jump through various metaphysical hoops. I certainly wasn't going to indulge him on the fairly paltry advance that I was getting. If they had paid me three times as much maybe I would have been happy to treat him like a bird (Moorish or otherwise, although I would have drawn the line at tongues). Additionally I would have duly pretended that the bitty scraps of sounds that he had initially given me were somehow Schoenbergian in their scope, or even on a par with the works of John Cage. Don't get me wrong about Eno; he is not, in my opinion, without talent. The atmospheric noises that he made with Roxy Music were first class, and his general sense of aesthetics is not without merit. Indeed, I bought *Another Green World* and *Here Come The Warm Jets* back in the seventies. He is the bloke most of the 'also-ran' ambient blokes and would-be record producers would love to be, because he is able to pull all kinds of strokes. He is the ultimate music business 'player'. They all aspire to be him. There are definitely no flies on Brian Eno. He plays for pretty high stakes (in music business terms at least).

The first record on my 30 Hertz label was not the *William Blake* album but *The Celtic Poets*. Similar to the Blake album, it was a mixture of spoken word and music (with a bit of singing). The Blake album had whetted my appetite in regard to poetry. I fancied doing something with an Irish theme. I was told that Ronnie Drew was performing spoken-word shows at that time. As chance would have it he was doing one in London a month or so later. I attended that show and was mightily impressed. One of the poems that he performed that night was 'The Dunes' by Shane MacGowan. I found the poem and Ronnie's rendition of it very moving. Ronnie had given me food for thought that evening. He is a truly charismatic performer, as much an actor as a singer or poet. A little while after that I found myself doing a spoken-word show on the same bill as Ronnie in Dublin. (I was performing the William Blake stuff as well as some of my own poems.) I had a chat with him and we got on very well. Ronnie came over to London and we recorded the session at Intimate Studios in Wapping. Ronnie brought his books of poetry and we sat down to select some pieces. 'The Dunes' was an absolute must as far as I was concerned. We also selected poems by Louis MacNeice and Brendan Kennelly. As well as those Irish poets Ronnie suggested a poem called 'Like Dust in the Wind', by the German poet Friedrich Ruckert. The Brendan Kennelly poem is about Paddy Kavanagh; it's called 'The Man I Knew'. The ideals expressed in that poem are everything that I honour in life. I can even identify with the desire to be buried in 'The wilds of Norfolk', with 'No commemorative stone, no sheltering trees, Far from the hypocrite's tongue and eye, Safe from the praise of my enemies'.

*On that session, among many things, Ronnie talked eloquently of one-armed men expertly hand-rolling cigarettes in Franco's Spain, the music of Brittany, and even the history of the Wapping Irish (it amazed me that he knew of that). It was such an honour to have him come and perform on the record. Ronnie came back a few months later and performed some shows with us. He played a show with us a couple of years ago in Dublin. Sadly Ronnie passed away recently. I'll never forget the man.*

My requiem mass was the second release on the label. Since then we have released twenty-six albums on the label as well as three EPs. It is a pretty diverse selection of music. The only constant in the various recordings is me. There are a number of styles represented on the 30 Hertz catalogue. One of those styles is the Molam style of music from Laos (and northern Thailand). Molam is quite similar to dance hall reggae. I thought that Molam music would suit dub mixing techniques perfectly. I went to work trying to find some Molam artists to work with. I thought that the best thing would be for me and my engineer of the time, Cai Murphy, as well as a couple of my musicians, to fly to Vientiane in Laos to do a bit of recording. However, Clive Bell again proved invaluable to me. He had found out about a group called Molam Lao in Paris. That made sense because Laos had been a French colony. I got Jean-Pierre to call them, because they did not speak English. They are a four-piece vocal group, plus they all play hand percussion. The leader of the group, Khampar, plays a khene (a sort of large bamboo mouth organ).

When Molam Lao arrived on Eurostar they were pretty nervous. Once we got the first track down Khampar and the rest of Molam Lao loosened up considerably. Copious amounts of whisky and beer aided that process for them. They all love a drink, that's for sure. When we added the delays and reverbs and all that to the music they went berserk. They loved it.

The party atmosphere suited the music down to the ground, because Molam music is just that: party music. Lyrically it is very bawdy and near the knuckle (just like a lot of early ska music). We became very friendly with Molam Lao and have performed shows in Europe and Japan with them. They still cannot safely return to Laos. Indeed, Khampar has not been back there since he escaped from captivity at the end of the war (he swam across the Mekong in order to make good his escape). You would never know that they have had such difficult obstacles to overcome. They are full of life and laughter.

1998's *Umbra Sumus* is a pretty deep and weird album. As well as Harry Beckett it featured a Bosnian singer called Amila Sulejmanovic (she also sang on the first Deep Space album). Marc Atkins did the photographs for the album. His photographs matched the mood of the music perfectly. I'd met Marc through Iain Sinclair, the writer. Marc supplied the visuals for some of Iain's books, as well as providing visuals when Iain did spoken-word performances. I was on the same bill as them a couple of times. I remember driving down to Brighton with them to do a spoken-word thing. I read some of my own stuff, as well as Blake and a couple of other bits and pieces.

*I did quite a few spoken-word shows around that time. Michael Horowitz got me to do a couple of the Poetry Olympics events in London. John Cooper Clarke did a couple of those events. Not only is he (still) a great poet, he is also a great stand-up comic. He had me in stitches. Roger McGough (formerly of the Liverpool group Scaffold) is another terrific poet/stand-up comic that I performed with at that time.*

I had contacted Iain in 1995 after reading *Lud Heat*. I had come across it in the Local History section of Bancroft Road library. He lived with his wife and family in a large and well-maintained Georgian house in Hackney. 'How can he afford this?' I wondered, as I walked up to his front door. At that time it hadn't quite happened for Iain, in terms of commercial success, although things were just turning for him. I was quite taken by *Lud Heat*. I was amazed that there was a writer living in East London who was writing about Hawksmoor and walking up the canals. Not only that, the book had been written twenty years earlier. I thought to myself, I'll have to hook up with this bloke. I thought that maybe he could supply some words and narration for a spoken-word album. I probably would have called it something like *Dialogue With The Godhead In The Lea Valley*. I was convinced that he was going to be an occultist and quite possibly a bit of a 'knower'.

When I met Iain I got a surprise. He wasn't even a Londoner but was a determinedly middle-class sort of a bloke from Wales. We got along OK, but I realised within a matter of seconds that he had no direct experience of the mystic. Nevertheless, I told him, slightly half-heartedly, about my plan for him to write some lyrics for an album. I thought to myself, you never know, it might still work. I gave him a copy of *Take Me To God*. Within a matter of weeks he had written some stuff. However, it wasn't that good. I recall that I suggested to him that he fuse the sorts of themes present in *Lud Heat* with the lives of living, breathing Londoners. However, what he came up with was pretty hackneyed and clichéd.

It seemed to me that Iain had no empathy for 'regular' people, especially the working classes that surrounded him. In fact he had what I felt was a rather sneering attitude to regular people. It dawned on me that this bloke had lived in East London for over two decades and probably didn't have any real contact with local people (then again, that's not untypical of gentrified London). He reminds me of some of the Victorian writers who acted as guides, for their genteel readers, through London's Dickensian labyrinth. Indeed, the middle classes love Iain. (And of course they are the ones who buy the books.) That whole 'London' literary thing that has been so big over the last decade or so is a totally middle-class scene. They are so divorced from the thing they discuss. I wonder if there is even one writer from that scene that actually grew up in an inner London environment.

I'm probably sounding like I'm completely critical of Iain, but that's not the case. To give the bloke credit he was doing his marginal crazy books for years before the world came round to him. I particularly like two of his books, one of them, the aforementioned *Lud Heat*, and the other one a work of non-fiction, *Lights Out for the Territory*. To give him his due he does put the pedestrian miles in. I bumped into him a few times on towpaths in the East End.

*Actually, there is a tale to tell regarding* Lights Out. *In that book Iain talks about a jogger, out for an early morning run, seeing a dead body floating just under the surface of the water. I knew that bloke; I had let him stay at my Dellow House flat for a while, when I was staying over the river. My mate Terry Penton knew him and had vouched for him. Apparently the bloke had not long come out of the army. He needed a place to stay in the East End. He was a half-Jamaican bloke. He used the name 'Mike' but I found out later that wasn't his real name. Mike told me that he had been a top sniper (marksman) in the British Army. I remember popping up to see him once at Dellow House. I happened to be passing and wanted to ensure that all was well. I couldn't believe what I* saw. He had thoroughly cleaned the place top to bottom, as well as applying a lick of paint here and there. Not only that but he was in the process of putting in a new kitchen. He was personally making the new parts (work surfaces and the like) for the kitchen as he was a skilled carpenter. I was happy that he had cleaned and applied a lick of paint here and there, but I wasn't happy about the kitchen. It was my flat and he should have asked permission. To be honest I wasn't terribly angry with him; as much as anything I was gobsmacked: it was a bloody council bedsit, the last thing I expected was for my temporary visitor to start making unauthorised home improvements.

I had made it clear to him at the outset that it was a short-term arrangement and that at the first sign of any problems he would have to leave. I specifically warned him about getting involved with one or two people around that estate. In my drinking days I'd had a pretty serious 'run-in' with one of those people. Even in those drinking days I'd had the good sense to give certain sorts of people a wide berth; however, although this bloke didn't even know me, he had taken an absolute liberty with me. I had got very upset with the person in question. I had subsequently dealt with the matter in a very forthright manner indeed, and that bloke never bothered me again.

Unfortunately Mike paid no heed to my warnings. I found out that he had been associating with the very people that I had warned him about on that estate. Not only that, but that he had now fallen out with them severely. Apparently automatic weapons had been waved about and all sorts. I really did not need that grief. At the time I was working on the Underground and trying hard to keep my nose clean. Yet again no good deed had gone unpunished, and I asked Mike to leave my flat forthwith, which he did. Unfortunately the kitchen never did get finished. To be fair he didn't strike me as a terrible lad, but then again I only met the bloke on three or four occasions. He had a sort of misguided vibe around him, a bit like Ronnie B and one or two other blokes that I *have known. Well, anyway, a year or two after that, I heard from my good mate Terry Penton that Mike had been murdered. When I read Sinclair's* Lights Out *I realised from the circumstances that the body in the canal that Sinclair referred to was that of Mike. May God bless his soul.*

# Chapter Fourteen: Farewell to All That

## WHOLE NEW LIFE

In 1997 I married Zi-Lan in Manchester. It was a nice relaxed day. I don't think either one of us was particularly nervous, but we were both happy, that's for sure. The whole day was a good-natured affair. We both simply did what we were comfortable with, a registry office ceremony followed by a sit-down banquet (of superb food) at our favourite Chinese restaurant of the time (the famous Yang-Sing). All the Chinese present commented that Zi-Lan's sometimes taciturn dad was 'all teeth, no eyes', i.e. he was very happy, as was her mum, a very easygoing woman who is a renowned t'ai chi teacher as well as being a first-rate cook.

The following year our son John was born. His Chinese name is Tien Chi. The Chinese simply call him 'Ti-Ti'. John was supposed to be born at the Women's Hospital in Liverpool. We are friends with a midwife who works there. However, John had other ideas and he made his arrival a couple of weeks early. He was delivered at the London Hospital, Whitechapel. My God, he was loud and angry as he entered this world. Upon his arrival he was thrust straight into my arms. He screamed like a screaming machine, looked up at me and went straight off to sleep. He had an ancient and eternal vibe about him.

*Of course, if you said that to the teachers at his school they would laugh. They would probably say that nowadays he has a very naughty vibe about him. John's ten now and is playing drums and percussion in a manner that is most promising. He recently did his first proper session for me, on glockenspiel. It was a fiddly little part but he nailed it.*

At that time we were still living in Bethnal Green. However, I was beginning to get a bit troubled by what I was seeing around where we lived. There were two things that I found particularly disturbing: the increased availability of class A drugs (and all the bullshit that goes with that), and simmering racial tension between the Bangladeshis and other racial groups in the area. When I had first moved into Corfield Street, in 1994, it had been one of the nicest streets in Bethnal Green. That's why I had moved there from Shadwell. I certainly saw no overt signs of drug dealing there at that time, unlike in Shadwell, which was already rife with drugs at that time. Unfortunately, by 1997 we had a crack house directly opposite us in the flats on the other side of Corfield Street. That meant that the poor old addicts would be literally queuing up a few yards away from our front door every morning and afternoon. You would hear them calling up to the dealer's window at all times of the night or day. Some of them looked in a right old state. You would notice other drug deals being done on the street at all times of day and night. I never once saw the Old Bill stop and search anyone on the street, let alone nick them. I also noticed more and more working girls plying their trade around where we lived. In the past they had tended to work only in Spitalfields and Shoreditch. So as well as needles it wasn't unusual to find used contraceptives littering the area.

However, none of that stuff had come out of the blue. Ever since 1992, the year that crack cocaine came to London, I had noticed things deteriorating rapidly in Tower Hamlets. I was still living in Shadwell at that time, and I would find all the various forms of detritus and paraphernalia that drug users tend to leave in their wake, discarded all over the stairwell.

It was obvious that a lot of street dealing was going on. Crack cocaine and heroin were the two most popular drugs. I quickly realised that it was those two drugs that fuelled the sudden upsurge of crime in the locale. What really surprised me was that it was the Bangladeshi youths that tended to be the worst offenders. As far as I know there was very little drug abuse in their community right the way up to the nineties. It was obvious that a lot of street dealing was going on. It was quite apparent that there was an epidemic of (class A) drug abuse occurring.

It was in 1992 that two crack cocaine addicts broke through the ceiling of my flat. The burglars had managed to break into the secured loft space that ran the length of the block. Apparently they had first tried to smash through the roof of my neighbour's flat. However, they had heard my neighbour's wife scream as they attempted to smash their way through. Rather than quickly scarper they simply moved on to my flat and smashed their way through. I had only popped out for about twenty minutes to have a quick swim at the Highway Baths, which was just around the corner. When I came back I quickly realised that something was wrong. When I tried to open the door it had been bolted from the inside. On that particular day I had no female company waiting in the flat for me so I knew something bad was up. My neighbour came out and filled me in on what had happened. It turned out that the burglars had also done another flat farther down the block, where a single mum lived with her young child. Apparently the council took ages to repair her smashed ceiling, which meant that the poor mum was left staring up into the black abyss of the loft, just waiting for evil faces to appear staring back at her. The council never came to repair the damage, even though I made several calls to their emergency number. In the end my mate Phil boarded it up for me.

It was funny really. Whenever I came back from a tour I would expect to see my steel door torn from its steel frame. Here I was going for a quick swim and they come through my ceiling. What can you do? I knew that it was a drug-fuelled crime. That was confirmed when the two crack fiends returned to try the same thing at the block lying adjacent to Dellow House. However, they came unstuck because some of the tenants apprehended them. They gave them quite a pasting apparently. In fact a geezer, a complete stranger to me, who lived over in that block, came over to my flat to ask me if I wanted to go and give them a few licks, before the Old Bill were summoned. I declined; what was the point? They were crack fiends in the throes of addiction. It wouldn't have served any purpose. It turned out that the burglars had just got out of prison, where they had served a sentence for similar offences. They would now be going straight back.

Those burglars hadn't even bothered with my telly or video. They only took a massive ghetto blaster (a very tasty one) and my passport. Losing my passport was a major drag because I had to go away again the following week.

*At the time I was still signed to Oval. To give Charlie Gillett and Gordon Nelki their due, as soon as they heard about what had happened they sent over another ghetto blaster. That was a nice thing to do. I will give them that.*

To be honest, I was so busy then that I didn't have time to get too upset about the burglary. However, I knew that 'something was stirring in the jungle'. Something wasn't right; you could sense it in the pit of your stomach. Something dark was looming. It was that darkness that surrounds substance addiction.

*Obviously I knew, from my own experience, about the nature of cocaine use. However, I had never taken it in the form of crack cocaine. It seemed to me that there was a certain twist of evil with crack cocaine users. It was as if a dark, malevolent force was 'in residence' within some of those users. Some of the levels of violence that I was hearing about were totally gratuitous. At first I would hear about those incidents – kneecapping, the use of hot irons on skin and the like – and I would be shocked. I had only heard about stuff like that being done to sex offenders, grasses or by gangsters looking to 'send out a signal' to would-be competitors. But some people in the 'crack circles' seemed to get off on extreme and excessive levels of violence, simply for its own sake. These smokers of crack cocaine generally seemed far worse in their behaviour than people who snorted cocaine in its granular form.*

## THE THORNY ISSUE OF RACE

In the seventies the incoming Bangladeshis had been the whipping boys (and girls) for white racists. Now the boot was on the other foot. I can still remember the first time that I heard about Bangladeshis attacking whites (yet again this was around 1992). Bobby in the corner shop told me about it. Apparently a gang of Bangladeshis had seriously assaulted two white geezers on the stairs of Shadwell station. They had used baseball bats on them. I said to Bobby, a British Asian (God, I hate all these terms; really to me he was just another English geezer), 'Yeah, but what did the white geezers do to provoke it?' 'Nothing,' he said, 'they were just walking past them, minding their own business.' I was quite surprised; I had never known the Bangladeshis to be senselessly violent in that way before. But then again, as Animal reminded me recently, as far back as the early eighties we had predicted that they (the Bangladeshis) would be the naughty boys of the future, simply because it was obvious that they would be the majority. So really I shouldn't have been that surprised. I'm amazed that their version of 'Ronnie and Reggie' hasn't yet made itself manifest to the wider community. It is only a matter of time, of course.

Within a couple of years it was not unusual for white and black people (especially Somalians) to be brutally targeted by very large gangs of Bangladeshis. It was also, by that time, quite routine for weapons like machetes, knives and baseball bats to be used by the borough's various Bangladeshi gangs in attacks on each other (often in turf wars related to drug-dealing issues), as well as in their racist attacks.

Additionally, at that time, Bangladeshis from the Borough of Camden, whose descendents hailed from Dhaka, would do battle with the gangs from Tower Hamlets, whose descendants largely hailed from Sylhet province. Sometimes white middle-class liberals would play down the racist attacks and claim that these were simply violent out-of-control gangs. On a couple of occasions I pointed out to representatives of the white chattering-class liberals that the old skinhead gangs used to do battle with each other as well as go 'Paki bashing'. 'So was I then mistaken,' I asked them, 'in thinking that the Paki bashing of the seventies and eighties was racist?' Predictably their answers were weak and contradictory. I recall one particularly appalling attack by a gang of Bangladeshis. Two Portuguese boys were in the process of visiting London while on their 'gap year'. Naively they found themselves in the wrong place at the wrong time, when they were accosted by a gang of marauding Bangladeshis, at Shadwell Docklands Light Railway station. They were both thrown into the path of an oncoming (driverless) train. The gang callously prevented them from scrambling to safety on to the station platform. One of the boys died from the injuries that he sustained. It was a truly horrifying attack.

Local people became angry that these violent, sometimes fatal, incidents were not reported widely in the media, particularly at a national level. People felt that if it had been gangs of whites beating up Bangladeshis it would undoubtedly have received widespread coverage across the media. It seemed to many of us, in the area, that large sections of the media chose to see, regardless of the evidence, all Asians as blameless victims and all working-class whites as racist bigots out for trouble. Broadly speaking you could call those people the white liberal chattering classes. They were still wedged tight in a 1970s 'right on' attitude. In their own way they were stuck in the mud, just as much as right-wing retired colonels living in mock Tudor houses in Surrey were. In a way that was fitting because they are of course often of the same bloodline as those colonels.

The PC mob also turned a blind eye to the rabidly racist posters that Muslim fundamentalist groups were putting up around the East End. I think that those posters really helped to fuel the flames of anger in the disaffected Muslim youth. At the time I couldn't believe that the people behind those posters were not brought to account. If a white power group had gone around putting up posters calling for a pogrom against the Jews and unbelievers, there would have been a massive outcry. It was also not unusual to see the slogan 'whites out' scrawled on walls around the area. The council would come and remove that sort of graffiti pretty quickly, far quicker than they would come to mend your leaking pipe (or broken ceiling), that's for sure. However, they (the council) never moved to tackle the real problem: the people putting up the graffiti. The whole problem of race was a hot potato that nobody in authority wanted to pick up. I noticed that by 1997 the white kids were too scared to 'play out' in the local area. Like the elderly they would venture out only when they had to, in a cowed fashion at that. It was sad to see. Whereas in the seventies I had found myself remonstrating with white kids to stop bullying Bangladeshis, now it was the other way around. Sociologists working in the borough at that time placed white boys as the bottom of the heap in regard to the various race and gender groups represented at schools in Tower Hamlets, in regard to academic achievement, self-confidence and expectations for their future. However, their reports were never highly publicised. But then again, who, in late-twentieth-century London, would stand up for poor working-class white boys? Certainly not the metropolitan elite, that's for sure.

*It didn't escape my attention that one hundred years or so after the East End was gripped by a Jewish-influenced secular political radicalism, an Islamic-inspired religious fundamentalism had now* taken root. The East End was still, I had to admit, an extreme and dynamic place. People still liked to throw stones and kick up a fuss. Of course, if I were a Muslim, I bet there's a fair chance that I would have some degree of sympathy with the new religious radicals. But I'm not, and the road they are going down is a very dangerous one for everyone. Of course, they would probably argue that many of the umma are already living in mortal danger every day, so what's to lose by being radical?

It came as no surprise to me when the BNP started to gain in popularity in Tower Hamlets. Hardly anybody in the media or politics gave a flying fuck about what was happening to poor whites (and blacks for that matter) there. Even I flirted with the idea of voting, out of desperation, for them (the BNP) in the election of 1997, so you can get some idea of how bad things had got. I thought that if enough people voted for the BNP in the area it would cause a stink and more might be done to protect us. There is one main and very obvious reason why I couldn't bring myself to vote for them. The BNP wouldn't want black or Asian people in their party. They only want white people. That for me does not fly. (And ultimately they would probably want to send my wife 'home' to China. Well, fuck that; I'd miss her. And more to the point, who would cook me tea?) Joking apart, one day there probably will be a British National Socialist Party with all races and creeds in it. I'm not saying that is a good or a bad thing, it's just the way things are going. I didn't vote for Blair in that election. I went for a truly independent left-wing option (along with about sixty others). It was either that or be a paper spoiler. I hated New Labour from the word go. They were ultimately vacuous, nothing more than a big PR company. They segued perfectly from Thatcherism. 'Things can only get better'; yeah, right. I couldn't believe the number of people I knew who bought into that bullshit at the time.

One or two other people that I knew in the borough, who came from either India or Pakistan, told me that 'these Bangladeshis are backward country people'. However, I thought at the time that that was a rather glib and easy explanation. I knew full well that the same thing had been said about my Irish ancestors. Those people were the first to advise me to get out of the borough way back in 1993. They guaranteed that it would get worse. Unfortunately they were right. It was a shame. My broadly socialist outlook had led me to believe that all races and creeds could, indeed should, get along fine, united we stand and all that. The big issue in this country, as far as I was concerned, was still class. All this race and religious conflict was, in my opinion, a red herring.

The Bangladeshis were the first immigrants into the East End that didn't seem to assimilate at all. One of the reasons for that was the fact that they didn't use local pubs. (In light of my own problems with alcohol, I can't criticise that.) Also the Bangladeshi women were not, generally speaking, as able as their non-Muslim counterparts to mix freely with wider society. I think that was another factor. They were also not able to freely associate with young men. That of course meant that the young men would, generally speaking, be denied the possibility of mixing with young girls from their own background, although from what I hear that is fast changing. I think that helped to nurture and accentuate the sort of 'all boys together' misogynistic gang culture that had become so pervasive in the borough. It also meant that women from other cultures would sometimes be seen in a very disrespectful way as mere sexual objects. They would be seen as girls (who incidentally were sometimes underage) that they would groom for and/or use exclusively for sex, but never consider marrying or having a respectful relationship with. That sort of outlook is part and parcel of cultural imperialism. White men have been doing it all over the world for years. I find it really ugly to observe. It is so psychologically and spiritually damaging for all concerned. One would have hoped that women's groups would have come through and said something at the time. But of course they would have been terrified of being labelled racist, and anyway, who gives a fuck about a poor white girl?

It started to feel increasingly weird living in an area where you didn't have any meaningful contact with what was now (in the Shadwell area) the majority of the population. Often on my forays up Watney Street market I would be the only non-Asian in sight. Apart from the architecture of the buildings you could have thought that you were in Dhaka. Sometimes I would make a point of going into Bangladeshi shops (to buy things like okra and coriander), but that was about the only contact I would have with their community, apart from my regular visits to my favourite curry house up Brick Lane, where I was friendly with the staff (however, to me that doesn't really count, because somehow it's too easy).

By the late nineties everyone I knew in Tower Hamlets was very concerned about the levels of violence that some members of the Bangladeshi community were inflicting on themselves and on those around them. Everybody that I knew had encountered problems. I'd had a couple of run-ins with smaller gangs when out walking by the canal, but it was nothing that I couldn't handle. However, like my pals, I knew it was only a matter of time before I encountered larger and therefore more aggressive gangs. And indeed that came to pass. I ended up defending myself from an all-out assault by a very large Bangladeshi gang, who were armed with knives, bottles, machetes and bricks. I had a proper row with them. I wasn't going to run away from anybody, especially not around where I lived, so I stood up to them. It really was one hell of a melee. I think they were quite surprised that I fought back with such determination. God was certainly with me that night. Incredibly I only needed a few stitches in a head wound.

In the A&E department, before stitching me up, the young doctor asked me the sort of questions that doctors put to anyone who may possibly be suffering from concussion (which I most certainly wasn't). She asked me what day of the week it was, what year it was and finally who was the current prime minister. I answered the first couple of questions sensibly. To the last question

I answered 'Rupert Murdoch'. She looked sharply up at me. I looked back at her in deadpan fashion for a few seconds before bursting out in laughter. I quite like myself sometimes. I had experienced a very scary incident and yet still had the ability to fuck around. (I like to think that one day, shortly after this life is over, I will meet St Peter at the pearly gates. I will then probably make a weak joke to him about being on the guest list or something.)

*The young doctor, who was very cheerful and pleasant, said that she also did A&E up the road in Hackney at Homerton Hospital. She said that the nature of the injuries she dealt with was often markedly different in the two hospitals. Where I was (the Royal London in Whitechapel) it tended to be knife and machete wounds, whereas at the Homerton (owing no doubt to its close proximity to 'Murder Mile') it was mainly gunshot wounds. So for once I was not the exception to the rule, not that night anyway.*

Anyhow, that attack was the straw that broke the camel's back in regard to me deciding to leave the East End. I had in the months leading up to that attack put my house on the market and then taken it off again (twice). Zi-Lan and I had already had a look at some houses in other areas of London in regard to finding another location to live in. I admit it: we made a few sorties out to Essex (I was just looking – OK?). However, I just couldn't bring myself to leave the East End. 'The Manor' still had me in its gravitational pull. Well, I now had to admit the game was finally up. I could no longer call it 'my area'. It was no longer, for the most part, populated by people of a similar disposition or culture to me. I knew in my heart of hearts that it was time to move on. I was in a very fortunate (financial) position, in that I could do that with no problem. I got two very serious propositions from people that I knew, offering to make serious retaliations on my behalf. I did not hesitate in declining those offers. I wasn't that bothered. Not much harm had been done; I'd stood my ground, and the local gang members were giving me a very wide berth. Anyway, I knew full well that reprisals would simply create new problems. That area could go up like a tinderbox at any time. I certainly didn't want to be the bloke responsible for making that happen.

By that time it was commonplace to hear the 'call to prayer' coming from the mosque up at Whitechapel Road. Funnily enough, at first I used to like hearing the 'call to prayer'. You could hear it all over Whitechapel, Stepney and Bethnal Green. Initially, I found its sound as calming as the resonance of church bells. But to be honest, towards the end of my tenure in the East End, I regarded it as the soundtrack to a foreign culture. One that was, generally speaking, more than happy to see my kind leave what was now 'their area'. Sometimes, to me, some of the Bangladeshis seemed as ludicrous and as out of place (and time) as many of the expat British do in Spain, with their *Daily Mail*s, all-day breakfasts and 'no Spanish food served here' signs.

Don't get me wrong. I know full well that if I told my tale of woe to a Palestinian, an Armenian or a Kurd, they would laugh in my face. I'm sure that they would love to put me straight about what it is to be truly displaced. However, it's my story, and you did say that you wanted to hear it. I'm also aware that there must be quite a few Asian people, Bangladeshi or otherwise, around my age and older, who could tell their stories of how they came to this country, with an open mind and a warm heart, and were then shocked at the cold and hostile reception that they received from the indigenous population.

Whenever I spoke to representatives of the chattering class at that time they were generally shocked at my opinions. Sometimes, from their reaction, you would have thought that I had informed them that I made a point, every year, of celebrating Adolf Hitler's birthday, and that 'by the way, the Holocaust never happened', rather than simply picking fault with the attitudes of some local Bangladeshis. Those middle-class dwellers of Clapham and Highgate tended to have been brainwashed by the unrealistic and unenforceable philosophies of multiculturalism and political correctness. I can understand full well why those philosophies came into being. I certainly wouldn't claim that no good has ever come from them. They were, at the beginning at least, a well-intentioned attempt to make a level playing field and protect the underdog. However, dealing with race and issues of equality is a difficult and complex matter (he said, stating the obvious). The crude application of multiculturalism tends to become reminiscent of the ways in which totalitarian regimes sometimes function. Multiculturalism begins eventually to work against itself. Instead of helping to achieve social harmony, it results, at best, in a lack of social cohesiveness, and at worst in serious civil disorder.

By the way, I wasn't expecting my Bangladeshi neighbours to join me for a 'good old cockney knees-up' and the enforced ingestion of jellied eels. All I wanted was the opportunity to meet them halfway, if only in terms of general attitude. Just a bit of eye contact and the willingness to return a smile would have done for starters. I knew full well that many of those chattering denizens of Hampstead, Islington and Chelsea would in time tend to see things the way I did. I knew the time would come when many of them would also feel threatened and affronted. Well, of course, that too came to pass. It is now not terribly unusual to see them, via newspaper columns and the like, getting all angry and indignant about the possible threat to their 'Western freedoms and values'. People such as the writer Martin Amis lead the charge for them.

*All that I have said is not a veiled rant against Islam in all times and in all places. It is simply an honest account of what I saw happening in Tower Hamlets at that particular time. It is also not a slur against all Bangladeshis. Ed Shipton (a mate of mine that I mentioned earlier in this book) has done very well for himself. He now runs a pretty large financial services company with one of his brothers. Obviously Ed is well aware of the sorts of problems inherent in Tower Hamlets. However, he ended up employing some people from Bangladesh. He was astounded at how positive the experience*

JAH WOBBLE

*was. He said that not only are they great workers, but they are also educated to a high standard, and scrupulously polite and honest. He says that they are his favourite race of people to employ. Eventually the situation in Tower Hamlets will level out. In fact it's changing now. The Bangladeshi community is being squeezed by the influx of eastern Europeans as well as the eastern encroachment of the City and 'Hoxton culture'. Even the curry houses are fast disappearing in Brick Lane.*

## IT'S NOT A PLACE, IT'S A LIFESTYLE

People like me were leaving the borough in their droves at that time. It wasn't just the white working class either. The first people to leave the street at that time were a black family who never caused any fuss. They were hard working and kept themselves to themselves. But they got fed up with their nice car being regularly vandalised. I now only know a handful of people in Tower Hamlets. Within a year of me leaving Terry Penton also (reluctantly) bit the bullet and departed the East End. Before leaving he featured heavily in a TV documentary about the changing face of the East End. I missed it but apparently Terry pulled no punches. He bemoaned what he saw as the deliberate eradication of his culture. With his impeccable left-wing credentials and mixed-race background it was impossible for anybody to dismiss him as a fascist. He criticised the process of gentrification that we saw going on around us.

There was now a dramatic increase in the number of young professionals buying and renting in the area. (By and large they didn't live on the tough council estates, of course.) Really they would have preferred to live up the road in Hoxton or Shoreditch, but those areas were already beyond most people's financial reach. The press was full of absurd manufactured stories about how there were now ten thousand artists living in the area. Artists my arse, it was a load of old bollocks. Any real artist would never want to live in an overpriced area with loads of other artists. I mean, where would be the inspiration in that?

*The East End was presented (by developers and estate agents) to the incomers (generally investors of one sort or another) as 'real', 'gritty' and 'edgy'. It was of course total and utter nonsense. It reminded me of what had happened in certain areas of New York, such as parts of Brooklyn and the Lower East and West sides of Manhattan. Yet again this country was following the American lead in regard to talking things up to the nth degree in order to turn a buck. It was like the eighties hadn't passed; it was yet another example of style over content on a grand scale. Admittedly I do still find the language of the property pages a jolly good wheeze. Why, only today I read one concerning the London postcode SE24 (that's Herne Hill in South London). The article in question said, 'It's not a place; it's a lifestyle.' Fucking tossers.*

*If it's not SE24, it's Hoxton or Docklands or Manchester's Northern Quarter or 'The Barcelona of the North' (that's Leeds to me and you). Of course, at the end of the cycle it will be the mug punters who will catch a cold. All the sharks are probably long gone. They are probably busy buying up property in Caracas or Slovenia or somewhere. Since the late nineties they have probably been through Bulgaria ('great potential'), Poland ('surprisingly good skiing'), Estonia ('excellent investment opportunity') and Dubai ('superb climate'). One thing's for sure: it will all end in tears.*

Anyway, all things considered it was time to go. That period was a crazy one for us. As well as preparing for the arrival of our second son, Charlie, and looking after John, who was a year old, we were also house-hunting and running 30 Hertz Records, which was really starting to take off. Additionally, I was by then in the third year of my BA course. If all that wasn't enough, I was also embarking on a pretty hectic schedule of live performances with my newly formed Deep Space group.

Initially Zi-Lan and I had intended to move to a bigger house in one of London's suburbs, or possibly a town such as Bishop's

Stortford, or even Brighton, which would have been within easy commuting distance of London. We had a look at a few places but nothing really took our fancy. To be honest, I should say my fancy, because Zi-Lan was pretty easygoing about it. As long as it wasn't an area like Tower Hamlets she was happy. (She wouldn't miss the handful of occasions when local Bangladeshi kids had called out 'Chinese bitch' as she walked up to Bethnal Green Road.) However, I started to rethink our plans. I started to get my head around the fact that we could within reason move anywhere. We even discussed going abroad to Australia or Canada. We both liked those countries. Even moving to Ireland was considered. But after a fair bit of thought I felt sure that a nice area in the north-west of England would make sense. I figured that it would be good for my sons to be near to their maternal grandparents. (Also, of course, you can't beat a nice bit of low cloud and heavy persistent rain.)

I knew that in all probability my boys would start attending the Chinese Pagoda Youth Orchestra in Liverpool (which they did). My father-in-law runs that orchestra. I wanted them to have a strong sense of Chinese culture (and indeed they do). I also had no doubt that I could introduce a lot of great English and Western stuff to them, which I have done. I simply wanted them to feel that they 'came from somewhere'. I wanted them to have a good sense of identity. As you will have gathered, I certainly feel that 'I come from somewhere'.

I also knew that by moving up North we could get a nice place, in a nice area, much bigger than we had been living in, without having to break the bank to do it. That in turn meant that I would not have to desperately chase a buck, doing work that I didn't like, in order to keep paying a mortgage. London property prices were beginning to go through the roof. I didn't fancy taking on an even bigger mortgage for a large house, just for the sake of living in London.

When I told Zi-Lan about my plans for us to move up North

she was shocked. She saw me as a total and absolute Londoner. She was convinced that it was a hare-brained scheme that I would regret. Also, to be honest, she was a bit sad at the thought of leaving London. She had strived hard to get work down there. London can be a tough city to make your home in, and just as she had got herself established I was asking her to leave. I told her that I was relaxed about it, and if she didn't fancy a move back North, no problem. We could just as easily go elsewhere. However, within a couple of days she started to see that maybe it could work. We looked in a few areas to start with, around the Wirral and Cheshire. Eventually we settled in a posh suburb of Stockport called Bramhall. While we were getting our house done up we stayed at my sister-in-law's house in Chorlton. Susan (Zi-Lan's sister) is very easygoing. We stayed at her house for about three months while our building work went on. On our first week there I took John for a walk. I passed a black woman in her thirties pushing a pram. She was done up in proper African dress. As I passed her she stared at me and asked, in a broad Mancunian accent, 'Are you Jah Wobble? What are you doing here?' I told her that I was staying with my sister-in-law. She laughed and said, 'Well, welcome, neighbour.' That was nice.

It was while we were living in Chorlton that Charlie was born. He is a very lively kid. Very lively indeed, and yet when he was born, at Stepping Hill Hospital, all he wanted to do was go back to kip. Similar to John, my elder boy, he has already done a session for me. He plays the gao hu, which is a Chinese instrument, not dissimilar to a violin. He is already the main soloist of the Pagoda Youth Orchestra. When we moved into our street in Bramhall practically all the neighbours signed a welcoming card, which I thought was very nice. After living opposite a crack den it made for a very pleasant change. People up North are generally quite chatty and sociable so I can't say that I felt in any way unwelcome (I just had to slow down my speech in order to be understood). I soon took to the hill-walking up here. I go up in the Peak District, which is near to where we live. At first I would start laughing to myself. Honestly, can you picture it? Jah Wobble in a flat cap and with a walking stick up in the high peaks. 'Fucking Hell; I live up North!' I'd say out loud to myself (the sheep would give me a funny look and move away). I love the silence up in the hills. All you can hear is the wind blowing (and some cockney bloke talking to himself).

## EPILOGUE

Well, I've been up North for ten years now. Somehow coming up here was a 'good luck move' for us (he said, tempting providence). We have earned a living and been happy. I don't regret not moving to Essex or the Home Counties. I still get down to London every couple of weeks or so. I generally stay in Chelsea when I come down (I owe that fact to my good mate, the artist and fellow Londoner John Freeman). You'll often come across me strolling by the river in that neck of the woods. I do creep over to the East End from time to time, sometimes to work (at Intimate Studios) and sometimes to socialise. However, most of the people that I knew have now left. In fact I probably know fewer than a dozen people in the borough. To be honest, I feel like a ghost when I wander around there so I tend to stay away. I still regularly punish myself by attending matches over at White Hart Lane, of course.

Obviously there's been a lot of water under the bridge since we moved out of London. Apart from writing this book I've done a ton of gigs with various line-ups. The mainstay musicians and singers have been Liz Carter, Clea Llewellyn, Chris Cookson, Clive Bell, Mark Sanders, Neville Murray and Jean-Pierre Rasle. As well as the players I shouldn't forget my live sound man Mick Routledge. They have been a terrific bunch to work with, they really have. In 2008 I augmented my regular line-up with a number of Chinese performers, musicians and singers, for the *Chinese Dub* tour. I did it in collaboration with Zi-Lan. It was initiated by the Liverpool

Chinese Dub

Capital of Culture Company, and we also got support from the Arts Council. The project really seemed to strike a chord with audiences. Westerners, so it seemed, were finally ready to brave the unfamiliar waters of Chinese tonality, albeit a tonality set in a rocking dub context. (I recorded some of the music that we performed on the tour for an album on 30 Hertz Records. It too is called *Chinese Dub*.)

Apart from all that, I have made a movie soundtrack, radio documentaries for BBC Radio and since 1996 I've written a number of book reviews for the *Independent on Sunday*. As well as all that I've been knocking out all manner of albums like there's no tomorrow. In fact in 2004 I decided that some sort of official retrospective/anthology was long overdue. By that time there must have been about twenty-five albums on 30 Hertz let alone the other twenty or so that I had made for other labels. I felt that it would be a good idea to get a major record company to release it. I knew that if I put it on 30 Hertz Records I would encounter problems in regard to licensing my older stuff from other majors. I was convinced that they would try to take advantage of me by charging me larger licensing advances than they would do to another major. Also, I knew full well that a major label, as long as they were well managed, would do a far better job than 30 Hertz could in regard to both international distribution and promotion, for a 'big record' like that. To cut a long story short, the anthology ended up being released by Trojan Records. I was over the moon. The first records that I truly loved were on the Trojan label. Those records were the first records that had deep bass parts that I could clearly hear. They were instrumental (no pun intended) in turning me on to becoming a bass player. It was a very big deal to me. To be on the same label as such great artists as Lee Perry, King Tubby, Dennis Brown, I-Roy, U-Roy and a host of others – well, that really was something special. It was as if the circle had been squared. The CD box set contained three CDs. I called it *I Could Have Been A Contender*. It was a tongue-in-cheek title. Many people, over the years, had said to me that I should have had far more commercial success than I had done, and that somehow it was unfair that I hadn't. I thought that the *I Could Have Been A Contender* title captured that sentiment in quite a melodramatic and therefore humorous way. It did, of course, conjure up images of Brando (as Terry Malloy) in *On the Waterfront*. Terry Malloy, of course, is forced to 'take a dive' and therefore loses his chance

This picture of Zi-Lan, John, Charlie and me, was taken in China in 2007

of a title fight. I must say that I love that movie. Brando conveys such a deep sense of brooding and resigned disappointment in it. In his job as a longshoreman Malloy comes up against all sorts of evils while working on the New York waterfront: corrupt union officials, extortion, bribery and murder. Well, there were many times in the music business that I felt a bit like Malloy. I never saw anyone murdered but, my God, have I met some corrupt and disreputable people. It is the main reason that I do not have so many pals in the (fast shrinking) music business. I have always kept my distance; that way you don't end up in anyone's pocket. Of course, ultimately the truth of the matter is that I could never have been a contender, not in the sense that I imply by the title. I simply don't have the temperament for it.

# Index

In this index JW stands for Jah Wobble